SPIRIT LED
WORSHIP

How to Follow Where *HE* Leads

By Karen M Gray

KMG

Dedication

This book is dedicated to the Bride of Christ. May she always be magnificently and beautifully clothed in pure & glorious Spirit filled worship, worthy of an awesome and most loving holy God!

Foreword

By Dr Mark Virkler

Spirit Led Worship by Karen M. Gray is training that is much in demand in the church of Christ. I believe we all understand there is a difference between singing songs to God, and entering into His presence where we worship before His throne, and are touched and transformed by His presence.

People come to church wanting to have an encounter with God. Will we offer them one? This heavenly encounter should be experienced in every part of the service. This includes the preaching, the worship, the body ministry and the release of the gifts of the Holy Spirit.

Karen's book trains you how to effectively be a Spirit-led worshipper who can lead a congregation into the presence of God to be touched and healed by Him. This book is both practical and spiritual. Karen covers every aspect of Spirit-led worship from the pre-service prayer, to the "what" and "why" we are even singing. We are here to come before His throne and worship along with the heavenly hosts.

John saw this heavenly host worshipping in Revelation chapter four. The nice thing about the Bible is that it is meant to be lived. If John can do this, so can we. Spirit-led worship will train you how to fix your eyes upon Jesus as you worship, sense the moving of His Spirit both individually and corporately, and move with His leading. Now church becomes fun, because it is a living encounter with the living God!

Read, learn, and practice the principles Karen shares and make your personal and corporate worship times, *encounters* with your heavenly Father.

Thank you, Karen, for this very unique, very special and much needed book on the "how to's" of *Spirit Led Worship*. May you as a reader of this book, be led to participate in Spirit-led worship.

- Dr. Mark Virkler
President of Communion With God Ministries
Author of *4 Keys to Hearing God's Voice*, which is available at:

www.CWGMinistries.org

Contents

The True Heart of the Matter

There is much one can say about effective worship leading but most of the chatter is usually about the mechanics of running the team, presentation, and so forth. Very rarely have I ever heard any teaching on **flowing with the Holy Spirit**, if at all. So like Dr. Mark Virkler who set about writing down how to hear the voice of God, I am undertaking the task of putting into words what I have always done intuitively as I have led worship, and what I look for in others as I have trained them to be worship leaders.

Before I launch into this discussion, I must begin with the fundamentals, otherwise the "how to worship lead" would be simply a formula, and not founded within a Godly perspective, as it aught to be. Yes, you could skip this part of the discussion, but I encourage you to stay with me through this discourse, as I strongly feel it has the potential to affect the way we approach worship, and thus, how we worship lead. So let's dive in together!

The Essentials

Jesus taught that true worshippers would worship "*in spirit and truth*". What does this look like? Does this mean worship can be totally free from the old physical forms of worship and left up to each individual to choose how to worship? No! Actually, to be God-pleasing, worship must observe a couple of God ordained constraints. (See also Chapter 2) He never said, "*Go and do whatever feels good to you*" but He did say to worship:

    1) From the heart

    2) In Truth

    3) In Spirit

    4) Him alone & with no other gods before Him.

(Note: this list is not in order of importance!)

1) Worship from the Heart

God's desire for man was always to have relationship with him. In the beginning, God walked and talked with Adam face to face in the garden. A picture of a loving Father talking to His son, answering Adam's innocent questions, and God teaching Adam and showing him what was pleasing and acceptable.

Adam knew nothing else. It had always been that way, but then came the fall. No longer did he have those close talks with God, his Father. Sin separates us from God. Now Adam would have suddenly realised the gravity of his disobedience and its consequences. (That was a hard lesson!) Disobedience had totally messed up something so precious – his relationship with God.

Though unable to enjoy his Father in the cool of the evening as he once did, I'm sure Adam often recounted his wonderful encounters and conversations with God. He obviously *did* describe to his children (who then passed it on to theirs etc.) the story of man's creation and life in the Garden of Eden, or we would not know this account for ourselves. His children may have sat wide eyed as he talked about God and life before the fall, or at least they would have learned much from Adam's recollections.

Enter the story of Cain and Abel! As already mentioned, it is unknown for certain whether God told them directly, or indirectly through Adam, that they should offer a sacrifice as means of saying thanks to God, or whether they thought it up themselves (unlikely as discussed), but in Genesis chapter four the Bible say:

> "*In the course of time Cain brought to the Lord an offering of the fruit of the ground, and Abel also brought of the firstborn of his flock and of their fat portions. And the Lord had regard for Abel and his offering, but for Cain and his offering he had no regard. So Cain was very angry, and his face fell.*" - **Genesis 4:2-5 ESV**

Cain was mentioned first as bringing his offering to the Lord. However, the verse gives the impression that both offerings may have been around the same time – we don't know, nor can we make assumptions. Did Cain think it up? Again, the fact is, we don't know.

What about his actual offering? Was something wrong with it? We don't know because the Bible does not say despite many teachers expressing their own personal point of view. All we *do* know is that it was *not acceptable* and Abel's was. This *may* have been because of the actual offering itself (the type of offering) although grain offerings were certainly acceptable in the Jewish Law, or the quality may not have been up to scratch, but equally plausible, its unacceptable nature may have resulted from the *way* Cain offered it – either physically or in Cain's attitude!

Let's take a look at a few "Sacred Cows" very often discussed today. I do this not to somehow take a poke at anyone, or to indirectly negate someone else's teaching on offerings, but to scrutinize Cain and Abel's worship. If we are to worship in Spirit and in truth, we need to understand, as much as can be possible, what exactly was happening here. Why did God not accept Cain's offering, and are we in breach of doing the same?

Was the problem to do with first fruits or the lack there-of? Frankly, the Bible does not say. Therefore we don't know for certain. We do know about agriculture though. Crops (not just wheat but vegetables as well – Cain's crop was the fruit of the ground) are usually harvested all at once. They are planted/sown all at the same time and subsequently sprout at roughly the same time.

Given that the crop would have been harvested by hand, the first sheaths cut could possibly be considered the first-fruit (as in Duet 26), but this also does not automatically make it the best quality either. Could the quality of Cain's offering been substandard? Possibly, but while there may be a few plants slightly better than others and vise versa, usually the entire crop is good, okay or poor. Again, Bible does not indicate that. Unfortunately, there was nothing written about it in Scripture for our instruction, nor was there any traditions concerning first fruits for Cain to follow. The fact is, we don't know! Anything beyond that is purely speculation and conjecture.

If the entire crop needed to be given (as some have argued) because it was the very first crop, it follows that Abel should have also given every lamb offspring, which is absurd! Despite the fact that they would have had nothing to eat for the year, Cain would also have had nothing to plant for the following year!

If, on the other hand, Abel's one animal was acceptable, why couldn't Cain have given one plant and how do we know that he didn't? Clearly, comparing the two offerings in terms of *amount* or *quality* is very silly at best.

All these discussions about Cain's crop in comparison to Abel's animal simply do not pan out logically, or have to include assumptions not found within the Scripture verses in order to support such arguments. Yes, of course we know that Abel's animal offering was the firstborn from his flock – it is stated – but to extrapolate that Abel's offering was accepted *because* his offering was the first fruit and Cain's was not, is to read meaning into the verse that is not there, nor supported by other Scriptures, all whilst ignoring all other possibilities.

Could the acceptability of Abel's offering lie in the fact that it was a *blood* offering and Cain's was not? We *do* know that grain offerings *were* acceptable offerings under the Old Covenant, and therefore, would also have been acceptable to God from the start. Was Cain's offering unlawful in some other way? There was *no* written or stated law at that time! So clearly he was not breaking any religious laws. What then made Cain's sacrifice of worship unacceptable?

There is a couple of old sayings that parents often recite to their children when they are unhappy with the way a task is carried out. "*It's not what you do but how you do it!*" and "*It's not what you say but how you say it!*" The parent is essentially telling the child that their attitude not their deed, needs a check. Perhaps it was

Cain's heart attitude that was the real issue here. Dod the Scriptures bear witness to this, or is this another assumption?

Let's read the passage taking particular notice of Cain's attitude.

> *"So Cain was very angry, and his face fell. ⁶The Lord said to Cain, "Why are you angry, and why has your face fallen? ⁷If you do well, will you not be accepted? And if you do not do well, sin is crouching at the door. Its desire is contrary to you, but you must rule over it." ⁸Cain spoke to Abel his brother. And when they were in the field, Cain rose up against his brother Abel and killed him."* - **Genesis 4:6-8 ESV**

Cain became angry (verse 5) that his sacrifice was not accepted. Now *if* his offering was substandard, and Cain knew so, he might have been a little annoyed at being caught out, or regretted his choice, but hardly angry – especially enough to murder his brother! Rather, a spirit of entitlement usually manifests when someone believes their effort is every bit as good as someone else's, and yet ignored or passed over. He would have worked quite hard tilling the soil, planting, and then keeping the wild animals away from the crop until it was ready. He obviously thought what he had to offer was just as good as his brother's, so why wasn't he also accepted?

God then addresses Cain about his offering. God has no favourites. If Cain does it right, he'll also be commended, but as it is, his attitude and thoughts of unfairness towards his brother could lead to sin. Cain did not take heed of God's warning. His anger turned to murder. This does not sound like someone who knew and loved God as his loving Father, and from that relationship, wanted to please Him. Rather, it sounds like someone who was doing something dutifully in order to receive affirmation – with a religious spirit, if you like.

When God then questions Cain about Abel's disappearance, instead of falling on his face and admitting his guilt and asking for God's forgiveness for what he had done, (consider King David's response when the prophet Nathan called out his murderous sin), or even trying to explain what happened, he brushes it off with contempt.

> *"Then the Lord said to Cain, "Where is Abel your brother?" He said, "I do not know; am I my brother's keeper?"* - **Genesis 4:9-10 ESV**

Clearly, he was not in step with God. There was no acknowledging God as supreme - the one who is above all. Surely he would have known even from Adam's accounts that God knew everything! To brush off God's question so contemptibly, indicates his heart was more for himself than for God, whereas Abel's actions demonstrate complete trust and love. True love gives and wants to please. Self-love wants to receive and give as little as possible. Clearly then, Cain only offered the sacrifice as an appeasement, or at most, as a dutiful offering that was action without heart.

Was Cain's attitude then the disqualifying factor? Cain had a form of worship but no love or heart felt praise for God.

Daniel I. Block wrote:

> *"We think that it is the sacrifice that makes the person acceptable to God; but actually it is the person that makes the sacrifice acceptable."*

The Scriptures agree with this:

> *"For the Lord sees not as man sees: man looks on the outward appearance, but the Lord looks on the heart."* -**1 Samuel 16:7b ESV**

The problem with Cain's offering was not the offering itself, but Cain's heart. He had an outward appearance of worship, but inside his heart was tainted. God just wanted Cain's heart, but instead He was given "straw" (or whatever the crop happened to be.)

Now Hebrews states that by *faith* Abel offered to God a better sacrifice than Cain, (Hebrews 11:4). We might then be tempted to think that this statement in Hebrews just negates all I've discussed thus far. How does faith even relate to the heart? It relates in every way!

Faith is not simply repeating, "I believe, I believe, I believe!" like a mantra. That is not faith at all, but purely an effort to convince oneself that God will grant us what we have requested. You can't simply "will" faith into being. Nor do we automatically have faith because we are now Christians. Faith must be based on something, or it is not faith at all!

Rather, real *faith is born from the knowledge of who God is*. It comes out of our relationship with Him. We don't just know about Him; we know Him. We know He is trustworthy. We know He is true to His promises and cares for our spiritual wellbeing. He cares for His sons and daughters. He will not abandon them nor leave them to struggle or suffer alone. We know this because we daily walk with Him. We have experienced His goodness and love towards us. It is a true "επίγνοσίς" (or epignosis using English characters) – the Greek word meaning real and full intimate knowledge of God, and the word Paul uses in Philippians:

> "9 *And this I pray, that your love may abound still more and more in real knowledge and all discernment"* – **Philippians 1:9 - NASB**

We have faith *because* we know Him. It is a complete and real knowledge based not only on the Word of God but developed through our relationship, Holy Spirit revelations, and experience with Him. It is the difference between reading a book about someone, and knowing that someone on a personal and even "intimate" level. (In this case spiritual intimacy or closeness.)

Thus, when we ask according to His will, we can boldly approach the throne of grace, knowing He hears us and that we have what we ask for. We know how He will answer, because in the same way we approached our earthly father and knew how he would respond to our request, we have faith in God, our heavenly Father, that He hears and will respond in a similar manner.

Jesus gave us further assurance when He told His disciples that two or three need only agree together in His wonderful name, and the Father would hear their request and answer them. Why – because He loves us too.

> *"¹⁹Again I say to you, if two of you agree on earth about any-thing they ask, it will be done for them by my Father in heaven."* – **Matthew 18: 19 ESV**

and

> *"²⁶In that day you will ask in my name, and I do not say to you that I will ask the Father on your behalf; ²⁷for the Father himself loves you, because you have loved me and have be-lieved that I came from God."* – **John 16:26-27 - ESV**

We have every assurance of God's goodness and faithfulness and that assurance (or faith) is based on love. Heart and faith are linked closely together, and therefore, Abel's faith had everything to do with his state of heart.

In John's first letter we read,

> "We should not be like Cain, who was of the evil one and murdered his brother. And why did he murder him? Because his own deeds were evil and his brother's righteous." - **1 John 3:12 ESV**

Does this disagree with the verse in Hebrews we have mentioned previously? No! Let's compare the two.

> *"**By faith** Abel offered to God a more acceptable sacrifice than Cain, through which **he was commended as right-eous**, God commending him by accepting his gifts. And through his faith, though he died, he still speaks."* - **He-brews 11:4 ESV**

The Hebrews explanation says that Abel was commended as

righteous, because of his faith, and therefore his gifts were acceptable. In contrast, the state of Cain's heart and consequential lack of faith, earned him the title of the *"evil one"* according to John.

To summarize this point: It was Abel's faith that made his offering acceptable rather than his brother's. However, Abel faith was obviously based on the revelation of who God really was through his *relationship* with Him. That is, because he knew and loved God, he gave extravagantly. His faith action response to his love and trust in God, was to give his first lamb (and more besides because love gives), which also proved he trusted God would care for him even though his flock was now incomplete and the number of reproducing animals for the following year would be diminished. His heart had responded lovingly and with faith in God as his provider.

Moving forward in time in the Bible to the next act of worship, and converse to Abel's heart felt offering and worship to God; we find another two vivid descriptions regarding what worship is *not*. They are:

> 1) that of the people who were alive at the time of the flood, and
>
> 2) the worship of those building of the Tower of Babel.

The people of Noah's time were described as having corrupted their ways (Gen 6:12) and

> *"The Lord saw how great the wickedness of the human race had become on the earth, and that every inclination of the thoughts of the human heart was only evil all the time."* – **Genesis 6:5 NIV**

In contrast to this, the Bible describes Noah:

> *"Noah was a righteous man, blameless among the people of his time, and he walked faithfully with God."* – **Genesis 6:9 NIV**

Noah did all that the Lord had commanded him, (Gen 6:22; 7:5) clearly demonstrating that he not only feared and reverenced God but that he trusted God would save him and his family. It is almost inconceivable that he and his family were the only righteous people who worshipped and obeyed God, while every other human being on the planet insisted on obeying every lust for evil and its diabolical practices – *all the time!* Self was number one everywhere. No wonder God regretted creating mankind. (Even so, in His great mercy, He still saved Noah and his family.)

In contrast to this, Noah's first act after disembarking from the ark was to build an altar and worship God.

> *"¹⁸ So Noah came out, together with his sons and his wife and his sons' wives. ¹⁹ All the animals and all the creatures that move along the ground and all the birds—everything that moves on land—came out of the ark, one kind after another.*
>
> *²⁰ Then Noah built an altar to the Lord and, taking some of all the clean animals and clean birds, he sacrificed burnt offerings on it."* - **Genesis 8:18-20 NIV**

Moreover, God was so delighted when He smelled the offering, He promised He would never again curse the earth and destroy all the living creatures upon it. All He desired was for people to love and worship their true God, and not themselves.

The Tower of Babel is exceptionally demonstrative of this point. As briefly mentioned in the last section, here, we see mankind literally trying to make a name for *itself*, not God. The construction was purpose built to give glory to man alone! There was no faith in God, only self-glorification. God does not share his glory like that! He *alone* deserves all praise! There is no life nor future in self glorification. Sure, man can achieve many things by his own reckoning, but this achievement has no eternal significance without God. Therefore, God had little choice but to destroy Babel and confound the languages.

The lesson here is that self-love and pride are an abomination to God. He created everything – even man. How can the pot presume to be greater than the potter who created it? **If we come to worship thinking about our own glory, we haven't just missed the mark – *God hates it!*** Conversely, I recently heard Chris Gore (of Bethel church in Redding, California) state that humility isn't merely denigrating oneself. Rather, humilty is thinking of yourself far less than you think of God! (That bears keeping in mind whilst on the platform!)

The next major worship milestone in the Old Testament occurs at the time of Abram. God called him to set himself apart and take his family to the land God would show him. God made great promises to him (Genesis 12:2-3) and Abram trusted or had faith in God, and responded in *obedience.*

Why did Abram do this? Why leave his family to sojourn in another land? Why would anyone obey if they didn't know God, or even know about God's greatness? Abram had to have had a revelation of just who God was, or why bother?

Could Abram have obeyed purely because he was afraid of what God might do to him if he refused? No! The Bible clearly states that Abram had *faith* in God. He believed that the things God had told him were true. He knew not only the stories his forefathers had told him, but somehow he *knew* God was trustworthy.

You don't choose to trust any strange voice that starts speaking to you out of nowhere, and especially one that says to a 75 year old man to leave your birth family, your country and all you know, to journey into some foreign land on foot. Even if the promise of becoming a great nation sounded appealing, he was an old man! Plus, it was no little ask. Abram was wealthy. He owned a great many possessions that would have to be transported on foot over many miles. Why trust this voice at all?

Nevertheless, Abram obediently took his wife and nephew, all his possession and servants along with their families, with him, and left for Canaan. It was a huge caravan and a major undertaking.

Also, because he took everything, he would have known he would not be returning. Why would Abram (or anyone for that matter) do such a thing?

It was four hundred years between the death of Noah and the call of Abraham – approximately ten generations. (Genesis 11:10-32) Though the people of the early earth would have known all about God the creator, 400 years later, those stories of God, if *not* handed down by parents to subsequent generations after the flood, could have easily been lost or corrupted by time. Nevertheless, it is conceivable that Abram's line *did* have knowledge of the early earth and the Creator. They may have even been the custodians of any early records – eg. The Book of Enoch – someone would have had to have kept it, or it would not have survived (assuming Enoch was in fact the author.)

The point is that Abram is likely to have known, at least, *about* the God of all things. Was knowledge of those early stories enough to convince him to travel to Canaan? Abram would also have had to have known that God could be trusted. How? - Because he not only knew about God, but knew God, Himself. He even knew His voice, which to me indicates that it wasn't the first time he had heard God speak.

In fact, Abram had such a revelation of God's character, that he was willing to leave his homeland and his father's house and relatives and chose instead to trust God.

Then, like Noah, the very first act in the new land was to construct an altar and *worship* God. (Genesis 12:7). Did God tell him to do this? No, it was Abram's response to God's goodness and faithfulness. God had delivered him safely to Canaan just as He said, and now reiterated His promise that this land now belonged to Abram and his offspring. The land was now Abram's despite its other occupants, and Abram believed God because he trusted that God's word was truth! He had a revelation of God's faithful, kind and generous character.

Abram responded to this display of goodness, with worship. It is the case that always God reveals Himself to us first, which in turn, elicits a heart/spirit response in us.

This *revelation and response* can be likened to a man romantically pursuing a woman. He approaches her. He talks sweetly to her. He asks her out on a date. He brings flowers and small tokens of affection. What is her response to his advances? At first she may not know what to do about his advances, but little by little trust begins to build, then attraction commences (though attraction can happen straight away, love generally takes time), and then eventually she loves him in return. This is a picture of how God woos us. He reveals Himself. He talks to us, gives gifts to us and makes wonderful promises. Our response is love and worship, and more so, as we receive greater revelations of whom He is.

In every case, God revealed Himself, and the great patriarchs of old responded in worship. Even in the Exodus account, we see God revealing Himself to a people who had been enslaved in a multi-theistic culture and who knew only stories of the God of Joseph. These stories must have seemed like bedtime stories because where was God now? However, God had orchestrated an amazing plan to show Himself as the one true God, above all their man made gods, and to establish His reputation once and for all.

> *"Some scholars have noted that every one of the plagues of Egypt was either aimed against the false gods of Egypt or the oppressive power structures that were revered with fanatical zeal. Some Egyptian deities, such as the Nile River, or the great sun god, were embarrassed directly by plagues of blood and darkness. Other deities were indirectly shamed by exposing their complete inability to do what they were supposed to do. There were gods who were revered as being able to deal with infestations of insects or to protect cattle from disease. The powerful religious elite was shamed. The deeply revered military was summarily annihilated."[1]*

> *"God had orchestrated the Exodus events so that He revealed His glory by establishing His name in a global way. Then, with the world watching, He drew the people to Him-*

self to establish a way of worship that all other nations could enter."[2]

"Through this experience it became clear that the God of Israel was first of all their Saviour-God. He had taken the initiative in their redemption. Their worship was essentially a response of gratitude to Him."[3]

James B. Torrance writes:

"The liturgies of Israel were God-given ordinances of grace, witnesses to grace. The sacrifice of lambs and bulls and goats were not ways of placating an angry God, currying favour with God as in the pagan worship of the Baali. They were God-given covenantal witnesses to grace—that the God who alone could wipe out their sins would be gracious"[4]

God had revealed and proven Himself to His people. He had redeemed them, and all He wanted in return was a grateful people who would love and worship Him. Moreover God gave them the task of leading other nations to the knowledge of Him. They'd seen God in operation. They saw His glory and power first hand. They heard His voice as it thundered on Mount Sinai. Who better than the first hand witnesses to His greatness, that He had redeemed from slavery, to be the very one's who could adequately proclaim His name throughout the earth.

*" [4] 'You yourselves have seen what I did to Egypt, and how I carried you on eagles' wings and brought you to Myself. [5] Now if you obey Me fully and keep My covenant, then out of all nations you will be My **treasured possession**. Although the whole earth is Mine, [6] you will be for Me a kingdom of priests and a holy nation.' These are the words you are to speak to the Israelites.' "* - **Exodus 19:4-6 NIV**

(Note: the use of the term "treasured possession" speaks loudly of God's great love for them!)

Then God made the covenant with the Israelites that if they continued to obey and worship Him alone, He would bless them abundantly. They had witnessed what He could do and knew that He indeed was the true and only God, and so they wholeheartedly agreed. They had faith in Him.

Unfortunately, with all the elements of the law and covenant in every day life, they still began to forget God's true nature as a lover of Israel, who had demonstrated Himself before all the nations as the one true God, who could and would redeem them all. If you forget the relational aspect of God, how can you love Him whole heartedly? It becomes religious piety and form without heart.

A few hundred years later we see King David appear on the scene. David through his psalms and love songs, showed us a glimpse of what love for God could look like. He was real with God. His words were not nice little ditties that his lifestyle negated. He displayed the praise and joy and the pain and sorrow in his heart, but always he responded to the negative situations with his complete trust in a God who is true, faithful, just and able to do all things. Those that followed after David, inherited yet another aspect of the character of God and how mortal man could love a faithful loving God with all his heart, despite the fact that he may never see Him face to face in this life.

David not only introduced love songs and worship music to the temple but David also desired to build God a temple – not only a place of worship but enabling God to live among them. He wanted God to live with them always in a tangible way. However, because of the blood David had spilled over the years, it was Solomon that fulfilled David's dream. We may be tempted to believe that it was David's idea to build God a house, but in actual fact, we see that it was already God's desire to live among men.

> *"But you shall seek the Lord at the place which the Lord your God will choose from all your tribes, to establish His name there for His dwelling, and there you shall come"* - **Deuteronomy 12:5 ESV.**

"God wanted to do two things in this special place. First, He wanted to reveal Himself by 'His name.' It would be a place of revelation as worshipers continually exalt His character and voice the stories and songs about His working. Second, God desired a place of encounter, of relationship, of dwelling. . . . To 'dwell' is a relational affair. It is consummated worship. God coming near His people as they come near to Him."[5]

We also know that once it was completed and they began to worship God, His presence so filled the temple, they could not minister. God did, in fact, come to dwell with them.

Although it was David who bought music into the temple worship, organising choirs and musicians, it was here in the temple of Solomon that ceremony combined with music to formalize the worship service. In fact, this worship music was the only thing that distinguished it from the worship of other gods in the pagan temples. The pagans also made animal (and sometimes human) sacrifices and observed certain feasts. They played drums and made enough noise to cover any screams from the parents whose child was being sacrificed. However, it was anything but musical. The worship of the Israelites, on the other hand, included music with instruments and choirs. God had introduced the arts into worship. It was no longer a cold ritual or intellectual act. It was from the heart and coloured by every expression of the heart that God had made available to man.

Unfortunately, after Solomon died, the heart of the nation grew cold. It was Jeroboam that rallied Israel to himself breaking away from Judah and king Rehoboam, elevating himself as another king. To prevent his subjects from travelling back down to Jerusalem to worship and there being swayed to serve Rehoboam instead, He set up his own altars of worship – even creating new gods (golden calves) for people to worship. It was a power play on his behalf, but thus, began the decline of people's worship to the one true God.

Judah eventually followed Israel's pagan practices. They forgot just who the real God was, and that He had taken the initiative to mightily save them from slavery in order to draw them to Himself. They forgot to sing the psalms with love like David. For those that still served God, even their worship became mechanical like that of the foreign gods, with form but no inner substance. So God became unhappy with their worship and rituals.

"²Has not my hand made all these things, and so they came into being?" declares the Lord. "These are the ones I look on with favour: those who are humble and contrite in spirit, and who tremble at my word.

³But whoever sacrifices a bull is like one who kills a person, and whoever offers a lamb is like one who breaks a dog's neck; whoever makes a grain offering is like one who presents pig's blood, and whoever burns memorial incense is like one who worships an idol. They have chosen their own ways, and they delight in their abominations" - **Isaiah 66:2-3 NIV**

God is clearly not happy with a form of worship *that lacks any real heart*. He hated their acts of worship. Isaiah records again:

"These people draw near with their mouths And honour Me with their lips, But have removed their hearts far from Me, And their fear toward Me is taught by the commandment of men" - **Isaiah 29:13 NKJV**

Jesus even quotes this when speaking about the legalistic Pharisees (who were never assigned or appointed by Moses, but who added many more laws of their own to those Moses had already given.)

"You hypocrites! Well did Isaiah prophesy of you, when he said: 'This people honours me with their lips, but their heart is far from me; in vain do they worship me, teaching as doctrines the commandments of men.'" - **Matthew 15:7-9 ESV**

The nation of Israel was enticed by the false religions of the surrounding nations, even though God repeatedly warned them about the dangers of idolatry and false worship. Imagine a parent constantly warning a child that if they continue their actions, there will be consequences they do not like. As every parent knows, there comes a time when punishment is the only course left. The behaviour of the Jews had continued despite the ongoing warnings from the prophets God had sent to them. Not only was this going to end badly for them, but their behaviour also brought ill repute to God's name and broke the covenant they had made with Him.

So with no other recourse left, God delivered the agreed covenantal punishment and destroyed Jerusalem, cursed the land surrounding it, and sent His people into exile. He was making good on His promises, and fulfilling His justice!

The people of Israel were to be priests to the nations, instead they had brought disrespect to His Name. Yet even this punishment became a testimony to the other nations.

> *"And many nations will pass by this city, and every man will say to his neighbour, "Why has the Lord dealt thus with this great city?" And they will answer, "Because they have forsaken the covenant of the Lord their God and worshiped other gods and served them""* - **Jeremiah 22:8-9 ESV**

Their worship and faith was to be demonstrated and as such bring the nations of the world into revelation of who He was: the great God Jehovah who had redeemed a people to Himself and had clearly shown that He was above all. Now their disobedience (i.e. worshipping false gods, disregarding the poor and being unjust in their dealings) and its consequences were their last great testimony to the world in accordance with God's original mandate for them.

However God is so redemptive that Ezekiel writes,

> *"And I will give you a new heart, and a new spirit I will put within you. And I will remove the heart of stone from your flesh and give you a heart of flesh. And I will put my Spirit within you, and cause you to walk in my statutes and be careful to obey my rules"* - **Ezekiel 36:26-27 ESV**

God would enable worship in a way that "*the Law, weakened by the flesh, could not do*" – (Romans 8:3). This He achieved by making our spirits alive in Christ, and by bringing us into relationship with Him.

So what is the point in me telling you/reminding you of all these things? It's to emphasise that right from the beginning God wanted worshippers to worship Him *right from their hearts*, and this Godly desire still remains the same to this day.

Let's take a quick look back at John chapter 4 - the story of the woman at the well. Jesus begins a conversation with this woman and explains that He is able to give her living water. He then reveals by word of knowledge that she has had five husbands and is now living with another man. Now realising that He is a prophet, the women tries to hear His opinion on a topic which was obviously hotly contested between Jews and Samaritans.

> "*Jesus said to her, "Woman, believe me, **the hour is coming** when neither on this mountain nor in Jerusalem will you worship the Father. You worship what you do not know; we worship what we know, for salvation is from the Jews. But **the hour is coming, and is now here**, when the true worshipers will worship the Father in spirit and truth, for the Father is seeking such people to worship him. God is spirit, and those who worship Him must worship in spirit and truth.*"" - **John 4:21-24 ESV**

Up to this point in history, the Jews had been given the job of being priests of God to reveal Him to the world. Salvation was of the Jews up until Jesus. However, Jesus said. "*But the hour is coming, and **is now here***". That is, things have changed. Now because of Jesus, salvation is through *Him* alone. Now true worshippers will not be reliant on rituals or other forms of worship, but from their spirits will automatically flow sweet sincere worship and adoration for a God who so loved them, He gave everything to save us from the bondage of slavery to sin. Now our hearts also cry out "*Abba Father!*"

God has peeled away the rituals in order for His people to come to Him as an issue or outflow of their hearts, and based on the revelation of who He is and the great and marvelous things He has done, not because this was the thing the law required.

In the same way that the people of the Old Covenant looked back to the Exodus when God showed Himself first as their Redeemer from slavery, and as the One true God, they responded with deep heartfelt worship, so too do we respond with an overflowing heart of praise, worship and thanksgiving for the cross, because the love of God was so great towards us, that He sent Jesus to redeem us from the slavery of sin. He was the complete fulfilment /requirement of the law on our behalf, and rising from the dead proved beyond all doubt that He also is God, and worthy of praise.

It is the heart that makes this sacrifice of praise pleasing, just as Abel's sacrifice was acceptable because it was given with a heart of love and worship, but Cain's sacrifice was unacceptable because his heart was not towards God at all. It was just a dutiful works-based ritual, much like that of the surrounding pagans whose hope was that their actions appeased their god or at least would afford them some divine favour. The truth is, God wants hearts more than form. A thorough search of the Old Testament in order to ascertain God's heart on the matter, has shown clearly that this truth has never changed. God has always wanted our sincere love and adoration, not our rituals or pretence.

Love is Expected

When Jesus was asked what was the greatest commandment of all, He replied,

> "And Jesus said to him, '*You shall love the Lord your God with all your heart, with all your soul, and with all your mind.*'" - **Matthew 22:37 NKJV**

> "*And you shall love the Lord your God with all your heart, with all your soul, with all your mind, and with all your*

strength.' This is the first commandment." - **Mark 12:30 NKJV**

"You shall love the Lord your God with all your heart, with all your soul, with all your strength, and with all your mind,' and 'your neighbour as yourself." - **Luke 10:27 NJKV**

It is obvious from the above verses that God expects His children to love Him. He has done everything to reveal His love to mankind. He expects our response will be to love Him in return!

"⁷Today, if only you would hear his voice, ⁸Do not harden your hearts" - **Psalm 95:7-8 NIV**

Our response to Him can only be love, unless we harden our hearts to Him! We were designed to love Him – God, our creator! It's who we are, and what we were created for!

Renowned prophet and teacher, Bob Jones, gave a testimony at a conference in Albany, Oregon in 2006, in which he related his time in heaven after he died in hospital:

While in Heaven, he saw two lines of people. One was filled with people who did not love God. These people were wrapped in the very things they had worshipped in life, and were being led bound by these things, straight into hell.

In the other line stood the believers. Here God asked each person only one question: ***"Did you learn to love?"*** Bob Jones pointed out that the question was not to do with what they did, because if you love God with all your heart and love others, you will automatically want to do the right thing. If the people responded with, *"Yes!"* Jesus opened to them.

Bob thought to himself that he would be ok – Jesus would surely let him in, but Jesus told him that He was sending him back. Bob protested that it was too hard and painful. Jesus told Bob straight that he was a liar and a coward. Nevertheless, Jesus acknowledged that Bob did love and had a heart for souls, so He gave him a choice: Bob had to look upon the line of people that was doomed for eternity. If he still wanted to be ushered in to heaven after seeing these poor souls, Jesus would open to him, but one look and Bob knew he had to go back.

Jesus didn't send Bob back because he didn't love but because He had a special task for him. However, the main point of me retelling this story is to re-emphasize that our ultimate purpose on this earth is to love God completely and to love others. See how this parallels what the above verses of Scripture say. It's worth quoting not just the single verse but the entire discourse in context.

> "28 And one of the scribes came up and heard them disputing with one another, and seeing that he answered them well, asked him, "Which commandment is the most important of all?" 29 Jesus answered, "The most important is, 'Hear, O Israel: The Lord our God, the Lord is one. 30 And you shall love the Lord your God with all your heart and with all your soul and with all your mind and with all your strength.' 31 The second is this: 'You shall love your neighbour as yourself.' There is no other commandment greater than these." 32 And the scribe said to him, "You are right, Teacher. You have truly said that he is one, and there is no other besides him. 33 And to love him with all the heart and with all the understanding and with all the strength, and to love one's neighbour as oneself, is much more than all whole burnt offerings and sacrifices." 34 And when Jesus saw that he answered wisely, he said to him, "You are not far from the kingdom of God." And after that no one dared to ask him any more questions." – **Mark 12:28-34 ESV.** (See also Matthew 22:34-40)

Jesus also commanded the disciples:

> "34 A new commandment I give to you, that you love one another: just as I have loved you, you also are to love one another. 35 By this all people will know that you are my disciples, if you have love for one another." – **John 13:34-35 ESV**

So not only are we commanded to love, but this love should be *evidence* that we belong to Jesus. It is not an option. We must learn to love during our lifetime. If we don't learn that lesson, perhaps we are not ready for eternity.

To extrapolate from this, since our main purpose here on earth is to learn to love, and the way to draw near to Him is through worship and intimacy, then worship should be number one on our priority list!! As we open up to Him, He reaches down and changes us. As we look into His face we are transformed from glory to glory into His image.

> *"¹⁸ And we all, with unveiled face, beholding the glory of the Lord, are being transformed into the same image from one degree of glory to another. For this comes from the Lord who is the Spirit."* – **2 Corinthians 3:18 ESV**

The one thing we need to learn above every other lesson on this earth, is to love. Love is our ultimate destiny. Moreover, He expects us to love Him above all else, even above family or those closest to us.

> *"He who loves father or mother more than Me is not worthy of Me. And he who loves son or daughter more than Me is not worthy of also Me."* - **Matthew 10:37 NKJV**

It doesn't stop there. Our love for Him must overflow to others, since He expects us to love others too. Consider this, we cannot possibly love God and hate our brother simultaneously. It is easy to state that worship is an expression of our love for God, it is harder to accept that it is also dependent on our relationship with one another. In John's first letter it says:

> *"¹⁹ We love because He first loved us. ²⁰ If anyone says, "I love God," and hates his brother, he is a liar; for he who does not love his brother whom he has seen cannot love God whom he has not seen. ²¹ And this commandment we have from Him: whoever loves God must also love his brother. "* **1 John 4:19-21 ESV**

If we are to worship in truth, we will be in right relationship with our brethren. Jesus instructed us in Matthew's gospel:

> "²³ So if you are offering your gift at the altar and there remember that your brother has something against you, ²⁴ leave your gift there before the altar and go. First be reconciled to your brother, and then come and offer your gift".
> - **Matthew 5:23-24 ESV**

We cannot worship effectively whilst there is bad blood between team members, or if we are critical of them. As Christians, if we do think that someone else's worship is offensive, we don't *react* to error, but *respond* with love, because we know God and therefore, know love. God is love. His language is love.

> "⁸ He who does not love does not know God, for God is love." - **1 John 4:8 NKJV**

> "And above all things have fervent love for one another, for "love will cover a multitude of sins."" – **1 Peter 4:8 NKJV**

Love overlooks wrongs. God is interested in a unified and loving bride. We must be in right relationship with one another when we worship. The end result of this kind of worship, i.e. when we are in unity (one accord), there is a blessing commanded for us – it is good and beautiful. As I mentioned earlier:

> "Behold, how good and pleasant it is when brothers dwell in unity!" – **Psalm 133:1 NKJV**

Worship and our love for God were always intended to be inseparable. You cannot have one without the other! If we do not worship from our hearts, we are not really worshipping at all!

2) Worship in Truth

If we have our hearts right before God, then our worship should naturally flow in truth, but what exactly does that mean? Let's again look at John 4:23. Jesus is talking to the Samaritan woman at the well who has just mentioned where people should worship. Jesus answers her and then adds,

> *"But the hour is coming, and now is, when the true worshippers shall worship the Father in spirit and in* **truth***: for the Father seeks such to worship him."* - **John 4:23 NKJV**

The Father is seeking those, who in spirit and truth, will worship Him, but what exactly does worshipping in *"Spirit and Truth"* mean?

Vines Expository Dictionary[6] gives this definition

> *"alethinos (αληθινοξ, 228), ... denotes "true" in the sense of real, ideal, genuine; It is used: ..... (g) His worshipers, John 4:23"*

Authenticity is essential in worship but even more so whilst on the platform and leading others. This is a difficult subject to broach. Nevertheless, as an individual worshipping in truth, all we do must be honouring to God and not just for "show" – otherwise, why bother! Who are we trying to impress if not God? Why are you there? Is our worship an outflow/outpouring of our hearts in response to Him, or just an "empty show" because that's expected on the platform – or worse, (for those in large ministry churches), because the camera happens to be pointed towards us? People are good recognizers of "fake" and insincerity, so don't be tempted to use clichés, pretend, or behave out of character because you think it's expected.

Smiling is not to what I am referring here. The Bible tells us not only to rejoice but that in His presence there is fullness of joy and at His right hand, pleasures forever more.

> *"You make known to me the path of life; in your presence there is fullness of joy; at your right hand are pleasures forevermore."* – **Psalm 16:11 ESV**

Smiling when you don't feel like it is not fake as much as stirring yourself up to rejoice and encourage others to do the same. We *decide* to rejoice - to enter into His joy.

Smiling is one thing, but as a worship leader, don't be tempted to be fake and to use clichés to stir up the congregation. Welcome the brethren to church, and invite them to journey with you. If not already done so by another, a prayer may be appropriate. Once you start, let the worship flow from your heart. Tom Inglis says:

> *"God wants our worship to be sincere, based on a personal relationship with the Holy Spirit and His word. Worship is the result of the Holy Spirit quickening God's word in your spirit and mind. This is what Jesus was alluding to above.* ***The Holy Spirit connects with your spirit and brings God's word alive in you so you can respond with worship.*** *For this reason worship cannot be manufactured, it has to be a response based on a genuine relationship with God and His word. Worship is such a personal thing between you and God. It removes all comparison and competition with others or judgment by them because no man knows the condition of your heart. You should never feel any condemnation when you worship, even though you might not be in a good place at the time."*[7]

This brings us to another point: Since worship occurs when the true Word is revealed to us through the Holy Spirit, (that is worship is our heart felt response to the truth of who God is) it suggests that the ***words we use in our worship songs must also be truth and in agreement with God's words.*** The Holy Spirit will not act on or through falsehood. Rather He guides us into all truth!

> *"[13] When the Spirit of truth comes, He will guide you into all the truth, for He will not speak on His own authority, but whatever He hears He will speak, and He will declare to you the things that are to come."* – **John 16:13 ESV**

The Holy Spirit reveals the truth of Jesus, and Jesus reveals to us the Father.

"6 Jesus said to him, "I am the way, and the truth, and the life. No one comes to the Father except through Me. 7 If you had known Me, you would have known My Father also. From now on you do know Him and have seen Him.

"11Believe Me that I am in the Father and the Father is in Me" – **John 14:6-7; 11 – ESV**

As we come to know Jesus more, we also see the Father, because Jesus is the express image of the Father. We begin to see His greatness and to understand the gravity of what He did for us. This makes our hearts grateful, causing us to stand in awe of the Creator of all things who also loves us so intensely. Moreover, as we behold Him (through the clarifying truth of the Holy Spirit's revelations to us), we are also changed into His image. (2 Corinthians 3:18) Can we, therefore, say that since we now live in Him and He in us, that it logically follows that we already live in truth and as such, must be worshipping in truth anyway? Jesus Himself tells us that when we abide in His Word we will *then* abide in that truth! It is be no means an automatic or given thing!

*"31 So Jesus said to the Jews who had believed Him, "If you **abide** in My word, you are truly My disciples, 32 and you will know the truth, and the truth will set you free."* – **John 8:31-32 ESV**

If we abide in His word we will know the truth. Further, if we do not abide in Him, we cannot do anything or merit – including worship!

*"I am the vine; you are the branches. Whoever abides in Me and I in him, he it is that bears much fruit, for apart from Me you can do **nothing**."* – **John 15:5 - ESV**

Apart from Him, *the* Truth, there is no way for us to worship as we should.

In summary thus far, now that it is no longer I who live but Christ who lives in me, I now have access by faith (Galatians 2:20) to the truth because Jesus, *the* Truth, lives in me. Nevertheless, I must also abide in this truth. To abide means to "live constantly within". Therefore, remaining and living in His love and truth is paramount. We abide by studying the word (not just reading but chewing the word over in are minds whilst asking the Holy Spirit to give insight and revelation) regularly and frequently, by praying and spending time with Him, and by being obedient to Him. These are essential to abiding in Truth. If we do not abide in Jesus who is the truth, how can we worship in truth?

When we love His truth and abide always in this truth, it will abide in us forever. We will know this truth throughout eternity.

> "*² because of the truth that abides in us and will be with us forever*" – **2 John 2 ESV**

Are we singing truth?

If we *know* the truth and seek to worship *in* truth, we need to be careful that the words we sing are also truth. Are the lyrics reflected in the Scriptures, or merely reflecting the doctrines and ideas of the songwriter? I am not trying to denigrate anyone's music or styles here. There is absolutely no reason why any song created for church worship, modern or old, cannot be totally in accordance with the word of God. (I'm not suggesting that every song's lyrics are a direct quote from the Bible - please hear my heart here - but that a song should *reflect* the truth the Bible contains. If it does not, why are you singing it in church?) We worship God for who He is. He is *the* Truth! The knowledge of truth comes from the *Word*.

Before I go on here, let me state up front that I am by no means suggesting that we become legalistic concerning the words we sing. However, as a music director, the words of the songs you sing from the platform are in essence another message that the congregation takes home with them each Sunday to sing again and again throughout the week. These words will be digested as truth and shape a person's thinking (even just by merit of repetition). It was Napoleon that said, "*Give me control over he who*

shapes the music of a nation, and I care not who makes the laws",
meaning that music has the power to indoctrinate, and therefore,
change the behaviour of people.

Naturally in a church setting, we want the singing of songs in
worship to have a positive effect on people's faith. Nevertheless,
if we are not checking what we allow to be sung on the platform,
while we may be preaching one thing, because the flock can be
singing words that may say something different (albeit a small
difference), are we not negating what is being taught? What then
does a person believe in a time of crisis – a time when the enemy
is throwing every lie at the believer in order to make him/her
succumb and give up? If I go home singing that I want more of
God, when hard times and crisis come, will I believe that God is
withholding and perhaps I need to be doing more to deserve
more, or maybe He doesn't really like me anyway? These are all
total lies that the enemy tries to feed us during a time of trial, but
could have easily been avoided had I sung truth in the first in-
stance.

It is true that God sees our heart as we worship, not the words
we sing. That's not in dispute here! However, as music director
you are also influencing the beliefs of those who are singing the
songs you choose for Sunday service! There is some measure of
responsibility required here!

Let me give you an example of the kind of words to which I am
referring, without naming the song(s). Under the New Covenant
our sins are completely washed away by the blood poured out on
Calvary. Jesus's sacrifice paid in full the debt that sin demanded.
Now that debt is paid, no one can bring to light your sins to demand retribution (now or any time in the future). Because these
sins have been dealt with, God remembers them no more.

However, there are songs that have the lyrics, *"He covers my sins."*
This may sound poetic but we are no longer under the Old Covenant, where the sacrifice of bulls and animals had no power to
eradicate sin. (Hebrews 10:4) Rather, we have been spiritually
birthed into the New Covenant, and we are now *completely* clean.

God won't one day uncover our old sins and point them out. That notion completely undermines the completed work of the cross and adds shadow to God's spotless character! (The verses in the *New* Testament that do deal with "*covering sins*" refer to a love between the brethren that refuses to see the sins of a brother/sister (i.e. "*love covers a multitude of sins*" – James 5:20; 1 Peter 4:8; and Romans 4:7) This brotherly affection continues to overlook the offence and to love even when we mess up, but this covering has nothing to do with how *God* deals with our sin.)

Okay, you might think that's a little nitpicky. Let's take a look at another example of untruths. Words that plead with God for more of His love, or that pleadfully stress, "*I want to be loved by You!*" Please note: **God does not withhold His love from us - EVER!** Rather, He gave everything, (Jesus) to show His love for us (John 3:16). His love has now been *shed abroad* in our hearts (Romans 5:5). The God who is love now lives in us. He is hardly going to reduce the measure of His love, after all that He has given in order to win you back to Himself, now. The concept that God will only give us a little more of His love when we behave or plead for it, is totally erroneous and not only undermines His character, but the power of the cross! God *so* loved! He constantly reaches His arms out to us in an invitation for us to accept it. It is *we*, His sons and daughters, that need to *accept* this love by faith. You are totally and *fully* loved!!

We are important to God. Now that Christ lives in us, do we really understand who we are in Christ? If we have not experienced this great love, perhaps we may need to check our own faith, (do we really believe we are loved) or even check our hearts (past hurts could have caused us to wall up our hearts), because the fault is certainly not God's.

> "*I have been crucified with Christ. It is no longer I who live, but Christ who lives in me. And the life I now live in the flesh I live **by faith** in the Son of God, who loved me and gave himself for me.*" – **Galatians 2:20 ESV**

> "[17] *so that Christ may dwell in your hearts through **faith**–*

*that you, being rooted and grounded in love, [18] may have
strength to* **comprehend** *with all the saints what is the
breadth and length and height and depth, [19] and to know the
love of Christ that surpasses knowledge, that you may be
filled with all the fullness of God."* – **Ephesians 3:17-19 ESV**

We must pray that we *comprehend* and *know* this love that surpasses knowledge, so that we can say with certainty in our own
minds that we are filled. Asking for more of the love you *already
have,* is just chasing feelings rather than truth.

Further, songs that plead using words such as "desperate", tar-
nish God's character as someone who would be stingy and only
give His love if we meet certain conditions. This is *far* from the
truth of God's word!

Sure, it could be that the composers, by saying, *"I want to be loved
by You"* or *"I want more"* or *"I'm desperate for You"*, are merely trying to express that they're not *satisfied* with their current level of
relationship with God. They want to *know* Him and His great love
more. However, the choice of lyrics suggests otherwise. To be
honest, not everyone who goes home singing those words will be
scrutinising the words before they sing them, and there remains
a strong probability that they will take the words at face value.
This means that for them, God has now become withholding,
stingy and waiting for them to measure up somehow - even if
only at a subconscious level that may spill out at a later date.

I understand also that songwriters are writing using an emotional art form, and thus, the songs are born out of the composer's emotions. However, *if we are saturated in the Word, the
songs that flow out of us will be based on the truth of His Word, because we know it.* It is living and active in us and in our hearts.

I make this point not because I have a bone to pick with song
writers or because I believe God will be angry and refuse to accept our worship – that's utter nonsense, but because you (the
music director) are also responsible for the spiritual food you
give the congregation each week! You are delivering words from

a platform of teaching and influence, and as such, you have a *"spiritual duty of care"*, to ensure there is no ambiguity, or corrupting doctrine within the songs we choose to use in our services. In fact James warns us, *"Not many of you should become teachers, my brothers, for you know that we who teach will be judged with greater strictness."* (James 3:1 ESV). You may not call yourself a teacher but a worship leader. Nevertheless, you are still instructing from the platform.

Just one little aside here with regard to song writing: When I was first saved, many songs flowed out of my spirit and onto paper as I read the word. However, as I began to grow in Christ I was also introduced to other doctrines that gave a different slant on things. Being rather green behind the ears and not knowing any better, I took the doctrine at face value and altered my songs accordingly. As I matured and studied the word in more depth, I soon realised that the initial words were, in fact, correct, so had to change them back. It was the Holy Spirit who had inspired me originally, but it was my *responsibility* to check this against the word of God, and had I done so initially, the changes would never have occurred.

Let me say again, as worship directors who are responsible for the kinds of songs we allow on the platform, we need to be so careful that the words we are singing are not in error but truth, and so avoid diminishing in our congregation's eyes, God's greatness and the power of His love towards us. Moreover, how can we tell God He is something He is not, or doing something that is simply not true? We honour God when we honour His truth and His character!

Therefore, the word of God should dwell in us richly. Paul instructs us:

> *"Let the word of Christ dwell in you richly, teaching and admonishing one another in all wisdom, singing psalms and hymns and spiritual songs, with thankfulness in your hearts to God"* - **Colossians 3:16 ESV**

We need the Word to dwell in us richly that we can admonish each other and sing psalms, hymns and spiritual songs. As I mentioned earlier, how much Word we have in us will be how much truth proceeds from our mouths when we admonish one another and sing songs of worship. These songs will even instruct the brethren!

To this end, some have argued that the lyrics of our modern worship songs are "*theologically shallow*". There may or may not be some truth in that statement. Some songs are padded out with copious "oohs" and "aahs", and have little to say, but conversely, the same can be said of older songs/hymns too.

To be quite blunt, there are, in fact, a couple of things *wrong* with the statement that modern church songs are theologically shallow:

i) Songs can contain Spiritual truth without being direct Biblical quotes:

I have heard some people say that the only songs that should be used in church should be word for word with Scripture and be predominantly from Biblical songs or Psalms. However, King David, himself, wrote from his heart – not from the writings of Moses, which were his Scriptures of the day! (Though I will add that his songs still contained the wisdom and truth from those Scriptures and he even borrows the occasional descriptive phrase from time to time – e.g. "*the blast of your nostrils*" Exodus 15:8; Psalm 18:15. David in turn, sings about the smoke or wrath of His nostrils in 2 Samuel 22:9)

Worship flows (or should flow) from the heart. It is a heart response as we have already discussed. Theology and the Word will naturally flow in songs created by those who *spend time in His word*. It may not be word for word, chapter and verse, but a summation of truth that the Bible contains nonetheless. The Holy Spirit can still use (and does use) these songs mightily.

Also consider where most of the *songs* in the Bible originate - the

Old Testament! Apart from those few prophetic portions that allude to the coming Messiah, none mention Jesus and what He has done. Apart from Mary's song (the "Magnificat") upon visiting her cousin Elizabeth, and Zechariah's prophecy/song after the birth of John the Baptist, what New Testament songs do we actually have? If we are insistent that our worship music should be only the songs from the Old Testament, then we miss out on lifting up the name of Jesus!

Another consideration is that these Old Testament songs are born out of the Jewish (OT) covenant and sometime can be in opposition to the New Creations truth of the cross. For example: There was a song from a few years back that can directly from Psalm 51:10-11. That is

> *"¹⁰Create in me a clean heart, O God,*
> *and renew a right spirit within me.*
> *¹¹ Cast me not away from your presence,*
> *and take not your Holy Spirit from me."* - **Psalm 51:10-11 ESV**

Firstly, our hearts have already been made clean by the finished work of Christ. Some will argue that even Jesus said that man's heart was wicked in Mark 7:21

> *"²⁰ And He said, "What comes out of a person is what defiles him. ²¹ For from within, out of the heart of man, come evil thoughts, sexual immorality, theft, murder, adultery, ²² coveting, wickedness, deceit, sensuality, envy, slander, pride, foolishness."* - **Mark 7:20-22 - ESV**

Jesus here is making a point about *trying* to be righteous by doing ritualistic practices, nevertheless, yes, the unredemptive man *does* have a wicked heart, but for the born again man, *"it is no longer I who live but Christ who lives in me"*. Christ has a pure heart! Therefore, the born again man has a pure heart too. Scripture agrees with this.

> *"And I will give you a **new heart**, and a new spirit I will put*

within you. And I will remove the heart of stone from your flesh and give you a heart of flesh. And I will put my Spirit within you, and cause you to walk in my statutes and be careful to obey my rules" - **Ezekiel 36:26-27 ESV**

*"Let us draw near with a **true heart** in full assurance of faith, **with our hearts sprinkled clean** from an evil conscience and our bodies washed with pure water."* - **Hebrews 10:22 ESV**

*"9 and He made no distinction between us and them, having **cleansed their hearts by faith.**"* - **Acts 15:9 ESV**

Not only is the born again heart clean but the born again man has a right spirit and will not be cast away from God's presence. Rather He calls us sons and daughters and tells us to draw boldly to the throne of grace!

This song (*"Create in Me a Clean Heart"*) is totally in opposition to the finished work of Christ, and if you continue to sing it in church, people will go home singing it, believing all that it implies. My old pastor back in Ballarat, instructed me (the then music director) to never sing that song in service because it was totally *not* suitable for any born again believer to be singing, and he was totally right!!

This is not to say that Scripture cannot be used in songs. On the contrary! If we take the truth of the Word and set that truth to music (that is, portions that are the complete truth under the New Covenant), it can be powerful union!

Indeed, singing the actual Scriptures is very powerful, and I personally loved the *"Scripture in Song"* albums when they were available a few years ago. Singing the Scripture not only helps people to learn the Word of God, but when used in worship, the Holy Spirit can take the Word (logos) and impregnate it with His power (dunamis). It is a bringing forth revelation that builds faith for miracles to happen – and they do! Singing God's truth should be our aim.

Ultimately though, remember it is not the amount of *theology* we sing in the worship, or the number of directly quoted verses that we sing, that pleases God! God is seeking those who worship in spirit and truth! He is looking for *genuine lovers* of God - sons and daughters who, like David, also delight in worshipping. These are the worshippers with whom He is well pleased.

ii) The Holy Spirit has NOT Become Silent!

The other issue with this mindset of "Biblical words only", is that it restricts and confines the Holy Spirit inspiration to the days of the early church and those of the Old Testament. The truth is that the Holy Spirit has *not* become silent! He still inspires, and still speaks prophetically to us today.

The Bible tells us that the gift of the Holy Spirit was not merely a Pentecost occurence but for us today as well.

> "*38 And Peter said to them, "Repent and be baptized every one of you in the name of Jesus Christ for the forgiveness of your sins, and you will receive the gift of the Holy Spirit. 39 For the promise is for you and for your children and for all who are far off, everyone whom the Lord our God calls to Himself."* – **Acts 2:38-39 ESV**

> "*13 If you then, who are evil, know how to give good gifts to your children, how much more will the Heavenly Father give the Holy Spirit to those who ask Him!"* - **Luke 11:13 ESV**

It is therefore, absurd to conclude that the Holy Spirit who leads us into *all* truth (John 16:13) (which suggests giving us greater depth of revelations and clarity concerning the Scriptures) no longer gives revelations, prophecies and words of knowledge! He was sent to guide us, and teach us to live as we aught; to tell us what to say as we stand before men. God who does not change! Why would He suddenly become silent?

I'm not talking about creating some new doctrine or teaching, (no way!) but to hearing His instructions and guidance. The proviso here is that we must be sure it is the Holy Spirit who is speaking - not the flesh, nor the demonic- and the test for the validity of the prophetically inspired message / revelation is whether what you hear Him say is *in agreement with Scriptures* or not. He will *never* contradict the Scriptures, because God's words are absolute truth, and He will not contradict Himself for that would suggest it wasn't truth to begin with. Therefore, any modern revelation must be seen first in the Scriptures and not be contrary to them if it is truly Holy Spirit inspired! This proviso does not mean the Holy Spirit does not speak today, but it is a test for us to ensure it is actually God who is speaking!

Since the Holy Spirit still speaks to us in revelation and prophecy, why shouldn't He use music to deliver that message? People are happy to receive prophetic revelation not just from a prophet but through day-to-day occurrences, or things they see or hear repeated. After all, God speaks in many ways. Music is just another conveyor of His messages. Yes, the Scriptures are the final authority, and the highest benchmark, but are not the only Spiritually inspired words.

As an example: The Holy Spirit did directly give me an entire verse and chorus of a song once - all the words and the music – chords, everything! I walked into my bedroom with view to worshipping on my guitar, but first headed straight over to the dressing table to brush my hair back out of the way before I began. (Had very long hair then.) I had hardly put my brush to my hair when it began to flow. Hurriedly I ran to my guitar and manuscript to try to jot this song down as fast as I could. It was definitely a prophetic song (or prophetic word set to music) that God was giving to me. The words were:

> Verse 1:
> *Can you hear His voice calling you?*
> *He's wanting you to come near.*
> *Can you feel His love pouring out from His heart*
> *- Love He died to give.*
> *He waits patiently for you to seek*
> *The springs of Living Waters.*

His voice echoes in the wind,
Can you hear His words of life?

Chorus:
"Yes, I am the Light that will never ever fade
And Mine is the joy
That will chase your pain away
My love for you is so great!"

Now some may say that this song can't have been directly inspired because it wasn't verse and chapter from the Bible, and besides, what's this *"voice echoing in the wind"* bit anyway! That doesn't sound Scriptural! The Holy Spirit has often been described as the wind of God, and He echoes the thoughts and words of God the Father to us. Also God's angels have been described as winds (*"He makes his messengers winds, His ministers a flaming fire."* - Psalm 104:4 ESV) who carry God's message – not their own. They too, are echoing His words! Any way you examine it, the message was in line with Scripture!

Besides, at that time I wasn't long saved, knew nothing about the prophetic other than in vague stories, and had no grid for any of this. All I know was that it happened without my intervention, and it was not only honouring to God, but when I sang it to some people on a Christian camp not long after I penned it, a young woman reported to me afterwards that it really effected her, touching her deeply on a spiritual level.

My point in sharing that event was again, not to make a big deal of myself, but to illustrate that the Holy Spirit can still speak through songs. They do not have to be word for word from the Scripture, **but** should nonetheless *be in accordance with the Scriptures* and definitely **not** contrary to them.

iii) Is modern worship, in fact, theologically shallow?

I have a science background. When I hear statements such as "Modern worship songs are theologically shallow", I wonder on what basis these claims are made.

Firstly, many of the *classics* that have survived the test of time do contain many thoughts and quotes from the Bible, and some beautiful poetry and sentiment as well. However, there have also been many hundreds to thousands of worship songs written through the ages that simple have *not* survived.

Some time ago I actually perused a very old hymnal and was surprised to see that there were many hymns I did not know, and whose words were quite frankly shallow and cliché as well. On the other side of the coin, there are modern songs, that like the classics, also carry those same Biblical truths. It would appear that this impression that the old was better, really depends on the songs to which you are currently listening and with which you are familiar, *and* your own personal preference and bias.

In fact, when analyzed in any depth, the "not theologically deep enough" complaint is itself a subjective and shallow one.

Secondly, where is the benchmark for how much theology is enough to take it out of the shallow category? I feel the real contention lies not with the amount of Biblical teaching, but between honouring Scriptures whilst still being true to the heart.

To be blunt: In order for the argument that "*modern songs are theologically shallow compared to the old Hymns*" to be true, someone would need to have conducted a proper comparison, not just give an *opinion* based on personal experience and limited personal observations.

This comparative study would firstly need to outline the benchmark: what exactly would be enough theology? Another criteria would be to set date limits. What fits the category of "*old*" hymns? Are we talking only those written by Charles Wesley, for example? Are we considering all Christian songs written from (let's just say) the time of Luther to the turn of the twentieth century?

What time frame are you using? You would also have to designate a time frame for modern Christian church music. Are you talking about only those written in the last year or so? If so the comparison is already biased – of course there will be more hymns if the time frames are so skewed.

Would a better comparison be the number of songs that fit the category as a *percentage* of the total number of praise & worship songs written year by year? And how do you decide over what period of years the study should scrutinize song lyrics? Even once you make that decision, you would still need to decide what years fall into the "old hymns" and "modern" categories! Further, once parameters for the study are set, a team of people would have to sift through and analyse every song written during those years, so that some true tally could be ascertained.

Besides being extraordinarily difficult to carry out, too many songs have been lost to antiquity and only classics have survived (as mentioned in my first point). Not only that but to compare with modern songs, you would have to be able to collect them all – old and new alike! Do you use only the most popular songs used and on what do you base popularity – record sales, lyric books sales, and/or CCLI licensing payments etc.? Is popularity even a consideration? What about songs that churches use frequently that are home grown and have never been published? Shouldn't they be considered in this comparison since they are modern too? How do you even begin to collect these?

Take this more recent song for example:

The Fountain of Life

Verse:
Your love, O Lord, reaches to Heaven;
Your faithfulness – to the skies.
You always hear the cries,
And the needs are not passed by
Of those You call Your own.

How precious is Your loving kindness;
You preserve all Your children
Beneath Your loving wings.
We're blest with all good things,
At the table of the King.

Pre-Chorus:
Your love;
It never fails to uphold,
It's priceless more than gold,
No matter who men are,
All find refuge in Your love.

Chorus:
You have the fountain of life.
In Your Light we see light to live,
Your light shines before us.

You have the well springs of joy.
Let the praise go on and on.
Jesus,
You are the fountain of life!

Compare this to Psalm 36. I think you would agree that this song contains much of that Psalm's sentiment and even some direct quotations, but you will never have heard this sung before. How do I know this? Because I wrote this for my congregation a few years ago, but was not interested in making records and albums, so it was never published or released to the world.

Many, many modern church bands write their own music. My example is only one.

iv) The Real Root Issue

As alluded to earlier, it is this "*theology versus emotion*" in church songs that appears to be the real root of the issue. For many, an outward show of emotion is uncomfortable, especially in a public setting. It is seen as a private display only between you and God. Emotionalism is even frowned upon by some people as unscriptural and too "me" focussed.

However, David wasn't ashamed to say how he felt, even if the situation was very dark.

"*I am weary with my moaning; every night I flood my bed*

with tears; I drench my couch with my weeping. [7] My eye wastes away because of grief; it grows weak because of all my foes." - **Psalm 6:6-7 ESV**

(As I will discuss emotion in worship in a later chapter, I will be brief here.) As we know, in David's Psalms, for every negative emotion he poured into His songs, he usually encouraged himself by the *"but God....."* before the end of the song! He always saw God as the answer. He trusted in God despite the circumstances. Despite this raw display of emotion, modern composers will generally avoid these kind of negative emotions and focus more on the positives, such as joy, love, hope etc., so that congregations are encouraged by them.

We see from the Psalms many examples, that emotion and "being real" with God in a song is perfectly fine with God, as He included them in the Scriptures for us to read and sing! I would add the caveat that in order for modern churches to use these songs, there is the proviso that the focus of the songs turn back to the amazing attributes of God and His abilities to rescue and overcome, because His character is perfect, His power and wisdom are infinite, and His love for us is limitless, AND it is also New Testament Biblical truth!

****

I hope through this discourse, I have shown that the *"theologically shallow"* argument **cannot** be substantiated in any way. It is very **subjective** in origin, yet many seem to have accepted it as absolute fact. In light of this, I believe we should be careful that we do not use arguments like these unsupported statements to take a crack at modern music because we have discovered yet another song we feel does not measure up to our own personal standards. This is rather divisive in nature, and something that I prefer to avoid when it rears its head in discussion. Enough said!

You are the worship leader – the music director of your church. It is your job to see that the songs you use for your worship contain only truth. It means you are responsible to check all the lyrics of all songs before usage to ensure Biblical truth. Remember, people will often go home singing the songs they hear at church and believe what they are singing because they heard it at church. Needless to say, the buck stops with you. You are responsible for what songs are played on the platform. Old or new is irrelevant! Too little or too much theology is subjective and really will just tie you up in knots. Choose wisely and under the guidance of the Holy Spirit. Let the truth of the Word of God and the leading of the Holy Spirit help you to decide. If you are not sure about introducing a new song, have a chat to your senior pastor.

In conclusion then: **Truth** is absolute because God is absolute - without any shades of grey, without any shadow or variation (James 1:17). If we are to worship in truth, there can be no error in who we say He is, and no pretense. Our worship needs to be authentic and genuine, based on the truth and the character of the One True God, and poured out of our hearts as a response to Him in gratitude and love.

3) Worship in Spirit

A most essential aspect of worship is that it is done in Spirit. Jesus stated that true worshippers would worship in *spirit* and truth. **The essential element in our worship is the operation of the Holy Spirit.** Note that Jesus did not say that worshippers would worship *from* their spirits but *in* spirit. It is a spiritual act and it is the Holy Spirit who reveals the Father to us and leads us into perfect praise. The Holy Spirit must be the ultimate worship leader.

> *"There is no work of God in which the members of the Trinity are not jointly operative. This is true of creation, redemption and worship. It is by the perfecting causality of the Spirit that the Church's worship offered in the Son reaches the Father. As a perfecter, **the Spirit leads us** to the Son, through whom our being and our act (worship) have free access to the Fatherly sanctuary in the same Godhead.*

*Only Spirit-perfected worship is **true worship**. Not only the Spirit joined through the Son to the Father is the proper object, but also the **causative agency of worship**, the one who exalts the community in Christ to the heavenly throne of the Father. . . . Worship as such is a gift of grace: what God begins in us He shall complete. God is the alpha and the omega of worship."*[8]

As mentioned already, praise and worship is not simply extolling God's marvelous virtues and greatness. Worship is Holy Spirit dependent. Paul says:

> *"For we are the circumcision, who worship God **in the spirit**, and rejoice in Christ Jesus, and have **no confidence in the flesh**."* - **Philippians 3:3 NKJV**

The Holy Spirit is our teacher and guide through life, but it is also the Holy Spirit who teaches and guides us in our worship to the Father.

> *"[14] He will glorify Me, for He will take what is Mine and declare it to you."* – **John 16:14 ESV**

Jesus also said in the breath before that verse that it is the Holy Spirit who would lead us into all truth.

> *"However, when He, the Spirit of truth, has come, He will guide you into all truth"* – **John 16:13a NKJV**

If we want our worship to be conducted in truth, surely we must follow the One who will *guide us into* all truth! The Holy Spirit is God. He knows all about God because He is God. He reveals this knowledge to us, and in response we cry out from our hearts, *"Worthy is God Almighty to receive all praise and honour!"*

> *" For what man knows the things of a man except the spirit of the man which is in him? Even so no one knows the things of God except the Spirit of God."* - **1 Corinthians 2:11 NKJV**

Because He is God, not only does He give us revelation that causes us to praise Him, but He will also show us how best to worship truthfully, and further perfect that worship if we but listen to Him and follow His lead.

I believe that without the Holy Spirit, we may be singing faithfully about God, and totally theologically correct, but it isn't really worshipping in spirit and truth as Jesus describes. We are just satisfying ourselves by fulfilling some sense of duty, rather than offering our genuine heart felt love and adoration in response to Holy Spirit revelation. If we want to truly worship correctly, we cannot possibly ignore the ministry of the Holy Spirit in worship!

Tom Inglis, author of "The Ministry of the Psalmist" [9], explains it this way:

> "*The Father wants the Holy Spirit to help us worship. He requires us to have dependency on the Holy Spirit for every worship service. It would be futile to consider leading worship without the Holy Spirit's help. The Holy Spirit is the one who comforts, guides and helps us to effectively live the Christian life. Without His presence in our lives on a daily basis, we could not pray or worship, as we should. Scripture says that the Holy Spirit knows the things of God. He knows how we can satisfy His heart with our worship at every meeting.*"

Further, just as Jesus only did what He saw the Father doing, so we too only do what we see the Holy Spirit doing (or should). Paul calls this walking in step with the Holy Spirit.

> "*24 And those who belong to Christ Jesus have crucified the flesh with its passions and desires. 25 If we live by the Spirit, let us also keep in step with the Spirit.*" – **Galatians 5:25-26 ESV**

We are spirit beings who are now fused with Christ and led by the Spirit, not the flesh. Our lives are not our own. We are expected to *follow*, to keep *in step with* the Holy Spirit, and be obedient to Him – not because God is a hard taskmaster, but because we love Him and want to please Him in all we do. Love gives! Love serves! In fact, obedience to God is a good test of our love for Him.

(In the chapter "*Worship Leading in the Holy Spirit Flow*" I will discuss just how we can worship in Spirit, (i.e. follow the lead of the Holy Spirit), and remain in that flow whilst encouraging the congregation in the same direction.)

4) No other gods / God Centred Worship

Even though the command to have no other gods before our God, was part of the Old Covenant, and even though we are now governed by the New Covenant, God's opinion on the matter has not changed, nor does He change His mind on such important issues. Let me state the obvious: He does not need our worship, but He knows that for us to worship Him, blesses us, and to worship anything else ultimately produces the opposite. In fact, worshipping oneself, human kind, or human thought, or worshipping demons and false gods, was forbidden because it leads to deception and death. Worshipping God with complete trust in Him, leads to life and life in abundance. Like any good father, He wants what is best for us.

Worship was rightfully for God alone, even before the Law came into play. It would appear God's thoughts on the matter have always been the same: Worship is for Him alone! (I will discuss these acts of worship in more detail shortly.)

When God gave Moses the Ten Commandments, God's first three instructions out of ten were to do with worshipping Him and Him alone. (Exodus 20) If you had the awesome task of writing up a list of laws for a group of people, how many of us would make the principal laws those to do with worship. But God thought it of primary importance.

The commandments stated that there should be no other gods before Him, there should be no idols, and that His name must not be used in vain. (Ex 20:2-7) It was priority for God.

"2 "I am the Lord your God, who brought you out of the land of Egypt, out of the house of slavery.

3 "You shall have no other gods before me.

4 "You shall not make for yourself a carved image, or any likeness of anything that is in heaven above, or that is in the earth beneath, or that is in the water under the earth.

5 You shall not bow down to them or serve them, for I the Lord your God am a jealous God, visiting the iniquity of the fathers on the children to the third and the fourth generation of those who hate me, 6 but showing steadfast love to thousands of those who love me and keep my commandments.

7 "You shall not take the name of the Lord your God in vain, for the Lord will not hold him guiltless who takes his name in vain." – **Exodus 22:2-7 ESV**

Jesus also repeats God's instructions when the devil tempts Him while fasting in the wilderness.

"And Jesus answered him, "It is written, "'You shall worship the Lord your God, and him only shall you serve.'" – **Luke 4:8 ESV**

God wants us to *so* worship Him until He becomes the very *centre* of our every day lives. Even in the wilderness the Israelites had to assemble their camp so that the tabernacle containing the Ark of the Covenant and the Holy of Holies should be right in the centre. God wanted them to be reminded of His presence constantly, no matter what they were doing. He was to be the centre of their lives.

Even today if you go to Israel, one thing that will strike you about the culture is that God is still the focus. The way of life is still set around Him! He is first in everything!

Likewise, He *must* be first in our lives! (If you feel that this is a given in your own life, consider: What is the first thing you turn to when you wake in the morning? Is it God or your phone? Does God have the same attention as your email, or social media etc.? Something to think about!)

The other problem you have as a worship leader is ensuring that He *is* the centre of the worship. The enemy of your soul hates this, and will try to distract you for listening to the Holy Spirit and worshipping in truth. The easiest and most effective method he employs is to needle our pride. He loves to whisper things about how wonderful you are when you minister, or how marvelously talented you are, or even how good it feels to be praised. You must be the best worship leader around! All the people come to church just to hear you!

It we are not keeping ourselves in check we can believe these things, and forge our identity around them. But we cannot - must not! God alone deserves all the glory. We are just His instruments, and therefore, must ensure that all praise is directed to Him and not our egos. It can be difficult when people want to congratulate or speak highly of your talents, but in your heart, that praise must go to God. I'm sure you have all struggled with this. In fact, I'm sure that every person who ministers on the platform has had to deal with this in some form at some time in their ministries. Just when you think you've got it under wraps, it pops up again. This is why we must guard our hearts with all diligence.

However, there is yet another sneaky way that the enemy tickles our egos, to encourage us to be looking for the glory as well. It is not so obvious as thoughts popping into our heads, and unless there is some attention drawn to it, you may never notice it.

Let me say first of all, that it is your job as worship leader to lead the music so that the congregation can set their hearts and minds on Jesus and give Him all the praise and honour He is due. If you do anything which distracts or detracts from that job description then you have failed as a worship leader! Sounds fair!

What are some of these distractions. The biggest one I see happen so often in churches, is worship leaders who want to change the melody line everytime they sing it. Why? The congregation cannot sing with you if they have no idea what changes or enhancements to the melody you are about to sing.

How many times has a congregation that had had their eyes closed and their hearts fixed on Jesus, been suddenly drawn back to look at what's happening on the platform because they could no longer join in.

You might be tempted to respond by saying, *"But I'm just embellishing it and making it sound better. After all, God deserves our best!"* We can justify anything with arguments that sound so altruistic, but the true motivation of the heart is what God sees. To be blunt: your job is to lead the congregation, not to ad lib embellishments or enhancements along the way.

If you and your team always sing it that way and the congregation are used to you doing that, there is no problem. They will follow without being distracted. Unfortunately, this has not been my observation for the most part.

Check your heart if you go "off on your own regularly". Are you really (perhaps even subconsciously) attention seeking? Do you want to hear people say how beautifully you sing, or how musically skilled you are? Does this make you feel good about yourself?

Our identities must be based solely on who God says we are. Do we look like Jesus? If your identity is in what people say about your ministry, be very careful. In the Old Testament, how did God feel about the worship *not* given to Him? He hated it! Has He changed? No! If *our* worship isn't for Him alone, He hates it too. This is a hard word, but it is of utmost importance for our sakes. Better to ensure our hearts are right before God than to be chastised by the Lord, because if we refuse to listen, it could be in a public setting that He chooses to open our eyes.

The Why, What & How

I have already discussed the four essentials that God requires as true worshippers. However, to some degree I have assumed that everyone reading this, (especially worship leaders), already understand completely what I mean by "worship". Unfortunately, as the term can be used to describe a number of activities, some clarification is required before I launch any further in this topic. As such, my discussion in this chapter will be centred around the "why", the "what is" and the Biblical "how" of worship. So for the sake of little to no ambiguity, it may be worth the time spent to read on, rather than to skip ahead. ☺

The Question of Why

As briefly discussed in the last section of the last chapter, we could argue that God already knows how good He is, so why worship? He is the Ultimate One – the Most Supreme God who is totally perfect in every way, and He has no one above Him or equal to Him. He is the ALL mighty God, who is from everlasting to everlasting. He doesn't need our worship. So why are we commanded to worship? Well, the answer is that *He* doesn't need our worship, but *we* need to worship Him for our own sake.

Let's look at some very good reasons to worship. (Though I have numbered the points for clarity sake, this numbering in no way represents an order of priority.)

Firstly, *He is worthy to be praised.* He is not some sugar daddy who is only there to bring personal fulfillment, or to fill our endless list of requests. Nor is He some tyrant in the sky that must be appeased. He is our loving Father, yes, but also creator of all things, who has/is ultimate power over all. He deserves our respect and honour! Such awesome power deserves acknowledgement and reverence.

He is also the One who is ultimate love and who cares for us as our Father, having even gone to extreme lengths to prove this love by sending Jesus as our ransom. He deserves our adoration!

Secondly, *we were created to love and worship Him.* Peter states in his first epistle our purpose here:

> *"But you are a chosen generation, a royal priesthood, an holy nation, a peculiar people; that you* ***should show forth*** *[declare]* ***the praises of Him*** *who has called you out of darkness into His marvelous light"* - **1 Peter 2:9 KJV**

We are to declare His praises. In John's Revelation, wonderful descriptions are given of heaven and the worship that is given to God eternally. We will eternally give Him praise and worship. It has been said that the only ministries in Heaven will be those of worship leaders. (An interesting thought though I'm not sure that that opinion has any Scriptural basis.)

Throughout Scripture the only times that God gets particularly angry is when people are either worshipping false gods or trusting in themselves instead of Him. His anger isn't born out of insecurity but because the reason we have been created has been violated, and we will ultimately hurt ourselves.

> *"The chief end of man is to glorify God and enjoy Him forever."* - **Westminster Catechism**

Judson Cornwall was quoted by Don McMinn[10] as saying:

> *"Worship is written upon the heart of man by the hand of God... In a broad sense worship is inseparable from and is an expression of life. It is not that man cannot live without worship, it is that he cannot truly live without worship..... man was made to worship as surely as he was made to*

breathe. We may restrict the expression of worship for a season, just as we may hold our breath, but there is an inward craving for worship that cannot be permanently stilled."

I love that description! We were created to worship God. That inbuilt ability is within each one of us. You can praise Him even though circumstances are bad and emotions are at an all time low, because we were created to worship the Lord. That ability doesn't disappear with the way we feel. It's part of our very being. We were created in His glorious image that we might reflect back that glory. If Jesus were to manifest Himself to us today, we couldn't help but worship Him. It's who we are, and what we were created for!

Thirdly, *it is our natural response to the divine revelation* of who He is, and all the wonders He has done. This is because we were created for worship! When we sing or speak of all His wonderful works, and even His marvelous and miraculous works in our own lives, it causes the praise and gratitude to rise in our hearts. Our worship is an outward flow of our inward man exalting Him. Our spirits cry out joyfully, "*You are worthy, Lord, to receive all honour, power and praise!"* It's not a matter of legalism but simply a natural response to who He is and what He has done!

Fourthly, *as we praise Him our faith in Him is built up and energized.* We remind ourselves of the great things He has done, that nothing is too difficult for Him, and of His amazing goodness towards us. We encourage ourselves in the Lord just like King David did.

As we worship, we abandon what is happening in this earthly realm, to focus completely on Him. Time spent in His presence worshipping during times of trouble, speaks of our complete trust in Him. He wants us to trust Him because that is faith. Without faith it is impossible to please Him. (Hebrews 11:6) He wants us to have faith in Him because He is completely faithful. Do we trust Him or our circumstances? As we worship, our faith is released. This faith or trust in God allows Him to step into our situations with power. (Compare this where Jesus could do very little because they lacked faith – Matthew 13:58) This brings me to the next reason.

Fifthly, *it is for our benefit* to worship. As previously stated, He doesn't need our worship. He knows that He is the ultimate One above all else. He has no insecurities that only our worship will overcome. He is perfect in every way. It is *we* who need to worship Him. We could just sit and talk with God, but it is we who would be missing out!! Imagine for a moment, husbands and wives just talking all the time, but never being intimate! Intimacy is on a much deeper level of knowing and sharing. Likewise, worship is a much deeper act of love than conversation/prayer. We are blessed in His presence! It is a joy to our souls! In every way, it is for our benefit to worship God. *He* doesn't need it, *we* do!!! This is His gift to us – not as a chore, but with delight.

Sixthly, *there is another layer of anointing available* when worshipping in one accord with the body of believers, that exceeds that of the solo act of private prayer and worship. Yes, that's a bold statement, but let me elaborate!

Private time with God is usually a very intimate time, and born out of our relationship with Him. We talk to Him about our deepest needs and desires and He talks tenderly back to us. We repent of any sins – deliberate or unrealized. We give Him thanks and praise, especially for all He has done in our own lives, and for all His promises to us. We intercede for others through the Holy Spirit and edify ourselves while we pray in tongues. It can be loud soft, singing or verbal but it is mostly very personal.

One the other hand, where two or three are gathered together, Jesus is in our midst.

> *"For where two or three are gathered together in My name, I am there in the midst of them."* – **Matthew 18:20 - NKJV**

So this infers another level of His presence, since He already lives in each one of us.

> *"I have been crucified with Christ; it is no longer I who live, but Christ lives in me; and the life which I now live in the flesh I live by faith in the Son of God, who loved me and gave Himself for me."* – **Galatians 2:20 - NKJV**

Was Jesus merely saying that there was more of Him collectively when we come together, since He lives in each one? It is doubtful! That interpretation also feels awkward and forced. Consider the verse from Psalms:

> *"Behold, how good and how pleasant it is*
> *For brethren to dwell together in unity!*
> *² It is like the precious oil upon the head,*
> *Running down on the beard,*
> *The beard of Aaron,*
> *Running down on the edge of his garments.*
> *³ It is like the dew of Hermon,*
> *Descending upon the mountains of Zion;*
> ***For there the Lord commanded the blessing—***
> ***Life forevermore."*** – **Psalm 133 - NKJV**

That blessing of life is a *result* of the unified gathering. Likewise, when we come togther whether to pray or for our church services, the *result* is that there He manifests in our midst another level or layer of presence. To worship as a church in this atmosphere is, therefore, greatly desirable.

I am also tempted to add, *"God Inhabits the Praises of His People!"* as it seems to be in keeping with the verse from Matthew 18. However, the psalm does not quite mean that which many people have interpreted and even used in their sermons and books. On first glance we see:

> *"But thou art holy, O thou that inhabitest the praises of Israel"* – **Psalm 22:3 – KJV**

But look at yet another translation (or several) and you will quickly see that the intention was quite different.

> *"Yet You are holy, enthroned on the praises of Israel."* –

Psalm 22:3 - ESV

In fact, any in depth study of the verse, renders it in keeping with the second translation and not the first. He is magnified as we praise Him, but that is quite different to God living in our praises, though I admit, I do like that thought. Actually the plain truth is that now we live in Christ Jesus and He inhabits *us*!

The Holy Spirit then crowns the corporate worship as He comes in power and blesses the Bride. It is like an explosion of power from the Heavenlies. I can confidently make this claim because after the coming of the Holy Spirit in chapter 2 of Acts, in chapter 4 Peter, whilst in the midst of the assembly, prayed for boldness and the Holy Spirit came and filled them afresh.

> *"29 And now, Lord, look upon their threats and grant to your servants to continue to speak your word with all boldness, 30 while you stretch out your hand to heal, and signs and wonders are performed through the name of your holy servant Jesus." 31 And when they had prayed, the place in which they were gathered together was shaken, and they were all **filled with the Holy Spirit** and continued to speak the word of God with boldness."* – **Acts 4:29-31 ESV**

This was the second Holy Spirit filling recorded, and not merely a filling for boldness alone. Those Holy Spirit fillings are blessings that bring healing to the many sick in the church; they can be of prophecies – encouraging, building up, and exhorting the body; they can be the deepening of faith with revelations of God as all powerful and for whom nothing is impossible. The blessings can also be a time of great joy and of healing of passed hurts and emotional bruising; they can be the setting of captives free of addictions and harmful habits, and they can forge greater unity and chords of love between the brothers and sisters in the body. During these times there can also be repentance and forgiveness, or whatever the Holy Spirit deems His Bride needs at that moment.

It is a deeper layer of anointing, often taking the people where they could not go in their own personal quiet time, especially when the Holy Spirit leads people to repent as a church, or heal possible rifts of division within the church.

Another example is when the Jews were all in one accord, gathered together simply to offer God their worship in the newly built temple of Solomon, the glory of the Lord fell among them like a cloud.

> "*10 And it came to pass, when the priests came out of the holy place, that the cloud filled the house of the Lord, 11 so that the priests could not continue ministering because of the cloud; for the glory of the Lord filled the house of the Lord*"
> – **1 Kings 8:10-11**

> "*13 indeed it came to pass, when the trumpeters and singers were as one, to make one sound to be heard in praising and thanking the Lord, and when they lifted up their voice with the trumpets and cymbals and instruments of music, and praised the Lord, saying:*
>
> *"For He is good,*
> *For His mercy endures forever,"*
>
> *that the house, the house of the Lord, was filled with a cloud, 14 so that the priests could not continue ministering because of the cloud; for the glory of the Lord filled the house of God."* – **2 Chronicles 5:13-14**

Yet another example: Remember Paul and Silas in prison. As they sang their praises to God, the prison doors opened and the chains fell off.

> "*23 When they had struck them with many blows, they threw them into prison, commanding the jailer to guard them securely; 24 and he, having received such a command, threw them into the inner prison and fastened their feet in the stocks.*
>
> *25 But about midnight Paul and Silas were praying and singing hymns of praise to God, and the prisoners were listening to them; 26 and suddenly there came a great earth-*

quake, so that the foundations of the prison house were shaken; and immediately all the doors were opened and everyone's chains were unfastened." - **Acts 16:23-26**

There is power in corporate praise!!

Seventhly, *it is a weapon of spiritual warfare.* Our praises leave no place for the enemy to reside or hide, and cause him to fear. In the Old Testament God instructed the Jews to praise Him as they went into battle. As the worship leaders and their band of singers and musicians, walked out before of the army into battle, God came down and smote the enemy.

> *"After consulting the people, the king appointed singers to walk ahead of the army, singing to the LORD and praising him for His holy splendour. This is what they sang: "Give thanks to the LORD; his faithful love endures forever!"* - **2 Chronicles 20:21 NLT**

Randy Felton author of *"Let Judah Go Up First"*[11] wrote,

> *"There were twelve tribes of Israel. Why should Judah be called upon to go up first? The Hebrew word translated as Judah is used many times in English as PRAISE. So the scripture could be translated as, LET PRAISE GO UP FIRST. This is good advice for us when facing struggles or battles. Let us first praise. This is both an act of faith and submission. Praise God before the battle is entered; anyone can praise when the battle is over and won. Only by faith can we praise at the start."*

As we praise Him still today, the enemy is completely routed. This means that chains fall off and people are freed from bondages – bondages of sin, bondages of torment and bondages of sickness - and the works of the enemy are destroyed. When there is an atmosphere of unified worship, many people are (and have been) miraculously healed without ever being prayed for by another. (The wonderful thing about these kinds of miracles is that God alone receives the glory and not the one leading the service, or the one praying etc.) More and more we are seeing these miracles happening amidst the worship of His people - testimony after testimony! Corporate worship can indeed be that powerful!

Finally, *the Bible tells us to do so* AND to do it with joy and thanksgiving.

> *"Enter into His gates with thanksgiving, And into His courts with praise. Be thankful to Him, and bless His name."* – **Psalm 100:4 - NKJV**

Indeed as the redeemed of the Lord, we have a great deal to be happy about. For us to rejoice as we praise and give thanks, demonstrates a true appreciation and gratefulness in our hearts, and trust that He will continue to care for us in every way. If we gave a very special gift to a loved one and they responded with a short, *"Thanks"*, and a lemon juice face, we would feel as if they were not too impressed with our gift, nor happy that we even went to the trouble.

Conversely, praising joyously speaks not only that we are truly thankful and appreciate God and all He has done, but again that we trust Him implicitly. We can lean back into Him without a care, knowing that He knows how to care for His own. Thanks Dad!

The Question of What

So much for the why, but what is *Biblical* worship? Every faith/religion has some form of worship. So what is it that sets Christian worship apart, or is there no difference in the manner in which worship is performed across all religions?

Obviously the word "worship" means different things to different people today. To some it's the quiet singing we do at church, to others it's the service we attend, or even our lifestyle. Others again would say it's something they do on their own, some would say in a group. Some say it's quiet, others loud. Some say being still, others jumping about. Worship brings different images to mind for different people, so can we say one thing above another? Obviously the answer lies within the pages of the Glory Book, (the Bible). Nevertheless, I'd like to start by stating the worship concepts I will not be discussing in any depth.

Worship as a Lifestyle

Let's start with the concept of "Worship as a lifestyle". After all, there are so many books written on the topic. Simply put, what most of these authors are advocating by using this phrase, is to honour God in all you do, and with all your heart, despite the cost, or as Paul exhorts us:

> *"I beseech you therefore, brethren, by the mercies of God, that you present your bodies a living sacrifice, holy, acceptable to God, which is your reasonable service."* – **Romans 12:1 NKJV**

(Some versions translate this as *"reasonable* worship" or *"acceptable* worship").

According to Vine's Expository Dictionary[12]:

> *"Reasonable"* = *logikos* (ιογικοσ, *3050), pertaining to* "the reasoning faculty, reasonable, rational", *is used in* **Rom. 12:1**, *of the "service" (latreia) to be rendered by believers in presenting their bodies "a living sacrifice, holy, acceptable to God." The sacrifice is to be intelligent, in contrast to those offered by ritual and compulsion; the presentation is to be in accordance with the spiritual intelligence of those who are new creatures in Christ and are mindful of "the mercies of God."*

From this and the writings of many Bible scholars/commentators, it appears that Paul was pleadfully stressing ("*I beseech you*") the importance for us to serve God with all that we are, no matter how hard His requests/demands of us appear, or what the cost. (We are the living sacrifice or thank offering). This is fully *reasonable* for us as a new creation in Christ. Other faiths embrace ritualistic worship as a form of pleasing God, but God wants our hearts as demonstrated by our willingness/attitude to serve Him obediently.

This verse, therefore, has more to do with loving service and obedience, than the kind of worship we offer God when we come together. I would also add that this is an *every day, every Christian lifestyle*, and not just pertaining to worship leaders and team members – to whom this book is written. It is God's expectation for all of us, and it is totally reasonable. We all should have a "*worship/service lifestyle*" because it is our reasonable service as Christians.

My intent here is to help worship leaders operate in the flow of the Holy Spirit. While it is true that music team members should also be thus yielded in their day-to-day lives, the kind of worship for which I write this book, is the kind we experience in our Sunday services and whenever we meet together to hear the Word, and share the Lord's Supper. Therefore, the terminology - "worship as a lifestyle" - only affords confusion to the discussion of church worship, and conversely, to the act of worship leading as well. Needless to say, I will not use that terminology again.

The "Act" of Coming Together?

I would also like to challenge the definition that the act of coming together is worship. Obviously worship can take place *after* we have assembled together, but is it really the *act* of coming together?

Many number of years ago, whilst in the mainstream church in which I was brought up, I mentioned to a fellow parishioner that my prayer life had slumped and this troubled me. His reply (with similar definition to the above concept) was that my very presence at the church was a prayer in itself. Well, he was into "New Age" thinking as it turned out, and really only attended church for the sake of his parents. His definition of prayer, filtered through his New Age lense, and though sounding deep and spiritual, I feel, is erroneous.

Prayer is talking with, or communicating with God. If I went to a friend's house and merely sat there with nothing to say, my friend might become most offended. True, it would communicate a message to my friend, but I doubt its interpretation would be positive! This silent treatment would also do nothing to further the friendship. This *act* of attendence is, in itself, empty!

Likewise, prayer isn't merely attending and/or sitting in church (nor is worship for that matter) but communing with God. There are many beautiful churches all around the world, that are visited by hundreds of tourists each year, but it is doubtful that you could call the tourist's visit a prayer, or worship. Clearly, this *act* of attendence is not worship, any more than sitting in church because of a sense of obligation and duty to attend, or because your parents dragged you along! Nor are we worshipping if we are not engaging our hearts but have our minds elsewhere, even though we may have wanted to come to church.

How easy it is to take on board these definitions without too much thought. Worship is adoration of God that comes from, or is a response to, a deep intimate knowledge combined with a Spirit born revelation of who God is (often from reading His Word), and must be done in Spirit and truth. While it is true that we may at times sacrificially come to church to worship God, and that He sees that act as honouring Him above our circumstances, it is not worship as defined within the Bible.

Note: Jesus said "true" worshippers will worship in spirit and truth. This not only suggests that there are false worshippers and perhaps even false methods and concepts of worship, but that only the true worshippers will worship as He prescribes. Care must be taken therefore, to not take statements (like the fellow's in my story) at face value no matter how pleasant they sound. Rather, *all things should be held up to the exposing light of the Word.*

Giving is Worship

Sacrificial giving and offerings are also a form of worship, that again demonstrates trust in God as our provider, but these are not to what I will be referring.

Not a Solo Act

Likewise, I have also heard many people claim that worship is a private part of our lives, and no one else's business. Although worship can be done alone, it also can and should be done corporately in the wider body of Christ. In fact, Biblical worship was something originally ascribed to the gathering of devotees, and not seen as a solo act at all. Let's examine the following Scripture references:

Old Testament Verses:

"Then he said to Moses, "Come up to the Lord, you and Aaron, Nadab, and Abihu, and seventy of the elders of Israel, and worship from afar." - **Exodus 24:1 ESV**

*"⁴ "Twenty-four thousand of these," David said. "shall have charge of the work in the house of the Lord, 6,000 shall be officers and judges, ⁵ 4,000 gatekeepers, and **4,000 shall offer praises** to the Lord with the instruments that I have made for praise."* - **1 Chronicles 23:4-5 ESV**

"⁶ The priests stood at their posts; the Levites also, with the instruments for music to the Lord that King David had made for giving thanks to the Lord—for his steadfast love endures forever—whenever David offered praises by their ministry; opposite them the priests sounded trumpets, and all Israel stood" - **2 Chronicles 7:6 ESV**

*"³⁰ And Hezekiah the king and the officials commanded **the Levites** to sing praises to the Lord with the words of David and of Asaph the seer. And **they** sang praises with gladness, and they bowed down and worshiped."* - **2 Chronicles 29:30 ESV**

*"I will tell of Your name to my brothers; **in the midst of the congregation** I will praise You"* - **Psalm 22:22 ESV**

*"All the ends of the earth shall remember and turn to the Lord, and **all the families of the nations** shall worship before You."* - **Psalm 22:27 ESV**

*"I will give You thanks **in the great assembly;** I will praise You **among many people.**"* - **Psalm 35:18 NKJV**

*"Let the peoples praise You, O God; Let **all the peoples** praise You."* - **Psalm 67:3 - NKJV**

*"**All nations** whom You have made shall come and worship before You, O Lord, and shall glorify Your name."* - **Psalm 86:9 NKJV**

*"And the heavens will praise Your wonders, O Lord; Your faithfulness also **in the assembly of the saints.**" And "7 God is greatly to be feared in the assembly of the saints, And to be held in reverence by all those around Him."* - **Psalm 89:5,7 NKJV**

*"Oh come, **let us** worship and bow down; Let us kneel before the Lord our Maker."* - **Psalm 95:6 NKJV**

*"Oh, worship the Lord in the beauty of holiness! Tremble before Him, **all the earth.**"* - **Psalm 96:9 NKJV**

*"I will praise the Lord with my whole heart, **in the assembly of the upright and in the congregation.**"* - **Psalm 111:1 NKJV**

*"7 Let **us** go into His tabernacle; Let **us** worship at His footstool." And "9 Let Your priests be clothed with righteousness, And let Your saints shout for joy."* - **Psalm 132:7,9 NKJV**

*"Praise the Lord! Sing to the Lord a new song, And His praise **in the assembly of saints.**"* - **Psalm 149:1 NKJV**

*"So it shall be in that day: The great trumpet will be blown; They will come, **who are about to perish in the land of Assyria, And they who are outcasts in the land of Egypt,** And shall worship the Lord in the holy mount at Jerusalem."* - **Isaiah 27:13 NKJV**

*"Stand in the gate of the Lord's house, and proclaim there this word, and say, 'Hear the word of the Lord, **all you of Judah who enter in at these gates** to worship the Lord!'"* - **Jeremiah 7:2 NKJV**

New Testament Verses:

"Then, as He was now drawing near the descent of the Mount of Olives, the whole multitude of the **disciples began to rejoice and praise God** *with a loud voice for all the mighty works they had seen"* - **Luke 19:37 NKJV**

"Now there were certain Greeks among those who came up **to worship at the feast"** - John 12:20 NKJV

"So he arose and went. And behold, a man of Ethiopia, a eunuch of great authority under Candace the queen of the Ethiopians, who had charge of all her treasury, and **had come to Jerusalem to worship"** - **Acts 8:27 NKJV**

"But when He again brings the firstborn into the world, He says: 'Let **all the angels** *of God worship Him.' "* - **Hebrews 1:6 NKJV**

"10 **the twenty-four elders** *fall down before Him who sits on the throne and worship Him who lives forever and ever, and cast their crowns before the throne, saying:*
11 "You are worthy, O Lord,
To receive glory and honour and power;
For You created all things,
And by Your will they exist and were created." - **Revelation 4:10, 11 NKJV**

(Note: the words of praise! Aren't they are glorious!)

"Then I was given a reed like a measuring rod. And the angel stood, saying, "Rise and measure the temple of God, the altar, and **those who worship there."** - **Revelation 11:1 NKJV**

*"**All who dwell on the earth** will worship him, whose names have not been written in the Book of Life of the Lamb slain from the foundation of the world."* - **Revelation 13:8 NKJV**

"Who shall not fear You, O Lord, and glorify Your name? For You alone are holy. For **all nations** *shall come and worship before You, For Your judgments have been manifested"* - **Revel-**

ation 15:4 NKJV

"5 Then a voice came from the throne, saying, 'Praise our God, all you His servants and those who fear Him, both small and great!' 6And I heard, as it were, the voice of a great multitude, as the sound of many waters and as the sound of mighty thunderings, saying, 'Alleluia! For the Lord God Omnipotent reigns!'
" - **Revelation 19:5-6 NKJV**

As you can see, worship was enjoyed when believers congregated together for the express purpose of glorifying God.

Biblical Worship

Now, rather than continuing to look at what worship is *not*, let's now discuss Biblical worship in more detail.

A definition is probably the best place to start. A secular dictionary is not the Word of God and as such can lack spiritual insight, but a Bible dictionary on the other hand, is a good place to start. Hopefully the work of many Bible scholars will be useful to us. Nevertheless, we will compare them with the Scriptures and fine tune or disregard the definition as we continue our discussion.

The New International Dictionary of the Bible[13] identifies only two words as worship: the Hebrew, '**Shahah**', as '*bow down or prostrate*', and the Greek, '***proskyneo***', as '*to prostrate or do obeisance to.*' It further says that worship

> *"is the honour, reverence, and homage paid to superior beings or powers, whether men, angels, or God. The English word means, "worth-ship" and denotes the worthiness of the individual receiving the special honour due to his worth."*

If you were to do a study of all the literal renderings of the word "worship" in Hebrew or Greek throughout the entire Bible (and infact there are several), you would discover that worship is something we do. It's an action. However, the most common Greek word translated as "Worship" means "*to kiss (the hand) to-*

73

ward" like blowing a kiss. This action implies a *heart attitude* as well, and an intimate one at that.

Tom Kraeuter[14] writes in his book "Worship is... What?!",

> "*Please understand that worship must originate from the heart, but it cannot be just heart.*"

Hence, this implies the "action" to which the literal translation refers. He continues...

> "*However, worship that is **action alone is not true worship**. God wants heart and action.*"

There was a book written by Bob Webber called "*Worship is a Verb*". The title making the point that we cannot sit back and observe or merely think about it in our minds. Rather, it infers we must be involved physically in some way as we engage our hearts. Worship is active. The concept of sitting quietly originates in Greek philosophy, not in the Old Testament. In fact, the references to silence in worship in the Old Testament, are very few. Rather, in the natural, when people are happily excited they become very loud and animated. It's the natural expression. Likewise in our worship, we can move around, dance, jump, clap, raise our hands, and provided it is done sincerely and respectfully, it will glorify God. It was the apostle Paul who said,

> "*Glorify God in your bodies!*" – **1 Corinthians 6:20**

Movement or the "*act*" of worship is by no means a modern addition to worship. Worship, as described in the Old Testament, was very animated. It is by no means a modern thing invented to entertain congregations, or even to attract the masses. It is as old as the Old Testament. Below are some Hebrew words translated as praise. This is an exert from Dr Roy Blizzard in his book - Let Judah Go Up First[15]:

> "*BARACH (Bar Rach) - To kneel, to bless, to adore with bended knee.*"

"HALAL (Hah Lahl) - The root is to shout, cry aloud."

"TEHILLAH (The Hi Lah) - This word for praise is also translated as "Psalm." "

"GADAL (Gah Dahl) - Often translated "magnify," it is used as a synonym of praise."

"ZAMAR (Zah Mar) — Meaning to make music to God."

"SHIR (Sheer) - Meaning a song - more specifically, vocal music."

"SHAVACH (Shav Ach) - To commend, to congratulate, to laud."

"RUM (Room) - The basic meaning is height and it is used to parallel many of the preceding words. Rum is used symbolically to express such lofty notions as glory, exaltation and to extol."

"RANAN (Rah Nahn) - To cry out, shout for joy or to give a ringing cry. It parallels joy, rejoicing, praise and jubilation in poetry."

"YADAH (Yah Dah) - The literal root is to throw or to cast. When used in text, it means to confess or declare Who God is and what He does."

Dr Blizzard also points out that "Judah" comes from the root, "yadah". Wikipedia[16] defines it like this:

"Yadah is the third person singular qal form of the Hebrew language verbal root ydh. Depending on its conjugation, it carries a range of meanings involving throwing or praising.

- *In the qal form, it describes the "shooting" of arrows in Jeremiah 50:14.*

- *The piel form means "throwing" (as in throwing stones at a person, in Lamentations 3:53) or "casting down" ("the horns of the nations," in Zechariah 2:4)*

- *In the hiphil form, it normally means "praising" (usually in the context of ritual worship) and occasionally for confessing one's sins.*

- *The hitpael form has a similar range of meanings, but the word most often means "confession" and less commonly "praise"."*[17]

Thus, when God was telling Judah to go first to the battle He was also reminding them to yadah! That is, to throw praise to their great and powerful God, - even confessing their own inadequacies apart from Him, and thus, acknowledging Him as the only way to true salvation – that is, the only way to win the battle. To me at least, this "throwing" of praise conjurers up images of wild abandonment – throwing any caution or hesitation to the wind, because they completely trusted that the One they worshipped would deliver them.

Imagine facing an army bent on your destruction. There may even be some fear and trepidation as you stand there face to face with your enemy. However, the Israelites decided they would trust in their God to deliver them, because they trusted His love for them and that He was indeed able.

Likewise, our willingness to worship should not be dependent on how we are feeling, but on God alone. He is always worthy to be exalted – always! In fact, when we praise God first, even in the worst of circumstances, it says to God,

> *"I may not know what to do or how to proceed, but whatever happens, I trust and believe in You and Your love and goodness towards me. You are still on the throne."*

King Jehoshaphat, when faced by a fierce invading army too large for him to defeat, sent the worshippers out first into battle. (I have already mentioned this in the "Why" section but it merits a closer inspection here.) King Jehoshaphat knew that by keeping his eyes on God and trusting in Him, God indeed would deliver them, and God did just that! What's more, not only were the invaders destroyed, but also the people were blessed by the sheer amount of spoils they collected after the battle.

"²⁰ Early in the morning they left for the Desert of Tekoa. As they set out, Jehoshaphat stood and said, "Listen to me, Judah and people of Jerusalem! Have faith in the Lord your God and you will be upheld; have faith in His prophets and you will be successful." ²¹ After consulting the people, Jehoshaphat appointed men to sing to the Lord and to praise Him for the splendour of His holiness as they went out at the head of the army, saying:

"Give thanks to the Lord, for his love endures forever."

"²² As they began to sing and praise, the Lord set ambushes against the men of Ammon and Moab and Mount Seir who were invading Judah, and they were defeated. ²³ The Ammonites and Moabites rose up against the men from Mount Seir to destroy and annihilate them. After they finished slaughtering the men from Seir, they helped to destroy one another.

"²⁴ When the men of Judah came to the place that overlooks the desert and looked toward the vast army, they saw only dead bodies lying on the ground; no one had escaped. ²⁵ So Jehoshaphat and his men went to carry off their plunder, and they found among them a great amount of equipment and clothing and also articles of value—more than they could take away. There was so much plunder that it took three days to collect it." – **2 Chronicles 20:20-25 ESV**

God loves our praise and worship especially when times are hard, not because He needs it, but because it demonstrates our trust in Him. It is relatively easy to tell someone you love them when things are going well, but another to demonstrate this in times of difficulty. It is our human nature to try to fix things ourselves. However, when we know there is no way out – that it is beyond us – and still we worship and praise Him, we show our complete reliance and trust in Him. It is proof that we truly believe He is who He says He is, and that we believe in His unfailing love towards us.

Judah was also the first tribe to set out after the Israelites broke camp.

> *"The standard of the camp of the people of Judah set out first by their companies"* – **Numbers 10:14a ESV**

Could this be God's way of reminding His people, that praise should precede all we do? In every circumstance, He is indeed worthy of praise.

The Question of How

A *"how-to"* description of worship may seem quite irrelevant for you, the worship leader, because not only do you already lead worship but also because you are looking to improve how you do so! (Or you would not be reading this book!) Therefore, I will make comments like, *"Worship is the natural response to God's greatness and simply overflows from our hearts"* and assume you will know to just what I am referring. If for some reason you do not, a simplistic description would be this:

As we focus on God, we call to mind His great worth, and all He has done – especially His benevolence towards us. We do not just praise for the sake of praise, however, since praise has to have substance – a basis. That is, we praise God *because* He is great and because He has done glorious things!

Therefore, we begin to verbally express these things. This could be reading a Scripture verse aloud, or singing a worship song, or to simply praising Him in your own words. Because our spirits have been made alive in Christ, and because we love Him, this retelling of whom He is and what He has done, excites our spirits. Our hearts can no longer sit quietly and be silent! Rather, both love and faith are activated, and begin to pour forth from us in the expression of worship. That is, worship is our spiritual response to who He is.

For some people, this response may not "feel" so automatic. The hurts and pains of life can shut the heart down, making it difficult to "feel" anything! Nevertheless, praise isn't reliant on how we *feel* in the natural. It's a *spiritual* response. Often times we are far too much in our heads to perceive just what our spirits are "feeling" or how they are responding. The important thing is not to wait to feel something in the natural before we dive in. My old pastor use to say that we too often are wanting to place the cart before the horse! That is, too often we expect to feel something in the natural before we decide to do something. Our natural emotions are not the cause of praise. It flows from our spirits! Our emotions may be evoked as we worship, but these natural feelings are not what initiates it!

We may commence by telling God (or singing about) how wonderful He is and how much we love Him no matter what the circumstances. We lift your hands in an attitude of humility. We praise Him simply because He is good. We let the flow of praise be genuine and from our hearts.

As we do these things, we may begin to sense our spirits rise with some excitement, which gives rise to the desire to worship Him further.

This action is what we were created to do. unfortunately, this eager response may not occur at all for those who have still to realise fully who they are in Christ, and especially just how much they are loved and accepted. Nevertheless, the more frequently you worship, the more you will begin to recognise your own spirit's response to His, and begin to enjoy worship. It was never meant to be chore, but a joy!!!

So much for my description of how to worship on a personal level! However, since we were created by God to know, love and worship Him, then surely it follows that the "*how*" of worship also originates with God. And where can we find God's guidelines? - within the Word. We have already discussed this at length in the chapter, "*The True Heart of the Matter*", but I now want to briefly conclude this discussion regarding the *outward* manifestations to which people refer, when discussing what happens during worship.

From the discussion so far we can conclude that worship in the Old Testament (and thus, the kind in which Jesus Himself would have partaken) was a noisy event. It was loud, boisterous and very animated. The crude analogy frequently used to encourage people to participate excitedly in the Sunday worship, is this: If we were at a sporting match barracking for our favourite team, we would shout and holler and give resounding, "Yay!"s. There would be punching of the air for every score, and rejoicing with our friends. The whole event would indeed be loud, boisterous and exceedingly animated. How much bigger than a mere sports team is God! Surely just the thought of His magnificence makes us want to shout, "*Hallelujah!*"

It is also unfortunate that the loud and animated worship of today has often been associated with images of unruly church-goers, "fleshing out", showing off, being disrespectful, and doing anything that "feels good", (including hanging from the chande-liers?) As a result, many churches have tried to restrict the kind of worship they will allow in their churches in order to avoid these excesses, and in many cases, regretfully, thrown the prov-erbial "*baby out with the bath water*". Both loud and animated worship are, in fact, Biblical after all!

Restrictions because of this can only be based on fear of what might happen in the worst-case scenario, but fear is not rooted in Christ who is love. In fact, fear is the complete antithesis of love, and is the enemy's most used weapon. Perfect love casts out all fear! (1 John 4:18) Since Biblical worship involves actions (as Paul instructs the brethren to worship "*in their bodies*",) then we are in danger of stifling the Biblically prescribed worship pattern out of fear!

If the individuals of our congregation really understood just how much they are loved and accepted by the God whose opinion is the only one that counts, they would surely not feel the need to impress others. If they also realised how much God hates our self-worship (as already discussed), they simply wouldn't do these things. When people "attention seek" during worship, it really suggests that we, as a church, have not sufficiently edu-cated our people about God's love and acceptance, and have assumed that worship was totally automatic rather than giving some kind of instruction about what God desires, and what is Biblical. After all, whose job is it to equip the saints? Is it not the role of the five-fold ministry, and in particular, the church appointed teachers!

Conversely, if we *have* equipped our congregation well, do we then love and **trust them** to worship Him alone, in spirit and truth, and with propriety? Or have our church "codes of conduct" created fear of reprisal, or of offending others if they do? Need it be said, there is only one person our worship should please – God – and that should always be the bottom line!

Too often it is our rituals, our set program, our traditions and even mindsets that can cause us to frown on those who worship differently – loud or quiet, still or animated. They do not fit our worship paradigm or church culture. How can those people possibly be worshipping if they act like that? And yet, if we were to take an unbiased closer look, we may just find that these noisy people are touching God! (A trip to the mission fields often changes rigid mindsets about worship. Other peoples may worship differently but God shows up in these mission meetings!)

Finally, I will let the Biblical description of worship – an altogether noisy affair - have the last say:

> "[1] *Praise the Lord!*
> *Praise God in his sanctuary;*
> *Praise him in his mighty heavens!*
> [2] *Praise him for his mighty deeds;*
> *Praise him according to his excellent greatness!*
> [3] *Praise him with trumpet sound;*
> *Praise him with lute and harp!*
> [4] *Praise him with tambourine and dance;*
> *Praise him with strings and pipe!*
> [5] *Praise him with sounding cymbals;*
> *Praise him with loud clashing cymbals!*
> [6] *Let everything that has breath praise the Lord!*
> *Praise the Lord!*" – **Psalm 150** ESV

Contentious Issues & Complaints

This is not the most pleasant chapter to write, and yet, in order for worship to be authentic and without doubts or man pleasing, these topics do need to be addressed.

Has Worship Really Changed?

Since *ritualistic* Old Testament worship has been replaced by worship in spirit and truth, what actions are still acceptable to God under the New Covenant? For example: New Testament worship no longer includes animal sacrifices since Jesus is our *"once and for all"* sacrifice, but is that all that has changed? What exactly does New Testament worship look like? Is there a place for movement such as dance, or physical posture such as kneeling, or lying prostrate? Or is the raising of hands the only action open to us? Does the Bible describe acceptable New Testament worship actions?

Remember that Paul in Romans 12:1 specifies that being totally surrendered is acceptable worship or service – like a sheep on the altar under the hands of God, but how does this play out in are Sunday services? Is this verse only referring to the every Christian lifestyle as previously discussed? What does modern worship look like?

In the New Testament Scriptures, while it is true that certain actions are translated as *"worship"*, some clearly lack adoration, and did not please God, such as in the case of the Gadarene demoniac.

> *"When he saw Jesus from afar, he ran and worshiped Him."*
> - **Mark 5:6 NKJV**.

While he had the form of worship, because he recognised Jesus as having all authority over him, he definitely had no love for God. Nevertheless, his stance/posture was one of submission before Jesus and that was translated as *"worship"*. Perhaps this action was common to pagan worship where appeasement or favour building with their god(s) was the aim. If the demoniac's actions were recognised as worship, this leads me to ask, *"Are there some actions that are expected of New Testament worshippers as they worship in spirit and truth?"* Obviously, some actions are, in fact, considered worship!

Jesus left no instructions other than to worship in Spirit and truth. He did not say, *"Quieten down when you worship!"* or *"Dancing is not allowed because you'll all just "flesh out" and make a show of it!"* or *"Flags and banners are irrelevant and could poke someone's eyes out - so don't use them!"* or *"Only instruments used in the Old Testament are acceptable!"* or *"Worship is a private affair!"* These are all man made constructs and not found in Scripture! Had Jesus said any of these things, we could easily claim that these attitudes are correct and true, but He did *not*! Moreover, most of these charges may simply be an over zealous attempt to ensure a sense propriety is maintained, but they do sound legalistic in nature nevertheless. (BTW, when He spoke about doing something covertly for the Father, He wasn't referring to worship but to giving, (Matt 6:4) personal prayer (Matt 6:6) and fasting (Matt 6:18)!)

The Old Testament gives many examples of worship. Nevertheless, after Jesus resurrection, there were very few to no instructions added regarding the matter. It is assumed the readers would understand how to worship because, apart from the sacrifice of animals, nothing about its form had changed.

So what Old Testament worship aspects/practices have not survived the transition to the New Covenant? As mentioned, one that has definitely been eradicated is the old system of sacrifices. It ceased with Jesus' *"once and for all"* sacrifice, (Hebrews 7:27; 9:12; 10:9-11). The debt of sin has been completely paid. Animal sacrifice is not only no longer required, but to continue would suggest that the offering of Jesus was somehow incomplete, which is nonsense, and Hebrews makes that very clear.

Has anything else changed? Putting the animal sacrifices aside from the Old Testament worship, what do you have left? You have loud shouts of joy and exultation, singing at the tops of voices, and noisy musical instruments with timbrels and drums. There are dancers and banners, people clapping and raising their hands. Then there times when people were bowed down, lying prostrate and with a posture that suggests submission.

Should we ignore certain aspects of Old Testament worship simply because some aspects may appear unpalatable? Again, no! Why should we! These things are only unpalatable to some any way! If God enjoyed these things in the past, He will not have suddenly changed His mind on the matter, especially without informing us. (However, keep in mind that He is already perfect and unchangeable, and therefore would not change His thinking regarding this!)

Further, we can hardly be expected to worship and not know how He prefers we do it! He loves us. He isn't about to trick us for the sake of catching us out! That weird thinking undermines His character! So the conclusion here is that apart from the sacrificial offerings, nothing about worship has changed!

In light of this, I would now like to discuss each aspect of our modern worship that has attracted criticism, in order to ascertain whether its *modern version* is still *Biblical* and uncorrupted, and therefore, relevant to our New Testament form of worship.

****

If we search the Internet in order to ascertain other people's findings on this topic (i.e. modern worship practices), we'll quickly uncover a great many judgmental websites that are heavily critical. Many of these websites also contain a great many negative labels and generalized opinions. I found this negativity unsettling, unloving, legalistic in nature, and far from building up the body of Christ. On the contrary, this was more divisive than unifying. Obviously, this is a very sensitive topic and within it, legalism and religion, together with temperament and artistic indignation, abound.

I personally have been raised in Christ within the modern worship paradigm, and as such, have sensed His presence during worship on most occasions – sometimes very profoundly and deeply. Sometimes the worship was quite literally life changing and healing. I've even been involved in services where healings actually took place during the worship, when all eyes were closed and on Jesus and there was no one laying hands or praying over people. So I'm sold!

However, to remain open to other points of view, I am more than happy to analyze and discuss the word of God to ascertain the truth of the matter. Does God enjoy our worship today, or does He condescend to turn up anyway? Is our worship corrupt, as some want us to believe, or in reality, conducted in spirit and truth? Let's now look at some various complaints of modern worship to ascertain whether modern worship has strayed from its original roots and God ordain intentions.

Worship & Preaching

In some churches, worship leaders are appointed, not because of their qualifications to lead worship, but to enable them to become accustomed to the pulpit before stepping into a preaching ministry. On that point, I personally don't believe the worship ministry should be used for that purpose. Nevertheless, this generally occurs where the worship is seen as relatively unimportant – something to warm up the congregation for the main part – and it is the sermon that takes priority over everything else happening in the regular Sunday service. Worship is then relegated to a small number of songs and usually a very short time frame, for example – 10 to 15 minutes, or less.

I have even heard the complaint that modern worship services have "*taken over*" the Sunday service, and the worship leader is not even part of the five-fold ministries that Jesus gave to the church! Firstly, while worship is not a five-fold ministry, Christians shouldn't need "*equipping*" in worship. (The five-fold ministry is for the equipping of the saints! (See Ephesians 4:11-13 ESV)) Worship is our *natural response* to God's many wondrous attributes.

I recently read another rather negative comment, which would seem to present some truth on first glance but on closer inspection is quite deceptive and overall feels more like having a swing at modern music teams, rather than offering anything constructive on the matter. In essence the author was making the point that we place too much emphasis on the music in "*its upfront dress*", (already an emotive description of showing off rather than worshipping) whereas we would be "*better served*" (although these words have an air of authority, they are subjective and opinion based only) expending this energy on intercession and study of the word, on sitting in silence and in prophesying. Of course we should be doing these things *as well*, but whilst it is true that the Scriptures can and do inspire our worship, to insinuate that worship is *less important*, is to ascribe a humanistic view to our faith that was never intended in or by the Word.

Secondly, worship has always been part of the service since days of King David.

> "*³¹ These are the men whom David put in charge of the service of song in the house of the Lord after the ark rested there. ³² They ministered with song before the tabernacle of the tent of meeting until Solomon built the house of the Lord in Jerusalem, and they performed their service according to their order.*" – **1 Chronicles 6:31-32 ESV**

People had always worshipped God, but David organised the musical kind within the temple service program. It was the Levites – specially appointed Levites – who were in charge of the music, and they were expected to keep the worship going day and night!

> "*³³ Now these, the singers, the heads of fathers' houses of the*

Levites, were in the chambers of the temple free from other service, for they were on duty day and night." – **1 Chronicles 9:33 ESV**

It was still part of the priestly duties of the Levites when Jesus walked the earth, and as such, He did not have to give it again to the church as a five fold ministry gift or any other gift. Since, we (the church of the New Covenant) are all now priests unto God, does that mean that we no longer need the worship service? No, it means that we are *all* worshippers and, in fact, worship is now part of our priestly "duties"!

That does not mean that the worship service is more important than the word of God. Some would argue that because we are here to learn to love God and one another from that overflow, that worship - being an activity of the heart - is far more important than hearing yet another message. Others would argue that unless you are properly trained in the Word of God, there is the capacity to stray into error and to follow one's own impulses and desires, leading to spiritual death.

It is not my place to argue one way or the other. Suffice to say that worship is an important component of the Sunday service; important to every believer, and also to the church. Preaching and teaching are part of the five-fold ministry Jesus gave to the church, and are also of vital importance! The truth is, we need both!

The Holy Spirit will use *both* the preaching and the worship as His vehicles to do His purposes if He is allowed room to speak to and minister to hearts. He gives us revelation about God through the inspired word, and our hearts excitedly jump and respond with worship. Sometimes the lyrics of the songs themselves will be Holy Spirit inspired and He will use those to raise the worship in response. The Word and the Worship work together in a divine dance.

Likewise, the worship leader is not more exalted, nor does he/she have more authority than the senior pastor. The worship leader does not run the service, or the church. Rather, he/she is a minister *under headship*, just as all the ministers are under that church authority.

I read one example where a music director complained that he should be receiving a salary because it was he that people were coming to see each Sunday and not to listen to the sermon. There are so many things wrong with that attitude! (Philippians 2:3-11) Clearly, that person needed a heart check!

Nevertheless, to reduce the time frame in which the Holy Spirit can minister through the worship (because some don't want the worship to be elevated above the Word), tells the Holy Spirit that if He wants to minister to people He's got to be quick! (Wow! Not the message I want to give God!) The Scriptures clearly tell us to walk in step with the Holy Spirit. It is *not* the Holy Spirit's function to walk in step with us, or to fit into our agenda!

Of course, even with our regimented service structures, the Holy Spirit *can* still minister to the congregation through the preaching of the Word, providing the preacher is willing for Him to do so, he/she is preaching truth, it is *the* God given message for the day, and the preacher has followed the Holy Spirit's lead in every aspect from sermon from preparation to execution.

The preacher's responsibility is no different than the worship leader's responsibility in that respect. Both worship and the preaching must be Holy Spirit impregnated. True Spirit led preaching may even mean that the preacher changes his/her message at the last minute if the Holy Spirit says to do so, or that he/she remains silent altogether and allows the Holy Spirit to minister. Seems the same rules apply to both the worship and the preaching, and both are vehicles that the Holy Spirit can anoint and use for His own purposes. To say one is more important than the other is preposterous! Both work together and both are essential! (However, I will add that if the message is a topical opinion piece, then I would suggest that the worship on that particular day probably was more important! In the same way, if the worship consisted merely of singing a couple of songs to warm people up, then the message probably *is* more important!)

The Purpose of Worship & Preaching Differ

One may or may not be more important than the other, but *each has a particular and differing function.* The sermon provides teaching, direction, clarity and revelation, whereas the worship provides intimacy and relationship building. That does not imply that the Word is not important or even less important than the worship. On the contrary, the Word is our guide, a light to our path and a lamp for our feet. It is sharper than any two edged sword and living and active in changing us, but the ***destination of our study/preaching of the Word, should always be the heart.*** The preaching of the word should be a *heart changer*, and therefore, a life changer, because it is (or should be) Spirit led and because ultimately God wants our hearts not our heads.

The command to love God with all that we are is not merely an Old Testament instruction that no longer applies to us. Even Jesus, when asked what was the most important commandment, summed the law into two; that is, to love God with everything, and our neighbour as ourselves. God wants our hearts above all other things. He did not say the most important commandment is to study the Scriptures, but to love God. Study of the Scriptures is important, of course, but ***the main aim of this study is to show us more of God so that we know, love and worship Him more in response.*** Otherwise, we are merely tickling ears and appealing to the minds of men without changing hearts.

Jesus, by restating the heart of the law to the Scribe, basically summed up the law now written on the hearts of born again believers. He did not come to abolish the law but to fulfil it. Now that the legal debt of sin is paid, the spirit of the law – which is love - lives on in us, enabling restoration of the Father's intended relationship with us! Love has always been and will always be, what God desires of us!

We were created to love and worship Him. Love and worship are extricably joined and cannot be divided. Further, when this world is over and we abide in Heaven, it is our love and adoration that will persist. Knowledge will pass away, and gifts of the Spirit will pass away. (1 Corinthians 13:8) It will only be our love relationship with God that will continue. In this world we can ever only know in part but in heaven we will see Him face to face and truly know Him (*we will see Him as He is* – 1 John 3:2). We will continue to worship Him in heaven, but the preaching will stop because God, Himself, will be revealing Himself to us and He will continue to reveal more of Himself throughout eternity!

Though we should definitely not stop or give less importance to the Word and study of Scriptures etc., our prime mandate on this earth is to learn to love and therefore worship, because worship flows when we love Him. This love grows, both through intimacy *and* study of the Word. Therefore, both the study of the Word and worship have an important role to play in every Christian's life but both differ in function.

Geoffrey Wainwright explains:

> *"Theology [is] a handmaid of worship, performing a service ancillary to a primary activity of the church."*[18]

JI Packer, author and theologian states that

> *"The purpose of theology is doxology. We study in order to praise."*[19]

Or the full version from J. I. Packer on the topic of theology:

> *"Theology, as I tell my students, is for doxology: the first thing to do with it is to turn it into praise and thus honour the God who is its subject, the God in whose presence and by whose help it (the Word) was worked out!"*[20]

Note that *doxology* literally means the study of praise. It arises from comes from the Greek doxa, ("glory, splendour, grandeur") and logos, ("word" or "speaking"). However, dictionaries usually define it as an *expression of praise!*

In other words, *the revelation we gain through the Word of God inspires us to praise and worship*, and not to make us better people or more righteous! Jesus already accomplished that part!

No doubt some will continue to argue: "*But we can worship alone anytime any place but Sunday church is a time for preaching and teaching.*" As we have already discussed, worship was never seen as a solo act in the Scriptures. It was always intended for corporate use. Nevertheless, as followers of Christ, we look to His example and leading. Therefore, what did Jesus and His New Covenant church do?

While it is true that Jesus early ministry consisted of teaching in the temple, and later preaching the kingdom in all kinds of remote places, no description or direction is given of the actual "service" proceedings that Jesus preferred, which may in turn imply that He was not changing the traditional temple service. However, one of the last accounts of Jesus time with His disciples did include worship. After eating His last meal with His disciples - having communion if you like - (and John's gospel gives more insight to the teaching Jesus also gave to the disciples at that time – His last sermon before He died), Jesus sang a Psalm with His disciples then went to the Mount of Olives:

> "30 *And when they had sung a hymn, they went out to the Mount of Olives.*" – **Matthew 26:30 ESV**

(See also Mark 14:26 ESV) Note: there was teaching, communion and worship!

I would also argue that *ultimately* God, as a relational God, is not interested in how much teaching we can absorb via our ears (science tells us that we retain as little as 10% of what we hear and even less as time progresses unless those words are repeated). God wants our hearts. The preaching should produce Holy Spirit inspired revelation and not just give knowledge, and then from that revelation, our lives and love will flow (or should flow) back to God and out to others. This kind of change does not happen through mere knowledge on a sermon topic. It is revelation that produces transformation (2 Cor 3:18), and from that eyes now opened revelation flows worship. It is love that is the ultimate goal. Without love we are nothing!

Spiritual Food to Go

Fortunately and unfortunately we have a multitude of preaching and worship music available to us today through our technology and availability of books - so much more than ever before - that we practically have them on tap. However, with the fast pace of life, it is growing more difficult for people just to *be still* and worship Him. To combat this, God's children resort to listening to preachers and worship music in their cars and hope that will suffice as part of their quiet time or Bible study. Better than nothing perhaps, but driving demands some level of concentration which means you are not totally focussed on God. People can still retain some level of knowledge from what they hear that way, but how much intimacy have they had with God?

Also as a result of this fast paced dynamic and take away ministries all ready to devour on the go, we've become less interested in the participation of worship, and even setting aside a regular quiet time with Him, but more interested in receiving. It's easier to sit and be fed, or to have our ears tickled, than to make time for Him.

It can be difficult to sacrifice our precious time, but true love gives and gives lavishly. (John 3:16) When worship becomes second place, our Christianity becomes all about "me" and the "doing". It's easy to skip our time with Him and tell ourselves we'll catch up in the car or listen to some music while we do some other menial job, but the truth is, that's no substitute for just being still in His presence and worshipping Him! When we worship we stir ourselves up as we are reminded of His goodness and love towards us. The less time we spend with Him the less we thirst for Him, despite our great need for a close relationship with Him. It's like we forget somehow. Conversely, the more we draw close in fellowship with Him, the more hungry we are for time in intimacy with Him, and the more our hearts cry out worship to Him. It is from this place that we begin to live out of the overflow of His great love.

In the same manner that worship is vitally important to us as individuals, it is also vitally important to the spiritual health of the church, more so now as we see His Day approaching. Therefore, to reduce it's timeframe in preference to the preaching of the Word, seems less than helpful - detrimental even. If the Holy Spirit moves during the sermon, no one would blink an eye if the preaching continued overtime. All eyes would be on what God was doing! Likewise, true Spirit led worship does not worship the clock, but continues for as long as the Holy Spirit desires.

Note here that I am not talking about a service that is not in order and out of control like the practice of the early Corinthian church to which Paul had to bring correction. You still have oversite of what is happening. Should there be any fleshly goings on, you are responsible to rein it in, and put the service back under the Holy Spirit's guidance. God is a God of order, not disarray or confusion.

Neither am I suggesting that if the worship lingers, that we should cut the sermon short or have none at all, (though perhaps if that is the way the service is headed, and everyone is doing carpet time before the Lord, insisting that the preaching of the word goes ahead, may just interrupt the flow of what God is doing.) God is perfectly able to speak to hearts Himself in these circumstances. *Everything* must follow the lead of the Holy Spirit. He is God, and we are there *for* God, not to be entertained or hear another message. Time frames and set schedules can at times be more a hindrance than a help to God's people! Who is meant to walk in step with whom?

To *remove* the time frame for worship is very scary for some worship leaders (and pastors), but again it has to do with the priority of each church. This is not to say that you cannot still have glorious anointed worship within a set time, but it is far more difficult to cut things short when the Holy Spirit is ministering to hearts, without grieving Him.

On the other hand, the worship leader should definitely not drag the song service out hoping that something will happen, or because he has a certain time allocation to fill, any more than the preacher should stand at the pulpit waffling to his congregation because his message was too short and besides it's Sunday! If God is not on it, the mature leader (worship leader or preacher) may even cut his/her platform time short to make way for something else that God can minister to hearts through! (e.g. Prayer lines, prophetic ministry, etc.)

It must be *all* Spirit led (worship and preaching) and has nothing to do with importance of one over another!

Music in Worship

So how does music fit into all of this? David as we know, brought music into the temple (1 Chronicles 6:31-32 listed above), but can we worship without it? Yes! Worship isn't music dependent but heart dependent. God is looking at our hearts, not the music. However, music in worship is Scriptural. If it was good enough for God in the Old Testament and used again in the New even by Jesus, why should we stop now? God obviously enjoys it!

Music is also an emotional art form. It has colours, tones and textures just like a painting. It sets a mood or expresses the emotions. It can be uplifting, exciting, aggressive, or calming, peaceful and so forth. Because music is a great conveyor of emotion and imagery, it becomes a wonderful vehicle we can use to joyfully express our love for God, and with which to enter His courts in praise.

Music can change the mood. You may not be ready to worship God then and there, but it can unconsciously set the tone, which we then pick up on, and choose then to enter in or not. It can pick us up and draw us in, or leave us sitting back watching others. Obviously you make the choice, but the music can encourage us to participate because of the emotion it illicits.

The Book of Psalms is not a "hymn book" as many would suppose but a collection of prayers, poems and songs, which were then organised into the book after the exile of Israel. Included within those pages are even prayers of Moses and Samuel!

However, well before the Book of Psalms was made a "book", David not only appointed choirs, instrument players and songwriters for the temple (1 Chronicles 25), but set many of the prayers and poems to music. As such, many of the Psalms are addressed *"to the choirmaster"*, *"to the tune of..."* or *"with stringed instruments"*, and so on. Basically they became songs – i.e. set to music – before they became the book as we know it today! This tradition of singing these songs and prayers then continued, as can be seen in Nehemiah 11:22-23.

"²² The chief officer of the Levites in Jerusalem was Uzzi son of Bani, the son of Hashabiah, the son of Mattaniah, the son of Mika. Uzzi was one of Asaph's descendants, who were the musicians responsible for the service of the house of God. ²³ The musicians were under the king's orders, which regulated their daily activity." – **Nehemiah 11:22-23 NIV**

Within the Book of Psalms the Psalmist says:

*"Shout for joy to God, all the earth; ² **sing** the glory of his name; give to him glorious praise! ³ Say to God, "How awesome are your deeds! So great is your power that your enemies come cringing to you. ⁴ All the earth worships you and **sings** praises to you; they **sing** praises to your name."* - **Psalm 66:1-4 ESV**

*" **Sing** aloud to God our strength; shout for joy to the God of Jacob! ² **Raise a song**; sound the **tambourine**, the sweet **lyre** with the **harp**."* - **Psalm 81:1-2 ESV**

*"Oh come, let us **sing** to the Lord; let us make a joyful noise to the rock of our salvation! ² Let us come into his presence with thanksgiving; let us make a joyful noise to him with **songs** of praise!"* - **Psalm 95:1-2 ESV**

"¹ Make a joyful noise to the Lord, all the earth!
² Serve the Lord with gladness!
*Comᵉ into His presence with **singing**!"* – **Psalm 100:1-2 ESV**

*"⁴ Make a joyful noise to the Lord, all the earth; break forth into joyous **song** and **sing** praises! ⁵ **Sing** praises to the Lord with the **lyre**, with the **lyre** and the sound of **melody**! ⁶ With **trumpets** and the sound of the **horn** make a joyful noise before the King, the Lord!"*

²⁴ Your procession is seen, O God, the procession of my God, my King, into the sanctuary –
*²⁵ the **singers** in front, the **musicians** last, between them virgins playing **tambourines**"* - PSALM **98:4-6, 42-25 ESV**

*"It is good to give thanks to the Lord, to **sing** praises to Your name, O Most High;*
² to declare your steadfast love in the morning, and your faithfulness by night,
*³ to the **music** of the **lute** and the **harp**, to the **melody** of the **lyre**.*
⁴ For You, O Lord, have made me glad by Your work;
*At the works of Your hands I **sing** for joy."* – **Psalm 92:1-4 ESV**

*"I will **sing** of steadfast love and justice; to You, O Lord, I will make **music**."* - **Psalm 101:1 ESV**

Further, Paul also admonishes the Greek communities to sing to the Lord together:

*".....speaking to one another in **psalms** and **hymns** and spiritual **songs**, **singing** and making **melody** in your heart to the Lord,"* – **Ephesians 5:19 ESV**

*"Let the word of Christ dwell in you richly in all wisdom, teaching and admonishing one another in **psalms** and **hymns** and **spiritual songs**, **singing** with grace in your*

hearts to the Lord." - **Colossians 3:16 ESV**

(Note: this singing was a *corporate* activity!)

Tom Inglis[21] also makes the point that Psalms are really prayers written to music, hymns are songs of praise (often based on personal testimony such as "Amazing Grace" or "Rock of Ages"), and spiritual songs are directly inspired by the Holy Spirit and spontaneous.

> *"A **psalm** is God's inspired word, found only in the Old Testament. As they are technically prayers as well as praise, it could be concluded that we should use them as a basis of prayer expressed as song."*

> *"The important criteria about **hymns** is that they are songs of praise addressed to God."*

> *The term "**spiritual songs**" "is not referring to the genre, style or cultural source of the songs, but to the divine origin, being the Holy Spirit."*

I'm not sure I *totally* agree with Tom's attempt to distinguish the various forms of singing that Paul mentions, (though it does sound rather neat and tidy) since a study of the Psalms will demonstrate that all these types of musical expressions are, in fact, within the psalms themselves.

Vines Expository Dictionary describes each this way:

> *"**Hymn** = (Humnos 5215) denotes "a song of praise addressed to God" (Eng., "hymn"), Eph. 5:19; Col. 3:16 ....*

> *Note: The **psalm** (psalmos) denoted that which had a musical accompaniment; the "ode" (Eng., "ode") was the generic term for a song; hence the accompanying adjective "spiritual."*

> *"'**spiritual songs**' are songs of which the burden is the things revealed by the Spirit, Eph. 5:19; Col. 3:16; 'spiritual wisdom*

and understanding' is wisdom in, and understanding of,
those things, Col. 1:9"[22]

The term "psalms" therefore, clearly incorporates hymns according to these expository definitions by W. E. Vine, and even spiritual songs can be found in the Book of Psalms.

From this we see that the songs the apostle Paul was actually instructing us to sing to each other, are songs that glorify God and are full of Holy Spirit inspiration and revelation! Yes, we are commanded to sing!

We can worship God verbally, yes, but it is clear from Scripture and our discourse thus far, that worship that is sung is both preferred and a delight to God. It is not merely a mantra, but an outpouring of our hearts. He enjoys us extolling His virtues in song!

An important thing to note here is that Paul commences the verse in Colossians 3:16 by saying. *"Let the word of God dwell in you richly."* Why? So that when we do use spiritual songs, the Word of God and the Spirit of the Word, can be poured out liberally and with accuracy upon our listeners! (See previous discussion in the section *"Worship & Preaching"*)

Since our worship songs should be impregnated with the Word, what Scriptures are appropriate song material? Should we rely solely on the Psalms as some people have suggested? To be honest, I'm not sure that that was what Paul meant.

A closer inspection of the Book of Psalms, reveals not only songs of praise to God, but many different types of songs with differing purposes, and some psalms may not be appropriate for worship at all! Let's take an in depth look at Psalms to see exactly what I mean by that statement. (I will give a few examples but will not include the whole Psalm every time as some are quite long, but I will at least give you the reference for you to check out! There are far more examples of each than those I have listed below, but you'll get the idea!)

Let's start with **songs of praise**: Psalm 8; 9; 19; 24; 93; 96; 97; 99; 103; 104; 113; 117 and so on. There are many! Here is one example:

> "*1 O Lord, our Lord,*
> *How majestic is your name in all the earth!*
> *You have set your glory above the heavens.*
> *2 Out of the mouth of babies and infants,*
> *You have established strength because of your foes,*
> *To still the enemy and the avenger.*
>
> *3 When I look at your heavens, the work of your fingers,*
> *The moon and the stars, which you have set in place,*
> *4 what is man that you are mindful of him,*
> *And the son of man that you care for him?*
>
> *5 Yet you have made him a little lower than the heavenly beings*
> *And crowned him with glory and honour.*
> *6 You have given him dominion over the works of your hands;*
> *You have put all things under his feet,*
> *7 all sheep and oxen,*
> *And also the beasts of the field,*
> *8 the birds of the heavens, and the fish of the sea,*
> *Whatever passes along the paths of the seas.*
>
> *9 O Lord, our Lord,*
> *how majestic is your name in all the earth!*" – **Psalm 8 ESV**

There are **love songs** to God that are very intimate in nature:

> "*1 O God, you are my God; earnestly I seek you;*
> *My soul thirsts for You;*
> *My flesh faints for You,*
> *As in a dry and weary land where there is no water.*
> *2 So I have looked upon You in the sanctuary,*
> *Beholding Your power and glory*
>
> *3 Because Your steadfast love is better than life,*
> *My lips will praise you.*
> *4 So I will bless You as long as I live;*

In Your name I will lift up my hands.

⁵ My soul will be satisfied as with fat and rich food,
And my mouth will praise You with joyful lips,
⁶ When I remember You upon my bed,
And meditate on You in the watches of the night;
⁷ for You have been my help,
And in the shadow of your wings I will sing for joy.
⁸ My soul clings to You;
Your right hand upholds me." - **Psalm 63:1-8 ESV**

There are **songs of thanks** and gratitude: Psalm 138; 75:1; 100:4;
92;

"¹ I give You thanks, O Lord, with my whole heart;
Before the gods I sing your praise;
² I bow down toward Your holy temple
And give thanks to Your name
For Your steadfast love and Your faithfulness,
For You have exalted above all things Your name and Your
word.
³ On the day I called, You answered me;
My strength of soul You increased.

⁴ All the kings of the earth shall give You thanks, O Lord,
For they have heard the words of Your mouth,
⁵ And they shall sing of the ways of the Lord,
For great is the glory of the Lord.
⁶ For though the Lord is high, He regards the lowly,
But the haughty He knows from afar.

⁷ Though I walk in the midst of trouble,
You preserve my life;
You stretch out Your hand against the wrath of my enemies,
And your right hand delivers me.
⁸ The Lord will fulfill his purpose for me;
Your steadfast love, O Lord, endures forever.
Do not forsake the work of Your hands." – **Psalm 138:1-8**
ESV

———————————————————

"We give thanks to you, O God;
We give thanks, for your name is near.
We recount your wondrous deeds." – **Psalm 75:1 ESV**

————————————————

"Enter His gates with thanksgiving,
And His courts with praise!
Give thanks to Him; bless His name!" - **Psalm 100:4 ESV**

Songs of instruction and wisdom: Psalm 1; 15; 111; 112; 127; 128; 133

"1Blessed is the man who walks not in the counsel of the wicked,
Nor stands in the way of sinners, nor sits in the seat of scoffers;
2 but his delight is in the law of the Lord, and on his law he meditates day and night.
3 He is like a tree planted by streams of water that yields its fruit in its season,
And its leaf does not wither. In all that he does, he prospers.
4 The wicked are not so, but are like chaff that the wind drives away.
5 Therefore the wicked will not stand in the judgment,
Nor sinners in the congregation of the righteous;
6 for the Lord knows the way of the righteous,
But the way of the wicked will perish." – **Psalm 1 – ESV**

————————————————

"1O Lord, who shall sojourn in your tent? Who shall dwell on your holy hill?
2 He who walks blamelessly and does what is right and speaks truth in his heart;
3 Who does not slander with his tongue and does no evil to his neighbour,
Nor takes up a reproach against his friend;
4 In whose eyes a vile person is despised, but who honours

those who fear the Lord;
Who swears to his own hurt and does not change;
⁵ Who does not put out his money at interest and does not take a bribe against the innocent.
He who does these things shall never be moved." - **Psalm 15:1-5 ESV**

We also find many **prayers of petition**: Psalm 25; 70; 126; 141

There are **prophetic psalms** – some even speak of Jesus: Psalm 22:16-18; Psalm 110:1-7

"¹⁶ For dogs encompass me;
A company of evildoers encircles me;
They have pierced my hands and feet -
¹⁷ I can count all my bones –
They stare and gloat over me;
¹⁸ They divide my garments among them,
And for my clothing they cast lots." – **Psalm 22:16-18 ESV**

"¹The Lord says to My Lord:
"Sit at My right hand until I make
Your enemies a footstool for Your feet."
² The Lord will extend your mighty sceptre from Zion,
saying, "Rule in the midst of Your enemies!"
³ Your troops will be willing on your day of battle.
Arrayed in holy splendour,
Your young men will come to You
Like dew from the morning's womb.
⁴ The Lord has sworn and will not change His mind:
"You are a priest forever, in the order of Melchizedek."
⁵ The Lord is at your right hand;
He will crush kings on the day of His wrath.
⁶ He will judge the nations, heaping up the dead
And crushing the rulers of the whole earth.
⁷ He will drink from a brook along the way,
And so he will lift his head high." – **Psalm 110:1-7 NIV**

There are **testimonial songs**: Psalm 18; 114; 116; 120; 124

There are **psalms of encouragement**: Psalm 34:7-10; 31:23-24; 68; 121

> "7 *The angel of the Lord encamps around those who fear him, and delivers them.*
> 8 *Oh, taste and see that the Lord is good! Blessed is the man who takes refuge in him!*
> 9 *Oh, fear the Lord, you his saints, for those who fear him have no lack!*
> 10 *The young lions suffer want and hunger; but those who seek the Lord lack no good thing.*" – **Psalm 34: 7-10 ESV**

> "*Love the Lord, all you his saints!*
> *The Lord preserves the faithful but abundantly repays the one who acts in pride.*
> *Be strong, and let your heart take courage all you who wait for the Lord!*" - Psalm 31:23 ESV

There are **psalms of *self*-encouragement**/self-talk: Psalm 43:5 and repeated again in Psalm 42:5, 7-8, 11; 103:1-5

> "5 *Why are you cast down, O my soul, and why are you in turmoil within me?*
> *Hope in God; for I shall again praise him, my salvation and my God*" – **Psalm 43:5 ESV**

> "5*Why are you cast down, O my soul, and why are you in turmoil within me?*
> *Hope in God; for I shall again praise him, my salvation*"

> "7 *Deep calls to deep at the roar of your waterfalls;*
> *All your breakers and your waves have gone over me.*
> 8 *By day the Lord commands his steadfast love,*

And at night his song is with me, a prayer to the God of my life."

11 Why are you cast down, O my soul, and why are you in turmoil with me?

Hope in God; for I shall again praise him, my salvation and my God." - **Psalm 42:5, 7-8, 11 ESV**

_____

"Bless the Lord, O my soul,
And all that is within me, bless his holy name!
² Bless the Lord, O my soul,
And forget not all his benefits,
³ Who forgives all your iniquity,
Who heals all your diseases,
⁴ Who redeems your life from the pit,
Who crowns you with steadfast love and mercy,
⁵ Who satisfies you with good
So that your youth is renewed like the eagle's." - **Psalm 103:1-5 ESV**

There are **psalms of declaration** over oneself: Psalm 101

There are **psalms of blessing**: Psalm128; Psalm 20; Psalm 67

"¹ Blessed is everyone who fears the Lord, who walks in his ways!
² You shall eat the fruit of the labour of your hands;
you shall be blessed, and it shall be well with you.
³ Your wife will be like a fruitful vine within your house;
your children will be like olive shoots around your table.
⁴ Behold, thus shall the man be blessed who fears the Lord.
⁵ The Lord bless you from Zion!
May you see the prosperity of Jerusalem all the days of your life!
⁶ May you see your children's children! Peace be upon Israel!" – **psalm 128 ESV**

_____

"¹May the Lord answer you in the day of trouble!
May the name of the God of Jacob protect you!
² May He send you help from the sanctuary
And give you support from Zion!
³ May He remember all your offerings
And regard with favour your burnt sacrifices!   Selah

⁴ May He grant you your heart's desire
And fulfil all your plans!
⁵ May we shout for joy over your salvation,
And in the name of our God set up our banners!
May the Lord fulfil all your petitions!

⁶ Now I know that the Lord saves His anointed;
He will answer him from His holy heaven
With the saving might of His right hand.
⁷ Some trust in chariots and some in horses,
But we trust in the name of the Lord our God.
⁸ They collapse and fall,
But we rise and stand upright.

⁹ O Lord, save the king!
May He answer us when we call." - **Psalm 20 ESV**

_ _ _ _ _ _ _ _ _ _ _ _ _ _ _ _ _ _ _ _

"¹ May God be gracious to us and bless us
And make his face to shine upon us, Selah
² that your way may be known on earth,
Your saving power among all nations.
³ Let the peoples praise you, O God;
Let all the peoples praise you!

⁴ Let the nations be glad and sing for joy,
For you judge the peoples with equity
And guide the nations upon earth. Selah
⁵ Let the peoples praise you, O God;
Let all the peoples praise you!

⁶ The earth has yielded its increase;
God, our God, shall bless us.
⁷ God shall bless us;

Let all the ends of the earth fear him!" – **Psalm 67 ESV**

There are **psalms of joy**: Psalm 122

There are **psalms of invitation**: Psalm 95; 100; 66; 98; 105; 134; 136; 147, plus many more!

There are **psalms addressed to angels**: Psalm 103:20-22

> *"20 Bless the Lord, O you His angels,*
> *You mighty ones who do His word,*
> *Obeying the voice of His word!*
> *21 Bless the Lord, all His hosts,*
> *His ministers, who do His will!*
> *22 Bless the Lord, all His works,*
> *In all places of His dominion.*
> *Bless the Lord, O my soul!"* - **Psalm 103:20-22 ESV**

There are **warfare/victory psalms**: Psalm 89:6-10, 13-14;

> *"6 For who in the skies can be compared to the Lord?*
> *Who among the heavenly beings is like the Lord,*
> *7 A God greatly to be feared in the council of the holy ones,*
> *And awesome above all who are around Him?*
> *8 O Lord God of hosts, who is mighty as You are,*
> *O Lord, with Your faithfulness all around You?*
> *9 You rule the raging of the sea;*
> *When its waves rise, You still them.*
> *10 You crushed Rahab like a carcass;*
> *You scattered your enemies with Your mighty arm.*
>
> *13 You have a mighty arm;*
> *Strong is Your hand, high Your right hand.*
> *14 Righteousness and justice*
> *Are the foundation of Your throne;*
> *Steadfast love and faithfulness go before You."* – **Psalm 89:6-10, 13-14 ESV**

Psalms as **prayers for mercy**: Psalm 123 (particularly verses 3-4)

*"3 Have mercy upon us, O Lord, have mercy upon us,
For we have had more than enough of contempt.
4 Our soul has had more than enough of the scorn
Of those who are at ease, of the contempt of the proud."* –
Psalm 123:3-4 ESV

A psalm in which **God speaks about Zion and Jesus**: Psalm 132:14-18

*14 "This is My resting place forever; here I will dwell, for I have desired it.
15 I will abundantly bless her provisions; I will satisfy her poor with bread.
16 Her priests I will clothe with salvation, and her saints will shout for joy.
17 There I will make a horn to sprout for David; I have prepared a lamp for My anointed.
18 His enemies I will clothe with shame, but on Him His crown will shine."* – **Psalm 132:14-18 ESV**

There are psalms in which **God speaks to His people**: Psalm 108:7-9; 81:6-16; 50:7-15; 75:2-5

*"7 God has promised in His holiness:
"With exultation I will divide up Shechem
And portion out the Valley of Succoth.
8 Gilead is Mine; Manasseh is Mine;
Ephraim is My helmet, Judah My sceptre.
9 Moab is My washbasin;
Upon Edom I cast My shoe;
Over Philistia I shout in triumph.""* – **Psalm 108:7-9 ESV**

––––––––––––––-

*"6 I relieved your shoulder of the burden; your hands were freed from the basket.
7 In distress you called, and I delivered you; I answered you in the secret place of thunder;
I tested you at the waters of Meribah.*   Selah

⁸ Hear, O my people, while I admonish you! O Israel, if you would but listen to Me!
⁹ There shall be no strange god among you; you shall not bow down to a foreign god.
¹⁰ I am the Lord your God, who brought you up out of the land of Egypt.
Open your mouth wide, and I will fill it.

¹¹ "But My people did not listen to My voice; Israel would not submit to Me.
¹² So I gave them over to their stubborn hearts, to follow their own counsels.
¹³ Oh, that My people would listen to Me, that Israel would walk in My ways!
¹⁴ I would soon subdue their enemies and turn My hand against their foes.
¹⁵ Those who hate the Lord would cringe toward Him, and their fate would last forever.
¹⁶ But He would feed you with the finest of the wheat, and with honey from the rock I would satisfy you." –**Psalm 81:6-16 ESV**

– – – – – – – – – – –

"⁷ Hear, O My people, and I will speak;
O Israel, I will testify against you. I am God, your God.
⁸ Not for your sacrifices do I rebuke you;
your burnt offerings are continually before Me.
⁹ I will not accept a bull from your house or goats from your folds.
¹⁰ For every beast of the forest is Mine - the cattle on a thousand hills.
¹¹ I know all the birds of the hills, and all that moves in the field is Mine.

¹² "If I were hungry, I would not tell you,
for the world and its fullness are Mine.
¹³ Do I eat the flesh of bulls or drink the blood of goats?
¹⁴ Offer to God a sacrifice of thanksgiving,

And perform your vows to the Most High,
¹⁵ And call upon Me in the day of trouble;
I will deliver you, and you shall glorify Me." - **Psalm 50:7-15 ESV**

God also **addresses the wicked**: Psalm 50:16-23; 2:5-6

"¹⁶ But to the wicked God says: "What right have you to recite My statutes or take My covenant on your lips?
¹⁷ For you hate discipline, and you cast my words behind you.
¹⁸ If you see a thief, you are pleased with him, and you keep company with adulterers.

¹⁹ "You give your mouth free rein for evil, and your tongue frames deceit.
²⁰ You sit and speak against your brother; you slander your own mother's son.
²¹ These things you have done, and I have been silent; you thought that I was one like yourself. But now I rebuke you and lay the charge before you.

²² "Mark this, then, you who forget God, lest I tear you apart, and there be none to deliver!
²³ The one who offers thanksgiving as his sacrifice glorifies me; to one who orders his way rightly I will show the salvation of God!" - **Psalm 50:16-23 ESV**

———————————————

"⁵ Then He will speak to them in His wrath,
And terrify them in His fury, saying,
⁶ "As for Me, I have set My King
On Zion, My holy hill." – **Psalm 2:5-6 ESV**

———————————————

"At the set time that I appoint I will judge with equity.
³ When the earth totters, and all its inhabitants, it is I who

keep steady its pillars.   Selah
⁴ I say to the boastful, 'Do not boast,' and to the wicked, 'Do not lift up your horn;
⁵ Do not lift up your horn on high, or speak with haughty neck.'" - **Psalm 75:2-5 ESV**

God even **speaks of David!** Psalm 89:20-37

"²⁰ "I have found David, my servant;
with my holy oil I have anointed him,
²¹ So that my hand shall be established with him;
my arm also shall strengthen him.
²² The enemy shall not outwit him;
the wicked shall not humble him.
²³ I will crush his foes before him
and strike down those who hate him.
²⁴ My faithfulness and my steadfast love shall be with him,
And in my name shall his horn be exalted.
²⁵ I will set his hand on the sea
and his right hand on the rivers.
²⁶ He shall cry to me, 'You are my Father, my God,
and the Rock of my salvation.'
²⁷ And I will make him the firstborn,
the highest of the kings of the earth.
²⁸ My steadfast love I will keep for him forever,
and my covenant will stand firm for him.
²⁹ I will establish his offspring forever
and his throne as the days of the heavens.
³⁰ If his children forsake my law
and do not walk according to my rules
³¹ If they violate My statutes
and do not keep My commandments,
³² then I will punish their transgression with the rod
and their iniquity with stripes,
³³ But I will not remove from him my steadfast love
or be false to my faithfulness.
³⁴ I will not violate my covenant
or alter the word that went forth from my lips.
³⁵ Once for all I have sworn by My holiness;

I will not lie to David.
36 His offspring shall endure forever,
   his throne as long as the sun before me.
37 Like the moon it shall be established forever,
   a faithful witness in the skies." *Selah"* – **Psalm 89:20-37 ESV**

There is a portion of a psalm in which **God speaks to Jesus!**

"You are my Son; today I have begotten you.
8 Ask of me, and I will make the nations your heritage,
And the ends of the earth your possession.
9 You shall break them with a rod of iron
And dash them in pieces like a potter's vessel." – **Psalm 2:7-9 ESV**

There is even a portion of a psalm that **God sings over *us*!** Psalm 91:14-16

"14 Because he holds fast to Me in love, I will deliver him;
I will protect him, because he knows My name.
15 When he calls to me, I will answer him;
I will be with him in trouble; I will rescue him and honour him.
16 With long life I will satisfy him and show him My salvation." – **Psalm 91: 14-16 ESV**

If you think that is odd that God should sing over us, consider this Scripture:

"The Lord your God is in your midst,
A mighty One who will save;
He will rejoice over you with gladness;
He will quiet you by His love;
He will exult over you with loud singing." - **Zephaniah 3:17 ESV**

Many of psalms cross categories. For example: Some psalms start with an invitation and then follow with praise. In another, David is praying desperately but before he finishes he is praising God or at least pointing to God as the answer!

> *"O Lord, how many are my foes!*
> *Many are rising against me;*
> *² many are saying of my soul,*
> *"There is no salvation for him in God."* Selah
>
> *³ But You, O Lord, are a shield about me,*
> *My glory, and the lifter of my head.*
> *⁴ I cried aloud to the Lord,*
> *And he answered me from his holy hill.* Selah
>
> *⁵ I lay down and slept;*
> *I woke again, for the Lord sustained me.*
> *⁶ I will not be afraid of many thousands of people*
> *Who have set themselves against me all around.*
>
> *⁷ Arise, O Lord!*
> *Save me, O my God!*
> *For you strike all my enemies on the cheek;*
> *You break the teeth of the wicked.*
> *⁸ Salvation belongs to the Lord;*
> *Your blessing be on your people!* Selah" – **Psalm 3 ESV**

There are many psalms similar to this: Psalm 3; 13; 22; 69; 102 (In fact, they are too numerous to list them all!)

In summary then, there are songs *to* God, and songs *about* God to others (e.g. testimonies). There are *exhortations* to others (even angels) to come worship God, to give thanks and praise, and songs sung to *encourage oneself.* Then there are psalms where *God speaks* to Jesus, to David, to Israel, to the wicked, and to those who love Him. Finally, there are *prophetic* psalms, and songs of *warfare!*

Wow! That's a lot of different kinds of psalms! I included them all not to draw this out laboriously, but to make a point. There is such a large spectrum of content and even audiences to whom the psalms are directed, as well as reasons for their singing! It is easy to put the Book of Psalms into the *"lovely little songs of praise'* category, but the Psalms are much, much more, and all were considered songs of worship.

Note: as mentioned however, not all types of songs and prayers listed in the Book of Psalms would be appropriate for use in the modern Sunday service. (cg. Psalm 88)

Nevertheless, with such a variety at our disposal, the ramifications here are that we too can use various kinds of psalms/songs in our modern worship services, as we sing to God, to our brethren, to ourselves, God to us, and combinations of these! In fact, these psalm elements/types are already present in our modern worship service! For example: We may open with songs like, *"Come let us go up to the mountain of our Lord"* or *"I will enter His gates with thanksgiving in my heart"*, then sing praise and declarations of God's mighty works, followed with adoration and awe - even very intimate songs, and finish in prophecy or the prophetic song. All are legitimate Biblically based songs or psalms.

I have often heard criticism about modern worship songs being too *"me"* focussed, but the psalms clearly demonstrate that our *own testimony* and even prayers for help are legitimate forms of worship! (As mentioned earlier, if you are composing something in this vain, I would add the proviso that it should produce yet another reason for the congregation to praise God! You could hardly have a song of "Whoa is me!" and leave it there. That would not glorify God but rather glorify the strife you were in!)

By the way, all these songs also involve *music* and are *corporate*. So although we *can* worship in our hearts without uttering a single word, and although we *can* worship verbally without music, not only are there examples found in the Old & New Testaments which set the precedence for the inclusion of music in a corporate setting, but Paul *instructs* us to do so. Why does he tell us use music? Because loving God involves passion, and music provides that platform, *and* because worshipping Him in love, adoration and joy is the ultimate result that God is looking for from each of us.

I can understand the complaint that modern worship music can appear as a performance to the uninitiated. It is usually presented first in the Sunday service and can occupy a large chunk of time, giving it an air of pre-eminence. Those who are a little more scholastic may feel this is, therefore, elevating music above the Word of God, or at least detracting from it. However, this conclusion comes from an analysis of the outward appearance only, and not the heart of those worshipping, or the worship itself. In addition to what is not taken into consideration and perhaps of most major importance, is the work of the Holy Spirit as He speaks and tweaks each soul who has his/her eyes firmly fixed on Jesus during the worship.

Finally then, the Old Testament, and indeed, the entire Book of Psalms, is full of prayer and praise put to music. Music and in fact, all the arts, are what we use we express ourselves in worship. A couple of quotes from Johann Sebastian Bach:

> "*Where there is devotional music, God is always at hand with His gracious presence.*"

> "*Music is an agreeable harmony for the honour of God and the permissible delights of the soul.*"

> "*The final aim and reason of all music is nothing other than the glorification of God and the refreshment of the spirit.*"

Music is an important part of worship. It was always God's intention for use in worship. Worship is a heart response to His greatness and goodness. Music is the carrier used to convey with potency our true heart towards Him in worship, because music has the capacity to put us back in touch with our spiritual and emotional side, as it connects and engages the heart and spirit, without the rational mind.

Music Styles & Genres

There are those that believe that certain music styles are satanic because satanists are reported to have used these styles (or similar) in their rituals, or to promote ungodly behaviour. I want to state up front that I haven't read one scripture verse where Satan ever created anything. In fact, he is described quite oppositely – as one who comes to steal, kill and destroy. Jesus also described him as a liar. He uses and copies and defiles, but does this destroyer ever create? Our Father – God Almighty – is the creator of all things. Satan was only ever a created being. He can use the gift of music but can he create it? On the other hand, we were made in God's image and now as born again believers, we have our creative God living in us. We now have the mind of Christ and are led by the Holy Spirit. We have, therefore, become creative beings just like our Father.

Satan can and does pervert men's creative ideas or pollute those ideas with lies or filth. Yes, Lucifer has been called the "top-dog" worship leader in heaven, but that does not automatically follow that he created all the music, though it is possible. If so, does he have any musical creativity now that he has been exiled to the earth? Perhaps it was only possible in the presence of a creative God. One thing is certain, he can use other people's creative ability to his own advantage – some singer songwriters even testifying to something *inspiring* them, pushing their pens as they compose the words, or giving them lyrics outright, but this is a *pollution* of creative ability and not the ability itself.

Yes, some songs can carry a very bad/evil anointing. There have been some secular artists that have openly testified in interviews that when they sang a particular song at a concert, violent fights broke out – some even ending in death. Was this more to do with the artists or the song? We could argue that either way, but the fruit was definitely bad. Therefore, we can definitely say that that particular song was very corrupted when performed by this band! However, that does not mean the entire genre is bad because of one song. We need to be careful that we don't again "*throw the proverbial baby out with the bathwater*", and label all similar styles of music as evil. I feel this is a reaction out of fear and legalism, rather than based on any good and sound reason, or founded in Scripture.

Besides which, is the God who redeemed man so small that He

cannot redeem something as trivial as a music style? For example: Jazz is said to have had quite lude beginnings, but there are anointed Christian composers who have used this style to create some wonderful anointed praise music that definitely inspires people to worship.

Because God is listening to our hearts, I personally believe the *style* of worship music used is irrelevant. Yes, I've watched those old documentaries that tried to persuade people that rock & roll music was totally satanic, but I remain unconvinced. There are many rock & roll style Christian songs full of the Holy Spirit that have captured the attention of the unsaved, even bringing some to salvation! Still, you need to be convinced in your own mind, one way or another.

For any of us to fold our hands and declare, "I refuse to sing that song because the style is satanic!" even though the words our honouring God and those who are singing it are worshipping wholeheartedly, we are the one's missing out! We have elevated our opinion's importance above the opportunity to worship in unity with our brothers and sisters in Christ. Insisting on our own way or the highway is not an act of love!

Nevertheless, if people object to certain songs, then perhaps the best place to discuss these issues is with headship, and in a loving and rational manner, without pointing fingers and playing the blame game! If it turns out that you can't use a particular song, so what! There are plenty of worship songs from which to choose. The last thing you want to do is to create division. Let everything be done in love. Just keep your own heart pure and submitted.

With regard to other modern styles, worship leaders should also be mindful that not everyone in the church wants to, or should have to keep up with the latest greatest songs. Just because a song is new, doesn't give it precedence as *better*. Remember that God is not interested in the style or the date, but the heart. Yes, the psalmist says to sing a *new* song to the Lord, but a little digging would reveal that the "new song" mentioned here is actually a spiritual song, led by the Holy Spirit.

Using an older song here and there has the potential to lift the worship: Not because old is better or more anointed, but because people know the song, they are able to close their eyes and focus on Jesus while they sing. They are free to connect with God without the distraction of unfamiliar words or music. Anything that helps facilitate worship is good despite its age.

Please don't misunderstand what I am saying here. I'm not advocating the use of old songs in preference to the new. No way! Introduce new songs by all means, but don't be in a hurry to introduce too many at a time. Be mindful that the purpose of these songs is worship, not distraction.

Finally, I've heard internet worship teachers instruct worship leaders to not pick anything but songs with simple melodies. The reason given is that the songs are too hard for the congregation to learn, and if someone new attends they need to be able to join in as well. Needless to say, there exists a trend for Christian worship songwriters to "dumb down" their songs to suit. As a result of this simplification process, a great deal of our modern church music has become droll and monotonous and very repetitive compared to many of the hymns of old. So many modern worship songs use only four chords or less, repeated over and over.

By comparison, some of those old hymns/songs were quite technical, with a myriad of chord changes incorporating the use of augmented and diminished chord arrangements. Again, I'm definitely not advocating hymns above modern styles. Not at all! I am simply pointing out that we need to give more credit to the ability of the congregation to learn songs. Consider the technical aspects of the old hymn, "Oh, For a Thousand Tongues!" composed by Charles Wesley (not to be confused by the more modern simplified renditions of the song. Here is the Youtube version of the original. https://youtu.be/4O9kw3cILpg. Note the trills, the counterpoints and amazing harmonies, not to mention the copious chording of the accompaniment!) Many congregations down the years have sung that song, including all its vocal parts and with great exuberance!

Again, I'm not advocating songs so difficult that even the music team struggles with them either. God forbid! Nevertheless, it seems to me that there are more musically competent songs in the secular world that people love to sing over and over as they go about their daily business. Why - because they are *catchy*. A catchy tag/chorus will have people sing along every time.

The idea is not to be unpredictable or even technical, but to introduce something that people can catch onto quickly and sing without looking at the screen. Technicality is not even the real issue here! The idea is to help them focus on Jesus and not to distract them with the song itself. I know of at least one church that only used choruses for that very reason!

So if you happen to be a songwriter, don't "dumb down" your songs because it's what you heard somewhere, but do try and make the tags catchy and easily memorable - not monotonous. Most importantly, allow the Holy Spirit to help you creatively, both musically and lyrically.

The Question of Volume

Worship can be noisy! The Word of God repeatedly instructs us to come before the Lord with shouts of praise, singing, music and joyful noise:

> *"Shout for joy to God, all the earth; [2]sing the glory of his name; give to him glorious praise! [3] Say to God, "How awesome are your deeds! So great is your power that your enemies come cringing to you. [4] All the earth worships you and sings praises to you; they sing praises to your name." -* **Psalm 66:1-4 ESV**

> *" Sing aloud to God our strength; shout for joy to the God of Jacob! [2] Raise a song; sound the tambourine, the sweet lyre with the harp." -* **Psalm 81:1-2 ESV**

> *"Oh come, let us sing to the Lord; let us make a joyful noise to the rock of our salvation! [2] Let us come into his presence*

with thanksgiving; let us make a joyful noise to him with songs of praise!" - **Psalm 95:1-2 ESV**

" Oh sing to the Lord a new song, for he has done marvellous things! His right hand and his holy arm have worked salvation for him. *² The Lord has made known his salvation; he has revealed his righteousness in the sight of the nations.* *³ He has remembered his steadfast love and faithfulness to the house of Israel. All the ends of the earth have seen the salvation of our God.*

⁴ Make a joyful noise to the Lord, all the earth; break forth into joyous song and sing praises! *⁵ Sing praises to the Lord with the lyre, with the lyre and the sound of melody!* *⁶ With trumpets and the sound of the horn make a joyful noise before the King, the Lord!"* - **Psalm 98:1-6 ESV**

"Make a joyful noise to the Lord, all the earth! *²Serve the Lord with gladness! Come into his presence with singing!* *³ Know that the Lord, he is God! It is he who made us, and we are his; we are his people, and the sheep of his pasture.* *⁴ Enter his gates with thanksgiving, anᵈ his courts with praise! Give thanks to him; bless his name!* *⁵ For the Lord is good; his steadfast love endures forever, and his faithfulness to all generations."* - **Psalm 100:1-5 ESV**

Note: this "noise" was a joyful exuberance. When Solomon's temple was first dedicated, the glory was so thick that even the priest could not minister. This occurred after very noisy and exuberant praise!

"¹³ and it was the duty of the trumpeters and singers to make themselves heard in unison in praise and thanksgiving to the Lord), and when the song was raised, with trumpets and cymbals and other musical instruments, in praise to the Lord, 'For He is good, for His steadfast love endures forever', the house of the Lord, was filled with a cloud, ¹⁴ so that the priests could not stand to minister because of the cloud, for the glory of the Lord filled the house of God." – **2 Chronicles 5:13-14 ESV**

Old Testament worship was often times very loud, with people joyfully shouting and singing, with shofars and trumpets blaring, and with drums and cymbals banging and clanging, as well as other instruments like stringed instruments and even flutes (See Psalm 5 directions to choirmaster or Psalm 150).

Now some might be tempted to argue that the noise levels are far greater today because of artificial amplification. The acoustic nature of the Old Testament worship, surely would have been more "tolerable", but anyone who has sat near a shofar when it is played will know first hand just how deafening they can be (or any trumpet for that matter). They were not usually played solo, or once only either.

Nevertheless, today many churches *do* use the latest, greatest sound amplification gear, and some *do* turn the volume up to deafening volumes. Though I personally don't have a problem with people shouting or raising their voices to God, or even with the volume being a *little* loud, I am alarmed when the volume is amplified beyond a comfortable hearing range for the greater part of the congregation.

Causing one's brethren discomfort is simply **not** "*loving* the brethren". Rather, what the sound technician is saying here is that his own personal volume preference is more important than the believer's comfort! Yes, I'm aware that the excuse in the past has always been that the volume in the house needed to exceed the volume in the fold-backs, but these day when earpiece fold-backs are common place, that argument no longer holds up.

Unfortunately, the simple facts are, that when people can't hear themselves sing, they won't! (I personally know of a study conducted by Dennis Prince of "*Resource Music*" here in Australia. He visited church to church with a DB meter, and noting the congregation's participation at various volumes. He discovered that over a certain DB volume people stopped singing! It had nothing to do with the music style, the popularity, or even the age of the songs – only the volume.)

Older people, in particular, find loud noises difficult to listen to because many of their hearing frequencies have deteriorated or have been completely lost, causing the music to sound to them like muffled noise! It can also literally hurt their ears!

Again, I know of many people that have left churches, not because they have any problems with the church, (many actually loved the church and preferred to stay if they could), but because the music was intolerably loud. This is no lie, and the numbers are not low! If people leave, or even have to wear earplugs to prevent hearing damage, then the music is probably *too loud!*

Some have argued that in order to set the various instrument and voice levels correctly, the volume must be loud. I understand this, however, that is suggesting that correct mix outweighs the congregation's comfort. What are we really saying here - that perfectionism in this ministry is more important than encouraging people to worship? What are we there for? Let everything be done with love for one another, and to encourage worship, not simply because by some worldly standard it must measure up.

You may not want to hear what I'm saying because you have your own opinions on the matter, but I do challenge you to do your own research, remembering that churches generally have people who are *all* ages, not just young people, and statistically, in Western societies at least, the populations are aging!

As the music director, the buck stops with you. If you have complaints about the volume, then you are directly responsible to check the merits of that complaint. It is then a further responsibility to *act appropriately,* and to ensure that all the members of the congregation are being loved and respected in every aspect of your ministry.

Conversely, if one or two find the worship music too loud, and after investigation they appear to be the only people with this complaint (and, in fact, most people are enjoying the worship at its current level), perhaps some earplugs would be in order for them. They do not block all sound, but lower the volume to acceptable levels.

When the volume is merely a matter of preference and not of discomfort or hearing damage, then we as a congregation need to grow up and button it!

Is Silence Part of Worship?

What about being still before the Lord? We often are quiet as we wait on the Lord for the operation of the Gifts of the Spirit. As I stated earlier, there are very few Scriptures out of the many dealing with worship that speak of silence during worship. There is reference made to silence in Psalm 62 but it refers to waiting patiently for God to save, not to worship in silence. Habakkuk 2:20 mentions silence before the Lord: *"But the Lord is in His holy temple; let all the earth keep silence before Him."* But on closer inspection it is in reference to other gods and idols. They cannot boast anything for they are nothing in comparison to our God.

The only New Testament reference where silence took place in worship was in the book of Revelation 8:1. Rather than insert the entire account here, (please re-read this account for yourselves) here's a brief outline.

In Revelation chapter 5, John describes a scene where no one was found worthy to open the scroll. However, when Jesus appears on the scene, the place erupts in praise for our Great King, for He alone is found to be worthy. Then the Spotless Lamb of God removes the seals from the scroll one at a time, and John spends the next chapter describing the devastation this causes on the earth. Then in chapter 7 John goes on to describe the sealing of the 144,000 and an uncountable multitude from every nation and tongue, standing before the throne praising Him. John asks who these people are, and is told that these are those who have come out of the great tribulation. Then in Chapter 8 Jesus takes the last remaining seal off the scroll and *then there is silence.* The seven trumpets are about to sound, and heaven is awe struck in anticipation of the fulfilment of God's purposes.

Silence can interrupt our worship when God is about to do something awesome among us. Note that it is not the worship that is silent, but that silence emerges as He is about to move. It is a divinely appointed time of anticipation – a gasp of *"What glorious thing is God about to do?"* If the worship leader were to tell the people to be quiet when it was not of God, perhaps to try and make something happen, or *"it happened last week I'll try it again this week"*, we'd probably be waiting for something, but nothing of consequence would occur, thus making the worship leader look foolish.

On the other hand, there are times when the presence of the Holy Spirit descends and everyone is so over-awed by the majesty of God, that no one is inclined to sing or utter a word. (This is no doubt what happened in Solomon's temple when it was first dedicated. The Scripture does not say it was silent, but that the glory was so thick, the priests were unable to minister! I can imagine that they were all on the floor doing carpet time!)

This time of silence is almost a personal time, where each person is totally transfixed on God, not wanting to look away – not wanting to miss a thing. A worship leader who feels like he needs to do something because he fails to recognise the silence for what it is, will miss this great opportunity for God to move, or even grieve the Holy Spirit by the fleshy distraction. There's a blessing to be had in the awe of that moment. It may not be for the worship leader, but many people will be receiving it.

On the other hand, failing to see the congregational signals that the moment has passed (e.g. people looking around or fidgeting uncomfortably or worse – bored!) could be just as detrimental. (It's great to have our eyes closed and be enraptured in the moment, but a worship leader's job is to lead the people, not to zone out on our own.) It takes a worship leader with an ear inclined to the Holy Spirit, and with wisdom, to negotiate these times of silence, and to allow the Holy Spirit to finish what He started, without letting the worship to decline or fizzle out.

Emotion in Worship?

Emotionalism appears to be one of the biggest criticisms about modern worship songs. Perhaps some of the arguments are warranted, but some certainly are not. Some of the common complaints seem to be centred on whether songs are about us or God, about how we feel, rather than extolling God's virtues.

Firstly, in answer to this, I again would like to point out that many of the Psalms are extremely emotional, and some psalmists even go to great lengths to describe the negative aspects of how they are feeling. Take Psalm 88 as an example:

Psalm 88 A Song. A Psalm of the Sons of Korah.

> "¹ *O Lord, God of my salvation,*
> *I cry out day and night before You.*
> ² *Let my prayer come before You;*
> *Incline your ear to my cry!*
>
> ³ *For my soul is full of troubles,*
> *And my life draws near to Sheol.*
> ⁴ *I am counted among those who go down to the pit;*
>
> *I am a man who has no strength,*
> ⁵ *Like one set loose among the dead,*
> *Like the slain that lie in the grave,*
> *Like those whom you remember no more,*
> *For they are cut off from your hand.*
> ⁶ *You have put me in the depths of the pit,*
> *In the regions dark and deep.*
> ⁷ *Your wrath lies heavy upon me,*
> *And you overwhelm me with all your waves.   Selah*
>
> ⁸ *You have caused my companions to shun me;*
> *You have made me a horror to them.*
> *I am shut in so that I cannot escape;*
> *My eye grows dim through sorrow.*
> *Every day I call upon You, O Lord;*

I spread out my hands to You.
¹⁰ Do you work wonders for the dead?
Do the departed rise up to praise You? Selah
¹¹ Is your steadfast love declared in the grave,
Or your faithfulness in Abaddon?
¹² Are your wonders known in the darkness,
Or your righteousness in the land of forgetfulness?

¹³ But I, O Lord, cry to You;
In the morning my prayer comes before You.
¹⁴ O Lord, why do You cast my soul away?
Why do You hide your face from me?
¹⁵ Afflicted and close to death from my youth up,
I suffer Your terrors; I am helpless.
¹⁶ Your wrath has swept over me;
Your dreadful assaults destroy me.
¹⁷ They surround me like a flood all day long;
They close in on me together.
¹⁸ You have caused my beloved and my friend to shun me;
My companions have become darkness." – **Psalm 88 ESV**

Note, that in some of these lines, this particular Psalmist even blames God for casting him off and not coming to his rescue!

David, the prince of psalmists, on the other hand, has his own desperation highlighted in his psalms (for example: "*Cast me not away from your presence, and take not your Holy Spirit from me.*" – Psalm 51:11 ESV), but David also saw God as the answer. He would cry out, but he would also encourage himself by singing of God's great works and love for His people

Modern worship songs too, are often born out of a person's own life experience. Composers pour out their emotions before the Lord through their musical art form. In this way they are very similar to David's Psalms. Many of these songs begin as Christian popular songs but later are adopted into the church worship repertoire. (e.g. the song *He is Jealous for Me*) Why? Because these songs resonate with people so much so that they want to use them to worship God!

To be blunt, there *is* an element of emotion in our worship because it is a heart/spirit response to Him, and we have a very intimate relationship with Him (or should have). This worship response or reaction is initiated *because* it has connected with us on a very deep spiritual level. We don't just suddenly decide, *"Oh, I guess I should worship God for that!"* It automatically flows out of our spirits as a natural response. Therefore, it will always contain some kind of emotion whether it is joy, awe, thankfulness, love, or something else.

That being said, let me state again, that while our Christianity is **not based on** emotion or emotionalism, but rather the finished work and blood of Jesus Christ, **neither it is devoid of emotion**. As I also stated earlier, worship and love are inextricably linked!

We have entered into a relationship with God, and are now an integral part of His family. There is a connection there that may have started as just an introduction, (more often than not it is an overwhelming realisation that God first loved us!) but as we've come to know God, we began to love Him more and more. This relationship is anything but emotion*less*. A marriage may be a contract in the eyes of law, but is far from emotion*less*. Marriage is a picture of Christ and His church! The church is His Bride. How then can it be devoid of emotions?

Love can be described in many ways, but all would agree that it is, for the main part at least, an emotion, and out of that emotion flows acts of service, obedience and giving. To borrow a phrase from Heidi Baker, *"We are compelled by love!"* It is the manifestation of the loving God who lives within us.

However, we are commanded to love regardless of our feelings because we have the love of God living in and available to us, that enables us to minister to others. It is God loving through us to others – if we allow Him to do so.

Of course, love also proves itself with *action*, but love that is action *without* any emotion whatsoever, or without the Love of the Divine flowing through us, is just works, duty and obligation.

Paul says in 1 Corinthians 13 that without love, our works are nothing! Take out the emotion and all you have are a set of rules and regulations and Christianity becomes no different to any other religion. If worship is just something we always do without emotion, how can it be said to contain love? Would it not then, according to Paul, amount to nothing!

Worship without love and indeed, without joy (another emotion), is dead! *In His presence there is fullness of joy and in His right hand are pleasures evermore.* - (Psalm 16:11) The Psalms mention "joy" nearly 50 times, and often exhort us to praise Him joyfully. Joy *is* an emotion. There is therefore, no surprise that when the Holy Spirit leads worship, it is not without deep feelings and emotions of love and joy, mixed with awe and reverence. No, we do not rely on those emotions but the Word of God! To worship because we want some emotion or feel good experience, is to worship worship, which is idolatry!

Rather, worship is our *response* to the God who is wonderful beyond description because we love and know Him, and He never ceases to amaze us with His greatness, beauty, kindness, patience, grace, mercy, and every other extraordinary aspect of His character. If we did not know and love Him (as non-Christians do), what He has accomplished and who He is would probably mean absolutely nothing to us. But we *do* know Him and our spirit cry, "Worthy!" No, worship that never knows emotion has missed the mark!

(Some have said that because worship is our response to the revelation the Holy Spirit gives to us from the Word of God, then it follows that the preaching should be before the worship each Sunday. However, if the worship songs contain Biblical descriptions of God and what He has done, then the same heart response will be present! Really it shouldn't matter when we have the worship. Surely such a complaint is trivial!)

Finally on this topic of emotion, we must be careful that we do not crush our brothers and sisters or make them feel ashamed, by labeling them as emotion seekers rather than God seekers.

Only God knows the true intents and purposes of our hearts. Besides which, since it is *"no longer I who live but Christ who lives in me"* (Galatians 2:20), any criticism we throw at other Christians is really criticising Christ. Think about it!

Respectful Movements?

Do physical postures such as raising hands, or dancing, or any other physical actions add to worship as people sing or speak the praises of God, or are modern versions purely disrespectful and irreverent? Are these things even Biblical or merely another way we are entertaining ourselves to make ourselves feel good about ourselves without reference to God?

Dancing

To answer that question, let's look at one such occurrence of dance used as worship in the Old Testament to compare: David danced before the Lord. He was zealous for God and rejoiced in God!

> *"12 Now it was told King David, saying, "The Lord has blessed the house of Obed-Edom and all that belongs to him, because of the ark of God." So David went and brought up the ark of God from the house of Obed-Edom to the City of David with gladness. 13 And so it was, when those bearing the ark of the Lord had gone six paces, that he sacrificed oxen and fatted sheep. 14 Then David danced before the Lord with all his might; and David was wearing a linen ephod. 15 So David and all the house of Israel brought up the ark of the Lord with shouting and with the sound of the trumpet."*
> 2 **Sam 6:12-15 NKJV**

Some will say, *"Yes, but he was being respectful. These modern dances are not at all respectful."* Some have speculated that David was naked but the Bible tells us that David wore only a linen ephod, a priestly garment, and not his kingly regalia, and this caused his wife, Michal, to describe him as vulgar, and shamelessly uncovering himself.

"How the king of Israel honoured himself today, uncovering himself today before the eyes of his servants' female servants, as one of the vulgar fellows shamelessly uncovers himself." – **2 Samuel 6:20 b - ESV**

Was Michal merely jealous of the other women watching him and slandered him as uncovered shamelessly to take a cheap stab at David, or was there something more to it? It is possible that the ephod was a little more revealing than expected as David danced about in it, and this, in turn, caused Michal to become upset – especially with the other women witnessing it. It was designed for priestly duties and not dancing, after all! Nevertheless, his dancing was described as shamelessly *uncovered!*

David was worshipping God zealously from his heart, and God was pleased. We humans tend to judge on the outward appearance, but God sees the heart, and His main concern is that very thing – the heart! There's a lesson in that story for us, I feel.

The most famous *early* Old Testament dance was from Miriam who danced in praise to God after He split the Red Sea open for the Israelites to cross them closed it up to destroy the Egyptians who were pursuing them.

"20 Then Miriam the prophetess, the sister of Aaron, took the timbrel in her hand; and all the women went out after her with timbrels and with dances." - **Exodus 5:20 NKJV**

In fact, in the Book of Psalms it says:

*"Let them praise His name with the **dance**;*
Let them sing praises to Him with the timbrel and harp." -
Psalm 149:3 ESV

"3Praise Him with trumpet sound;
Praise Him with lute and harp!
*4 Praise Him with tambourine and **dance**;*

Praise Him with strings and pipe!
⁵ Praise Him with sounding cymbals;
Praise Him withe loud clashing cymbals!
⁶Let everything that has breath praise the Lord!
Praise the Lord!" – **Psalm 150:3-5 ESV**

Dance and worship are frequently coupled together in the Old Testament. Obviously dance was accepted as the normal worship practice. Like music, dance is an artistic form of emotional expression – a way we convey our love and adoration to our mighty Father and God. In fact, many of the references to dance in the Bible, refer to dance as an expression of joy. How wonderful then is it to worship with expressions of joy, and how much this speaks of our trust in Him!

Dance, just like the lyrics of a song, can also deliver a story or testimony, or carry a message. Both of these aspects of dance (i.e. emotional conveyance and message delivery) provide another layer to the worship, highlighting that which the Holy Spirit is saying. Dance can also carry amazing anointing when led by the Holy Spirit. So why stifle that which is both Scriptural and pleasing to God?

Some may object to the *kind* of dancing done. My daughter, Amelia, is a very anointed Spirit led dancer who often uses flags as well. When I asked her about dancing styles, her reply was that "*Style doesn't really matter so much. God will use whatever you have in your repertoire of movements, whether trained or untrained.*"

If you are still wondering whether particular dance movements or actions are not acceptable, a good rule of thumb is surely, that if the dancing is disrespecting others and/or the personal space of others, or is a distraction to others, (or worse, lude or crude), then it is selfish and not honouring to God or to others, and as such, should cease. However, if it is none of these things, and the dancing is done in the Holy Spirit, then, really, the *style* or the kind of dance should not be an issue.

You, the music director, may not have considered the dancers and flag bearers as part of your worship team, and yet these people are bringing yet another aspect of worship, which carries its own anointing if led by the Holy Spirit. It's analogous to a canvas that is being filled by the Holy Spirit with different colours and textures. All these different worship aspects are being painted together to bring an amazing picture of what God is saying to His church that day! (Let me add here that even actual artists can be used to paint a prophetic picture during the worship, thus adding yet another dimension/aspect to the Holy Spirit message!)

As such, you will need wisdom to know when you should highlight them on the platform and when they should remain in the congregation to minister from there. If you let just anyone up at anytime, you may just be adding a distraction to the worship, so ensure it is Holy Spirit appointed before allowing this.

Because flags and banners can add yet another dimension to worship and are frequently employed by dancers, it may also be pertinent for you to know exactly what the various flags mean, and how they administer the anointing to the meeting. To that end, I will include a brief description flags and banners, that I hope will widen your vision for your worship group, and enrich your church's worship experience! :-)

Banners and Flags

According to *http://bonasdancesite.homestead.com*, in the Old Testament the most common Hebrew words used for banners were:

- *Degel* means to be conspicuous (Strong's 1713/1714)
- *Nace* means a signal (Strong's 5251)
- *Owth* also means a signal (Strong's 226)

Modern users are by no means suggesting that banner wavers commandeer the spotlight, but that when the people do see the banners, their attention is immediately pointed back to Jesus – the reason why we worship! They also show the enemy to whom we belong, instil fear into the enemy, and proclaim the Kingship of Jesus! The reasons to use banners in worship are many. (Much of this information is readily available on many websites on the internet and in books and articles on the subject! I cannot cite one in particular as a source for the following, over and above the rest as they all pretty much say the same things.)

1) Banners **suggest a rallying point of truth:**

> "⁴ *[But now] You have set up a* **banner** *for those who fear and worshipfully revere You [to which they may flee from the bow], a standard displayed because of the truth. Selah [pause, and calmly think of that]!"* - **Psalm 60:4 Amplified Bible, Classic Edition (AMPC)**

2) Banners **rally His people from across the globe;** calling them to come.

> "*He will lift up a* **banner** *to the nations from afar, And will whistle to them from the end of the earth; Surely they shall come with speed, swiftly."* – **Isaiah 5:26 NKJV**

> "*He will set up a* **banner** *for the nations, And will assemble the outcasts of Israel, And gather together the dispersed of Judah From the four corners of the earth."* - **Isaiah 11:12 NKJV**

> "*Lift up a* **banner** *on the high mountain, Raise your voice to them; Wave your hand, That they may enter the gates of the nobles."* – **Isaiah 13:2 NKJV**

> "*Set up a* **banner** *in the land, Blow the trumpet among the nations!"* – **Jeremiah 51:27a**

3) Banners **proclaim & mark the establishment of Jesus glorious reign.**

> *"And in that day there shall be a Root of Jesse,*
> *Who shall stand as a **banner** to the people;*
> *For the Gentiles shall seek Him,*
> *And His resting place shall be glorious."* – **Isaiah 11:10 NKJV**

> *"Go through,*
> *Go through the gates!*
> *Prepare the way for the people;*
> *Build up,*
> *Build up the highway!*
> *Take out the stones,*
> *Lift up a **banner** for the peoples!*

> *[11] Indeed the Lord has proclaimed*
> *To the end of the world:*
> *"Say to the daughter of Zion,*
> *'Surely your salvation is coming;*
> *Behold, His reward is with Him,*
> *And His work before Him.'"* - **Isaiah 62:10,11 NKJV**

4) Banners **put fear into the enemy.**

> *"'He* (speaking of Assyria) *shall cross over to his stronghold for fear, and his princes shall be afraid of the **banner**,' Says the Lord whose fire is in Zion and whose furnace is in Jerusalem."* - **Isaiah 31:9 NKJV**

5) God Himself raises His banner against them. He is our salvation and deliverer!

> *"According to their deeds, accordingly He will repay,*
> *Fury to His adversaries*
> *Recompense to His enemies;*
> *The coastlands He will fully repay.*

*¹⁹ So shall they fear the name of the Lord from the west,
And His glory from the rising of the sun;
When the enemy comes in like a flood,
The Spirit of the Lord will lift up a standard* (or **Banner***)
against him.*" – **Isaiah 29:18,19 NKJV**

6) Banners **declare to whom you belong:**

> *"Everyone of the children of Israel shall camp by his own
> standard (or **Banner**), beside the emblems of his father's
> house; they shall camp some distance from the tabernacle
> of meeting.*" – **Numbers 2:2 NKJV**

> *"Your enemies roar in the midst of Your meeting place; They
> set up their **banners** for signs.*" – **Psalm 74:4 -NKJV**

They were used in warfare for the same reason. In declaring to
which army you belonged, the banner became not just a rallying
point, but a symbol of fear for the enemy, (as the above Scriptures
illustrate).

Used in a modern setting, banners can be very powerful instruments of warfare. They tell the devil in no uncertain terms that
we rally to Jesus the King, that we belong to Him and His banner
over us is His love!

7) One of the names of God is Jehovah Nissi or **"*The Lord is my
Banner*".**

> *"⁵ And Moses built an altar and called the name of it, The
> Lord Is My **Banner**"* - **Exodus 17:15 ESV**

We are under His protection and rally to Him alone! His banner
instils fear in the enemy.

8) Further, **His banner of love extends over us.**

> *"He brought me to the banqueting house, and His **banner**
> over me was love.*" – **Song of Solomon 2:4 – ESV**

We are not just His army under His headship, but His people whom He loves. He is our fortress and shield, our strong tower to which we run in the time of trial. He covers us with His feathers and draws us close under His wing. This banner then, is a comfort to us, and a reminder that we are not alone.

9) It is **God who sets up our banners.**

> *"May we shout for joy over your salvation, and in the name of our God set up our **banners!**"* – **Psalm 20:5 ESV**

As you can see, these are some great reasons to use banners, but even more so when the Holy Spirit specifies not only their use, but also the use of a particular banner. As mentioned, the various colours and designs also have different meanings and as such carry specific anointing when used under the guidance of the Holy Spirit.

Here are just a few flag colours and their meanings but the list is not exhaustive (again these lists can be found all over the internet):

Silver:	Wisdom, Word of God, Divinity, Refined / Purified, Righteous,
Transparent:	Water Baptism, Wind of the Spirit
White:	Purity, Holiness, Innocence,Righteousness, Surrender, Salvation, Worthiness of God, Honour to God, Bride of Christ, Completion
Green:	New life, New beginnings, Born again, Restoration, Healing, Flourishing, Growth Prosperity, Praise
Yellow:	Joy, Celebration, Praise, Glory of God, God's Light, Divine Fire
Gold:	Kingship, Glory, Anointing, God's Presence, Deity, Tested, Sanctification

Brass:	Testing Fires, Purification
Orange:	The Fire of God, Warrior God, Revival, Harvest, Deliverance
Copper:	Washing, The Tabernacle Altar, Offering.
Bronze:	Strength, Atonement
Red/Blood:	The Blood of Christ, Blood Covenant, Cleansing Forgiveness, Salvation, Atonement, Consuming Fire, Warfare
Pink:	Intimacy, Heart of Flesh, First Love, Childlike Faith, Humility, Faithfulness
Wine:	New Wine, New birth, Filled, Multiplication, Overflow, Mercy
Royal Purple:	Kingship, Royalty, Majesty, the Throne of God, Kingdom, Dominion, Authority, Mediator, Honour, Wealth, Inheritance, and even our identity as kings under the King of kings
Royal Blue:	Holy Spirit, Heavenly/Spiritual Authority, Priesthood
Light Blue:	Peace, Grace, Living Water/The River of God, Revelation, Prophetic, Heaven, Prayer, mercy
Rainbow:	God's Promise, Covenant, Hope
Black:	Death to Self, Judgement, Sin, Bondage, Affliction, Darkness

(To be honest, I'm not sure when the use of a black flag would be appropriate!)

Many flags are also multi-coloured in appearance and carry a mixture of meanings from those above, in order to present a more precise meaning. For example: Fire can be comprised of yellow, orange and red. Because each of these colours represent fore, this combination reinforces the message, and further removes any ambiguity. There is now no mistaking this for the other meanings with which each colour is associated.

Some flags also incorporate symbols that carry an obvious meaning (again this list is far from exhaustive):

Crown =kingship,

White dove = Holy Spirit,

Pitcher pouring gold = glory of God being poured out,

Flames = the fire of God

World Map – call to pray for the nations

Wheat sheaf = harvest

Other symbols will be significant to the one/church who made them.

There are also different types of flags. Besides the normal everyday flags, there are long thin flags or elongated triangular flags that are more like standards used in battle. These can be used in warfare or victory, or even for healing – crushing the work of the enemy. There are billows and thin streamer flags. People even use a piece of fabric without a pole/stick/handle. Whatever the Holy Spirit says is appropriate to use, someone, somewhere has made that version!

If a single flag waver has only one set of flags, the Holy Spirit may still choose to use them, but the focus may be more on the dance or the way the flags are used. (For example, the windmill flag maneuver is said to carry quite a warfare anointing.)

The Holy Spirit will use whatever is in your worship toolbox for His purposes and ministry. Dancers and flag bearers therefore must also be in tune with the Holy Spirit and prepared to follow His lead. Otherwise, just like the music, it can be yet another performance and distraction.

Unfortunately, there have been complaints in the past that flag and/or banner waving is simply unnecessary, so lets just avoid problems and leave out flags and banners (and this has occurred in many churches). Some churches refuse to include flags and banners because, in the past, flag wavers who were dancing with their eyes closed, have inadvertently whacked other church patrons. On the other hand, sometimes this happens when people are walking around and not giving these worshippers a wide berth, or there is little to no spatial provision made for dancers with flags and banner bearers.

Using flags and banners effectively, demands that a space for flags should be designated out of the way of the through traffic – especially the traffic to and from the toilets/bathrooms. Flags may be considered by some to be an unnecessary instrument of worship, but keep in mind that flags are Biblical, and add an extra dimension to the worship.

In conclusion to this discussion, modern worship hasn't changed much at all from Old Testament worship. Dancers, flags and banners all have their place in worship according to the Bible. Further, under the Holy Spirit's direction, all these elements and ways of worship, add to a glorious God encountering worship service. Yes, it may look different to the era when people stood both motionless and without passion in their seats whilst singing from a hymnal, but modern worship is nonetheless Scriptural!

Be a Leader Worth Following

Character

What's Your Motivation?

It is said that your gift makes way for you, or may propel you into a position of influence. However, it is your ***character*** that will sustain that position. Your character needs to remain strong and uncorrupted in order to continue to give God all the glory, despite the myriad of compliments and the proclamations of praise you may receive. Those that easily fall prey to pride will see themselves hurled out of their ministry as quickly as God may have advanced them. No wonder the Bible tells us to guard our hearts with all diligence (Proverbs 4:23).

Now I need to become a little hard on you, so I apologise in advance. The goal here is to encourage worship leaders to do some soul searching and become totally committed to giving preference to the Holy Spirit. It is a loving friendship forged in obedience and trust. You want to ensure God receives all the glory so that He is able to manifest His glory among the saints. To that end, you must be the vessel He can use.

The first question to ask yourself (and hopefully you have already asked it) is, *"Why do you do what you do?"* Why are you music director? Is it so that you will become the next big international worship leader of renown? If so, quit! Is it to create and sell worship albums? If so, quit! If you are on the platform because you need to make yourself feel good about yourself, quit! If you desire the worship ministry more than you desire Him, that's idolatry - quit! Likewise, if you see worship as a step up into your "professional" ministry, quit!

If you are not totally sold out to ensuring God gets all the glory, get out of the way so that He can, because all the glory belongs to Him. If you're too full of yourself, or too larger than life on the platform, the Holy Spirit has no room to manoeuvre, and all that you're producing is entertainment or showing off. God can use people who have a heart after God like David, but not those full of themselves.

If you are more than happy to run the music department faithfully, humbly, with all your heart, and to your best ability, even if it's a small, unknown church of less than 100 people in the middle of nowhere, then your attitude is correct and will enable the Holy Spirit to use you all the more. He is not interested in elevating your glory unless by doing so it elevates God's!

You need to decide before another moment passes, what your priorities really are regarding this ministry. Is God your first love - above and beyond leading worship itself? What if you were asked to step down from ministry tomorrow – would you be devastated or continue to praise God? Job who suffered so much, was still able to say, "*Ye though He slay me, yet shall I praise Him!*" Do you want Him before any other person, position, thing, fame or career? Do you want to bring glory to Him alone?

What are your priorities? If before you walk onto that platform, you "*reckon yourself to be dead*", but "*alive to God in Christ Jesus our Lord*" (Romans 6:11), and if your desire is for Him above all else, you are the right person with the right character for the job.

As music Director, your number one goal is to ensure all the glory is given to God, as He so rightly deserves. You do this because you know and love Him, you have the skills to enable you to do it well, and have been called to this position. It's not about your popularity. As John the Baptist said when his disciples pointed out that Jesus had more people following after Him that John did, "*May He increase and I decrease!*" If you can live with that notion, you're in the right ministry, and your team will be effective under your care.

Don't misunderstand me here. I am not saying that you have to "prove" yourself to God before He will respond to you, or that God can't use you unless you reach a level of holiness. That's simply a "works mentality".

> "*8 For by grace you have been saved through faith. And this is not your own doing; it is the gift of God, 9 not a result of works, so that no one may boast.*" – **Ephesians 2:8-9 ESV**.

We have been made completely righteous by the blood of Christ Jesus, and now we can boldly approach the throne of grace, placing our petitions with expectancy and anticipation, before the Almighty God and Father. You are totally clean, and God loves you to the full measure of His love. In fact, He offered this to you in full at salvation. You didn't need to earn it, because He gave it freely. He so loves you!!! (John 3:16)

What I am discussing is your *character* not your righteous standing before God, your salvation, or even whether you are loved by God – those are given – end of discussion! It is your character that sustains your ministry, and it is your character that will cause you to seek God's glory before your own. It is also your character that will let you down and destroy your ministry if you do not guard your heart!

Guard Your Heart!

You may rightly consider that pride is not the problem for you. You constantly keep that in check, asking the Holy Spirit to remind you when it starts to raise its ugly head. You also have regular sessions with your headship or a close brother/sister to whom you remain accountable, and who loves you enough to tell you when you're out of line. This is brilliant! Well done! So far so good, but pride can manifest itself when we take our eyes off "who God says we are" and choose to develop other things in preference to our relationship with God.

As a friend who was praying under the anointing once stated as he prayed about pride, "*When there is no separation between a per-*

son and God (speaking of relationship), pride is unable to squeeze in between." I love that statement! Also, when a person's identity is one of a beloved son or daughter of the one true living God of all things, (and all that implies), there is no other identity with which a person would desire to align him/herself. Why would we want to be called the world's best worship leader, when God desires and loves us so intensely? God even thinks good thoughts about us! Just whose opinion trumps that!

Pride is a major pitfall and much talked about for those involved with platform ministries of any kind, and as such may also be relatively easy to spot. Not so the little day-to-day issues that arise which have the potential to trip us up unexpectedly. How we deal with them is where character is tested.

For example: The enemy loves to intervene the very morning we are scheduled to lead worship. It only takes a small misunderstanding, or a sharp word here or there and you can be at odds with your family, or a team member. So if you do have something against your brother before you bring your gift of worship to the altar, make sure you make your peace first as Jesus instructed, and Paul pleads with the church:

> "*23 So if you are offering your gift at the altar and there remember that your brother has something against you, 24 leave your gift there before the altar and go. First be reconciled to your brother, and then come and offer your gift.*"
> - **Matthew 5:13 ESV**

> "*18 If possible, so far as it depends on you, live peaceably with all.*" - **Romans 12:18 ESV**

Remember that unity and fellowship are important to God as well. Don't take any angst onto the platform. Keep your heart clear of any clutter, and deal with the issues, as much is as possible, as they arise.

If you are unable to deal with an issue beforehand, even though you want to do so, thankfully we can still turn to Jesus and know that we are fully accepted and fully loved. We are still sons and daughters of the most High God. Therefore, pray for that person and offer this upset before the throne and leave it there, having every intention of renewing your relationship with your brother or sister as soon as humanly possible (see Matthew 18: 15-20). Don't let the sun go down on your anger, (Ephesians 4:26). Forgive and bless! Be of one mind in unity with one another. (Philippians 2:2) Guard or "*Keep your heart with all diligence, for out of it spring the issues of life.*" (Proverbs 4:23) This is living like Jesus and developing character. A person of Jesus' character will leave no issue other than love between him/herself and his/her brethren, and love between him/herself and God (if you happen to feel let down by God in some way!)

That is not to say that if things have happened and you're in a mess that you cannot fix nor avoid, that you can't still lead worship. If you are willing to listen and be used of the Holy Spirit, He will lead you because you are a son/daughter and made perfectly righteous by the blood of Jesus. However, it is often *hard to hear* the Holy Spirit when thoughts about situations keep bombarding our mind, or there is dis-unity in the worship team.

This of course, is just one example out of many. Honesty, faithfulness, integrity, reliability, responsibility, trustworthiness, transparency, being able to forgive and overlook any unfair treatment, and most of all love, must undergird all you do as a leader in God's Kingdom. You must be in tune with the Holy Spirit at all times, be organised, be able to delegate as needed and be able to make the hard decisions. These are all the virtuous characteristics you will need to sustain your ministry.

If you have the right character (and can handle it), God may just highlight you to a well-respected position within your church movement, or perhaps even escalate you onto the world stage, but then again, He may not. Don't go looking for it unless you are 100% positive – you know that you know that you know - that He has called you to that kind of ministry.

So you're expertly skilled musically – I'm sorry but this is not the required qualification! Check out what happens on the mission field. God still shows up there without music experts! That's not to say that some level of skill is not important. You would not have been called to this position if you had no skill at all! Even David used skilled musicians and singers!

However, the biggest qualification to allowing the Holy Spirit to lead worship is your willingness to allow Him to give all the glory to God. He wants genuine hearts that are pliable in His hands. Do you have a heart like David's? If so He can use you too!! :-)

If it turns out that you are in fact called to an international or inter-church music worship ministry, He will always deal with your heart, character and motives first while you are working on your skills etc. in the place of insignificance. That is, if you allow Him to do so. If, on the other hand, you try to run ahead, you may be heading for disaster. Better to fail a few times in the hidden places than on a world arena!

This growth in character can sometimes (and very often does) include a few very heavy trials to ensure the dross is cleaned off. (I think I can safely say that the majority of people who have always known they had a bigger ministry awaiting them, had to walk through their own fiery trials before they were ready to step into that ministry.) Only an impeccable character full of integrity and motivated by love, will keep you spiritually buoyant. Without character you will fall! Skill can only take you so far.

The bigger the spotlight, the brighter your character flaws and failings will appear. If you are not a person of Christian principal and integrity where no one else can see, the spotlight will eventually catch you out. Integrity in every area of your life is so important. This is amplified within the secular realm, which can and will "eat you up" if you are not completely dependant upon Him, and know who you are and your place in Christ.

You may think you are pretty strong and resilient already, but both the flattering and the nay-saying voices, and the temptations for pride building, will push you relentlessly in an effort to make you fall. In light of this, spending a little more time in the secret place, where God can mature you in His love and His word, is a wise course of action.

Don't rush, or force the doors open into ministry unless He is telling you to do so. If your headship is saying, "*No!*" don't assume he/she is in league with the devil – even if you've received prophecies about a big music ministry and you believe it's time! It could simply be that your pastor sees something negative about your character that you do not, and is trying to help you. Ask your pastor about this. Perhaps your pastor does not want to lose you, which you feel is a truly unfair restraint, but then again you may just need to raise up someone to take your place.

It could also be that someone has misrepresented you to your headship who has not heard your side of the story at all. Again, the only way to clear this up is to discuss this with your headship. Above all, pray about this. Ask for Holy Spirit guidance and wisdom, and whatever you do, be honouring and respectful to your headship and to your church.

As a leader, it is also worth keeping in mind that those you train will carry the same spiritual "DNA" (at least in part but it's often a very striking resemblance). In church ministry, the spiritual flavour is always top-down. If you have the wrong motives, or a self-serving character, you are going to develop worship leaders after your own kind. They will lead like you and will ultimately possess the same motives and ambitions. It is worth remembering that leaders are responsible before God for what they teach His children!

> "*Not many of you should become teachers, my brothers, for you know that we who teach will be judged with greater strictness.*" – **James 3:1 ESV**

You are their living example and this speaks louder than any teaching material you present! So the lesson here is to check yourself first!

To Hear & Follow

Jesus said that His sheep would know His voice. He hasn't stopped talking to us. However, we have so much noise coming at us from all avenues of life, that His still small voice can be blocked out, or go unrecognised. Is it any wonder that we are told to *"be still and know that He is God"* (Psalm 46:10)! We learn to hear Him in the stillness and quiet of the secret place. The more we stop to listen, the more we will hear. The more we hear and obey, the better worship leaders we become. We are "perfecting" our skill.

(If you have no idea what I am talking about, and haven't already done so, I suggest Ps. Mark Virkler's book, *Dialogue with God*[23]. He has also created a video teaching series that is readily available if you don't like reading. In his teaching sessions you will learn how to hear God clearly. From there it is a simple step from hearing in your daily prayer time to hearing God during worship.)

In truth, hearing God in worship is more about your relationship with Him, than perfecting your music, or bands, or harmonies. It is your relationship with the Holy Spirit that will help you enter the heavenly places, and will more than capably help others do the same. Being able to hear and obey is one of the most crucial elements of worship leading. (John 14:15) The other is the desire to worship alone and to come away to your secret place whenever possible.

Your own ability to worship God where no one sees – worship leading to an audience of one as the popular saying goes - the One – will be reflected in your abilities to lead a congregation in worship. If you fail miserably worshipping alone, you'll fail even more miserably in front of the whole church. The truth is: God wants you more than what you think you can do for Him. (I hope this message has shone through in all the discussion thus far.)

The best worship leaders are those who worshipped where no one else can see, worshipping and sitting in the Throne Room of

Heaven. There are no short cuts. As it is often said, "*You can't invite people to go where you have not been yourself.*" As Mark Virkler states, "*Those that have been filled by the atmosphere of Heaven, are more able to breathe it out and release it*".

Again, please don't misunderstand. I'm **not** talking about works (i.e. having to do or be something in order to have God move through you.) You are a spirit being who is alive in Christ. You carry God in you already, but in my experience, the most anointed worship leaders are those who worship regularly in the Holy Spirit in their private times. You can talk mechanics of music and music teams until the cows come home, but merely leading with the music team mechanics rule book won't touch or heal or set free anyone in your congregation. You want to work with the Holy Spirit because only He can do these things.

Note here that a person who spends a lot of time in the throne room worshipping God, can sing just about anything and the presence of God will still enter the room with such anointing. These people are glory carriers and what every worship leader should aspire to be.

While it is not difficult to hear the voice of the Holy Spirit, to say that worship leading is easy is rather trite. Hearing the Holy Spirit's directions in the midst of Sunday worship will always be more difficult than in your secret place. There are always many distracting elements combined with the tasks of leading the team and coordinating the music. So much is happening on the platform. You are singing, possibly playing an instrument as well. You are also listening to what the Holy Spirit is doing, leading the team (some leaders use signals, others give verbals), and always you are conscious of where the congregation is at (are they following or looking at you incredulously? If the latter, you'll need to pull back and take it more slowly).

This is why it is essential to practice the technical stuff at home until it's second nature and thus, affording you more time to listen to Holy Spirit rather than thinking about how to play the next passage or remember the words of the next verse.

In the secular realm, every seasoned performer knows that unless you can perform a piece without thinking, it could easily fall apart once on stage. That is why even professionals rehearse as much as they do. It is therefore, vitally important that the playing and singing of the songs is so well known to you, that it is second nature, or it also becomes a distraction.

On the other hand, if for some reason your mind *is* distracted and you are not sure what the Holy Spirit is saying, it is very important that you can lean back into that place of rest, and just listen. Let it flow naturally and not from a place of fear or striving.

Obedience

Hearing God also depends your obedience. If you constantly block out His voice so that you can do your own thing, you'll eventually have a hard time hearing God's voice at all. It is those that listen and obey as part of their everyday life, who will also hear and obey on the platform. It just doesn't make sense to suppose that a life of disobedience to the Holy Spirit will change suddenly on Sunday morning. So to restate – your ability to hear God more will depend on your every day willingness to obey when He directs you even in the little things.

Choices, sometimes even the smaller ones, have the capacity to impact our lives, to unexpectedly redirect them and change them. No, I don't mean which brand of breakfast cereal to buy unless purchasing that brand impacts others. God did give us likes and dislikes and the ability to choose. This is not to what I am referring. I heard this analogy once:

Sometimes our Good Shepherd leads us on a very narrow path and we need to follow His lead very closely – only putting our feet where we see Him put His, (or to speak plainly, to only do those things He is telling us to do!) If we don't, it could be to our own detriment. (E.g. The Holy Spirit might tell you to take another route home from work. Seems a little thing until you hear on the evening news that there was a major accident on the usual route and many people were killed. Now you realise that He just saved your life!)

At other times, the Good Shepherd leads us into lush wide pastures and allows us to eat, run, explore and play. These are times He allows us to learn and there is reasonable scope for us to choose things for ourselves provided that they do not lead us away from Him or the flock.

We are His – He bought us with a price. The words He speaks over you are, *"You are Mine!"* That is profound! (The first time I heard Him say that, I was deeply impacted.) Because we our His, we are His to command. It is only right that He expects our obedience. However, we obey not out of obligation, but because we love Him and know that He loves us. We also trust that what He asks us to do is right and good. Obedience speaks of both love for God and trust in Him. If we love, we will obey!

> *"15 If you love me, you will keep my commandments."* - **John 14:15 ESV**

> *"21 Whoever has My commandments and keeps them, he it is who loves Me. And he who loves Me will be loved by My Father, and I will love him and manifest Myself to him."* – **John 14:21 ESV**

Jesus obeyed His Father because He loved Him, and so that the world would know that He loved Him. You may not have considered this, but Jesus actually preferred not to have to endure the Roman cross. In the garden He actually asked His Father if He would take the cup from Him. Nevertheless, He desired to obey His Father over and above the torture that awaited Him. He chose obedience and sacrifice because He loved the Father above all else!

> *"I do as the Father has commanded me, so that the world may know that I love the Father."* – **John 14:31 ESV**

The choice to obey is always correct. However, choices can be right for you and wrong for someone else. Our backgrounds, experiences and maturity can determine why this is so. Therefore, if we are to be obedient like Jesus was, and walk solely in step with the Holy Spirit, we must ensure we are listening and following God's choice for us, not merely doing as others do or have done in the past. Jesus only did as He saw the Father doing.

> *"So Jesus said to them, "Truly, truly, I say to you, the Son can do nothing of his own accord, but only what he sees the Father doing. For whatever the Father does, that the Son does likewise."* – **John 5:19 ESV**

Likewise, He expects us to follow that example to follow only that which we see the Holy Spirit doing - not to be presumptuous and do what we think, but to hear His thoughts on every choice, and then with love, do without hesitation. (On that point, the Holy Spirit will never tell you to do something that disagrees with the Word of God! This is a great test of whether what you heard was from God or not.)

Honour Your Headship!

You have been entrusted with leadership of the worship team because your headship saw something in you that God could use. You are there to serve. (The meaning of the word "ministry" is service!) I realise that we are all one under God and it is really His church not any one man's, but the members of your team and indeed the members of the congregation have been placed under the headship of the senior pastor who often will be the "father/mother" – i.e. the person who established the church. He or she was given the vision and mandate by God for your church. Respect that, especially whilst on the platform. When you honour your headship and serve faithfully, God honours you.

Don't belittle your headship when talking to your team in the back room, even to make a small joke at their expense. Likewise, honour their decisions and directives without complaint. If they say only two songs today and you've prepared a huge list, don't make a fuss! It doesn't matter how much time you and your team have spent preparing, or how disappointed you may be, it's not your church and you are there to serve! This is your ministry because it was your privilege to be given it, not because it was your right. Do not allow that spirit of entitlement to raise its ugly head.

Further, if you honour your headship even should this occur, God will honour you also in the future. He does not forget. Therefore, be humble! Be faithful! Do everything without grumbling and complaint.

"[14] Do all things without grumbling or disputing, [15] that you may be blameless and innocent. children of God without blemish in the midst of a crooked and twisted generation, among whom you shine us lights in the world." – **Philippians 2:14-15 ESV**

Lead by example! If you grumble all the time, your team will grumble too, but it could just be you they grumble about. However, if you inspire them with your integrity and faithfulness, and motivate them with the joy and love only Jesus provides, they will indeed follow your example and leadership!

Who do we represent?

Our lives will demonstrate Jesus either in a positive or negative light. It has been said that we are the only Bible some people will ever read! If we demonstrate love, integrity, sincerity, and joyful obedience, we also reflect the nature of God to others. Our obedience to God will show others how much we love and trust Him, and also how trustworthy our Father really is.

Further, you do not just represent God to the world, but your also represent your church, your church leaders, and even to a lesser extent, your church movement - especially if the visitor has never had anything to do with your church movement in the past. People will judge God in you by what they see in your character every time you step on that platform. Moreover, those that do not know God – those you meet every day outside of church - will either be drawn to God because of what they see in you, or turned off completely. This means you are accountable before God for the image of Him that you portray. Therefore, your integrity, honesty, and character are of great importance to you, especially because of whom you represent as you stand on that platform. You are accountable to ensure you guard your heart and character, to be honest in all things, and pure of heart before God. You may do well to ask yourself if your actions do honour or dishonour those you represent as you lead the congregation.

If your church also video streams the service over the internet, (or simply films the services to use at a later time) not only is the reputation of the church, and its leaders on display but even that of Christ and the church at large, and globally! Who can say who will be watching! Are you reflecting a good image of Christ to people?

Remember, God is also watching you. As Bill Johnson stated, would you change the way you speak or behave if you had a dove (the Holy Spirit) on your shoulder? Well you do have the Holy Spirit, and you have Christ – the King of Glory - living in you.

The flip side is that without integrity, honesty, and the many other character traits I have mentioned; without a Godly character, the likelihood of failing is particularly high. These things are foundational to any ministry. Without solid foundations, Jesus taught us (while He spoke on obedience to Him), the house will fall as soon as the wave of strife beat upon it.

The good news is that even if you have failed in the past, God is gracious to forgive, and will let you start over. His mercies are new every morning (Lamentations 3:22-24). He wants you to be perfect as He is perfect. He wants you to realise who you really are in Him, to expand your potential as you invest your gifts, and fulfil your destiny. However, the only way to reach this is through obedience and character.

Be Teachable

As well as training others, you must ensure that you, too, are always learning, especially from the Holy Spirit, but also from other worship leaders who worship lead and navigate the Holy Spirit stream well. The best teachers will always be the Holy Spirit and the Bible, but that's not to say you cannot learn from others with more experience than you as well.

When you learn from others what things to avoid, you will be spared making their mistakes. You can leap from the elevated floor they have provided you, instead of climbing from the basement. Needless to say, this requires discernment on your behalf to choose carefully those leaders whose teachings will help you advance in your worship skills, without diminishing your dependence on the Holy Spirit.

The best teachers will be evident by their fruit. Besides being able to navigate the flow of the Holy Spirit well, they will also demonstrate humility, integrity, and be encouraging and building up others. I personally would avoid those that easily slander or put down other ministries. (James 3:8-12 warns us that worship and evil speak should not proceed from the one mouth!) Being a "big star" isn't the qualification you are looking for in a spiritual mentor either, but a leader's ability to flow with the Holy Spirit.

There is always plenty of material about running a band/music group and practical tips on how to run a team efficiently and effectively. There are excellent books about leadership as well. These are all useful if you are to build up and treat your team well. However, keep in mind that the goal is not about the "doing", but the **"resting and reliance"** on the Holy Spirit. Learning to follow the Holy Spirit far outweighs the need for you to improve your leadership skills. As He teaches you, He will advise you how to handle the group, and it will be in such a way that His people are built up and encouraged with love.

It is your relationship with the Holy Spirit and your ability to hear and obey that are the most critical skills you will ever learn! You are the only person who can develop this. It happens in your prayer closet and while you worship alone. It happens when you are still and listening – giving Him priority in your day-to-day life. Yes, there may even be sacrifice. You may have to say "*No!*" to some activities that you enjoy, in order to give Him first preference to that time slot, but oh the rewards!

Worship Leading in the Holy Spirit Flow

Jesus said that His sheep know His voice, and so hearing the voice of the Good Shepherd (and indeed our Father and the Holy Spirit), is paramount to us as Christians. How does this relate to worship? When we come together corporately, the Holy Spirit has an agenda far more glorious than ours. As well as give glorious praise and honour to our great and deserving God, the Holy Spirit wants to draw our hearts to the Father's, and in so doing set captives free, bring wholeness (physical, mental, spiritual and emotional) to the broken, sometimes to even bring correction (especially where division has crept in), encouragement, and new direction. Sometimes He causes spontaneous intercession to break out in the knowledge that God both hears and is able to intervene. Sometimes He speaks to the hearts of individuals - causing some people to weep, others to rejoice, and so, so much more.

This is **not** about "ushering in" the "presence of God". When we gather together, Jesus is already in our midst. Further, we all carry His presence since it is no longer I who live but Christ who lives in me. (See the seventh reason why we worship from the first chapter, regarding the levels of the anointing/presence the Holy Spirit in corporate gatherings.) Rather we are giving Him the worship leading reins.

I have already discussed what worship is and how God expects us to worship – to worship Him above all else in spirit and truth and from the heart. Worship leading, on the other hand, is not just about facilitating an atmosphere where people want to worship and give glory to God, (as opposed to a time where their minds are distracted or bored) but most importantly about partnering with the Holy Spirit and allowing Him to move, and do whatever He wants/needs to do in our meetings. (See the end of the first chapter.)

As a worship leader it is your responsibility to create space for the Holy Spirit to move. The simple truth is that He can't move if you're intent on doing it your way. When we insist on our way or the highway, or the structure of the service is prohibitive, there is little happening spiritually as well. We are His! It's His way or nothing!

It All Starts Before the Service Begins

Long before the service begins and even before the song lists are made, it is important to already be asking the Holy Spirit for guidance and direction concerning the up and coming service. Is there a special word, prophetic song, theme, or Scripture verse that He will be using? Don't forget to ask for wisdom and discernment, and the anointing. Yes, there seems to be contention over this word, "anointing", and what exactly is meant by it, and whether it really is anything more than the presence of God. Well I am not about to argue semantics. All I know is that I was reluctant to worship lead without the Holy Spirit and, as a result, always prayed for the anointing. What's more: He never disappointed me in this area.

To be blunt, we are all His children. He lives in each one of us and we have received the Holy Spirit in full measure because our Father does not give us His Spirit in half measures. Nevertheless, when some people worship lead, you feel transported into the very throne room of God, while when others lead and it's more, "Meh – nice song!" True it can have something to do with people's attitude and expectations as to whether they are open to the Holy Spirit, but when you are fully prepared to enter into worship, and have never met or heard of the worship leaders and therefore, have no preconceived ideas about them, you will be able to sense whether or not something is going on in the spiritual realm. Maybe we just "click" with some worship leaders, but

I'm more inclined to believe that these people have spent hours in the throne room worshipping God and as such, carry something over and above those who simply worship lead for a season because they want to use this platform ministry as a stepping stone to the preaching ministry. The anointing is real!

So to wrap this up, preparing yourself (that is, worshipping alone with Him and spending time with Him to hear what He is saying) is the first step to good worship leading.

The Song List

As a general rule of thumb, I personally believe a mix/range of old and new songs will suit most congregations, but honestly, are we about choosing songs to entertain the palettes of a select few, or to select songs that are not only honouring to God, but are His choice and can be effectively used by Him? How can I know the Holy Spirit will use them - because I sat in prayer before hand, listening to His voice, His choice, and His opinions on the matter.

And that is the key for you who are making up the song list. Obey your leadership's music/song requests and be respectful – of course – but also (as much as your headship deems permissible) choose songs you have prayed about and discussed with the Holy Spirit. It's not about our particular tastes, or what we think the congregation should learn because after all, this is the latest greatest worship song, or it was amazing last week in your church or the church down the road. We are there to please His heart ultimately, and unity is more important to Him than our favourite style of music or song!

Creating the song list can often be tricky, but you do need to be prepared – don't just show up and expect everyone to just follow without some direction and some time for them to prepare as well. Sure you all may be experienced and skilled musicians and singers, but a last minute "throw together" can end up in disaster, with people looking for cues rather than focussing on the Holy Spirit, and making distracting mistakes because they misinterpreted what was next.

You simply must sit with the Holy Spirit well in advance to hear what He has planned. It may help to have your songs listed in categories. For example: victory songs, or songs of joy, or songs of intimacy. Then it's simply a matter of hearing the Holy Spirit's topic for the day and then asking Him to choose from those particular songs. The Holy Spirit may give you the entire list, but more often He'll give you the theme that you can fit songs around. He works with you and leaves room for you to present your thoughts and ideas – at least to a point. At other times He may give you one particular song, possibly two or more, and you'll have to fill the gaps with similar themed songs or transition songs.

It's not the number of songs that matter, but whether the Holy Spirit can and wants to use them. You may have as little as three songs on your list. If that's what the Holy Spirit wants, go with it. You may be all on your faces before God before you even get to the last song! On the other hand, because of issues occurring within your church, it may take time for people to get out of their heads and focus on God. At these times you may need a few more songs.

There may be those times you can't hear Him select any song at all. If you are in that position, I'd personally choose songs that highlight God's greatness – real praise encouraging songs. You could even start with thanksgiving because the Word tells us to enter His courts with thanksgiving in our hearts. This is a great encourager for people to settle in and take their minds off the distractions of life. When we are all focussed on Him, Holy Spirit can easily steer us (if we are open to this of course!)

The problem can be finalising the list. You will be required to give lists to not just other people in the platform team, but to those running the electronic media – word projectionists etc. and even the dancing group if you use them. These people must also be prepared, so don't give them the list last minute.

Coping with any last minute alterations really depends on how skilled and how able to cope with changes your people actually are. If they are not that skilled, you may just have to spend more time in free worship than adding in another song – unless you are really sure your team know it extremely well. Having a few extra similarly themed songs on the list as a standby can be a good idea to help facilitate this, especially if you have a short list and are not sure if you have heard correctly. This is why it is important to have at least a rough idea about where the Holy Spirit will lead you on the day.

Please note that if the Holy Spirit makes changes, He is not trying to trick you. Holy Spirit's final selection might depend on whether particular people decide to come or not come at the last minute. We simply don't know! Perhaps you have too much going on in your own head at the time of selection, to hear Him accurately.

Providing room for the Holy Spirit to move is important. Depending on how the congregation is responding to the Holy Spirit in their worship, Holy Spirit may go on a different tack, or want you to repeat a verse or two. So be prepared to be flexible with your list. Naturally, if the Holy Spirit has given you the complete list beforehand, and you are sure there will be absolutely no variation – great! However, be flexible none the less.

God will not *force* people to do anything. He has given us free will. As mentioned, He wants to work with you and the congregation. If the congregation, or even you as a worship leader, are unwilling to follow Him or to listen to the message He wants to bring for that day, then what would be the point? On the other hand, if there is unity and all the people just want to set their hearts on Him, worship can be gloriously blessed.

So with all these various factors coming into play, be as prepared as you can be, but also be prepared for the unexpected – as much as this is possible.

A final note on making the list is that if your church is open to it, make sure you leave room for free worship, the Song of the Lord, prophetic songs, a Scripture verse, and prophetic utterances. It is not you who are not running the show, but the Holy Spirit. As much as possible within your church's service framework, give the Holy Spirit free reign. It's not about the number of songs you have prepared, (though it's not a bad idea to have more than you require as I said). If the Holy Spirit is on a song, just keep it going until He says to change it. You may end up only doing a few songs for the entire worship set, but if Holy Spirit is leading, you'll have glorious worship anyway.

Worship Leading in Service

O.K! Moving on to leading worship in church: As mentioned several times already, this should simply be an extension of what you've been doing at home. The worship leader who is looking for and listening for the Holy Spirit is, in a sense, operating in the prophetic realm. This leader is listening for what sounds will come next, how the music is to flow, if there is a particular style of music or beat, if there is a prophetic song, if the next song is one that will adequately carry His message or heart for this particular gathering/service, and so on. Sometimes the leader will "see" where the music is heading as well.

Some of you may be a little skeptical and thinking, "*Sounds and beats! What rot! Worship is worship and anyone can extol God's virtues! You don't even need music to worship God!*"

While that's true, we don't need music or even to be in church to worship, there is so much more to be had. (I've already discussed "*Music in Worship*" earlier. If you've jumped forward to this section you may wish to read that discussion now!)

We've become such a left brain society that it is often difficult to get out of our heads. Music and the creative arts are a right brain activity – far more in tune with the emotional AND the spiritual. You can worship without music and it too can be glorious, but for those struggling to get out of their heads, and for those who remain distracted by the many things in their lives that are vying for attention, music (and also praying in tongues) is a great way to quiet the thoughts and focus on God.

Spirit led worship carries a corporate anointing that's unlike the personal anointing. As previously mentioned, in this atmosphere, Holy Spirit can do amazing miracles. He doesn't run by our rulebook. We may not understand what He's doing, but understanding is not required; obedience is. So if Holy Spirit says, "*Sing!*" or "*Shout!*" or "*Dance*" why do we become offended? He's running the show. Embarrassment speaks of pride and the expectations of others taking priority. Obedience speaks of humility and trust.

I'd like to draw your attention to Scripture where Jesus deviated from the norm and did something highly unusual. Let's turn to John chapter 9.

"Jesus Heals a Man Born Blind

¹ As he went along, he saw a man blind from birth. ² His disciples asked him, "Rabbi, who sinned, this man or his parents, that he was born blind?"

³ "Neither this man nor his parents sinned," said Jesus, "but this happened so that the works of God might be displayed in him. ⁴ As long as it is day, we must do the works of him who sent me. Night is coming, when no one can work. ⁵ While I am in the world, I am the light of the world."

⁶ After saying this, he spit on the ground, made some mud with the saliva, and put it on the man's eyes. ⁷ "Go," he told him, "wash in the Pool of Siloam" (this word means "Sent"). So the man went and washed, and came home seeing.

⁸ His neighbours and those who had formerly seen him begging asked, "Isn't this the same man who used to sit and beg?" ⁹ Some claimed that he was.

Others said, "No, he only looks like him."

But he himself insisted, "I am the man."

¹⁰ "How then were your eyes opened?" they asked.

¹¹ He replied, 'The man they call Jesus made some mud and put it on my eyes. He told me to go to Siloam and wash. So I went and washed, and then I could see.'" – **John 9:1-11 NIV**

We all know that Jesus could have healed this man's sight with a spoken word. We are talking about the same God who spoke the world and the heavens into being. Later, He simply commands Lazarus to come forth and Lazarus emerges from the tomb, fully alive, after being dead four days! It would seem a little odd that for this particular miracle He chose to make mud and put it onto the man's eyes.

There could be many reasons why Jesus did this. Perhaps the man's faith was lacking. He desperately wanted to be healed but perhaps he only had the faith to believe if Jesus actually did something. Then again, dead people don't have any faith and He still raised them. Or perhaps Jesus just wanted to demonstrate something with the mud to His disciples – old mind-sets need to be washed away if the blind man was to retain his sight. Who knows? This is all conjecture and supposition. And do the "why's" really matter anyway! The fact is that Jesus operated in a completely different way. He broke the mould.

We've all heard of unusual miracles. I met a woman in dance ministry who related this story to me. One night the pastor of her church called for the sick to come forward for prayer. There was one very sick lady who came forward. At that moment the Holy Spirit told the dancer to dance around this sick woman, so she did. Some other dances then came out and joined her. They were very anointed dancers and God used them powerfully that night. When they finished dancing, the woman was healed.

These are unusual miracles but they are "of God" nevertheless. Many, many people are often healed during worship. As they open up to God, He is able to come in and set people free – free from sickness, emotional hurt, mental problems or whatever the bondage they suffer. He knows what is required for each one of us. He can use whatever, however, and whenever. He is God! He can even use flags to set the demonic running and set people free. Sounds crazy even, but He is in charge and it's His power that heals, not us.

So if the Holy Spirit instructs you to make a particular sound on your instrument, or sing a particular musical phrase, who are we to question Him? It could be that we've been listening to the wrong stuff too long and He just wants to clear it away so that we can hear Him. Who knows? All I know is if Holy Spirit says to do it, do it! It's the worship leader's job to follow Holy Spirit and to, hopefully, encourage the congregation to do the same. The caveat here is to be sure it is the Holy Spirit speaking and not the flesh, but the more you do this, the sharper you become!

If we listen, we can hear the sounds He gives. Those that are musical may understand this better. However, it only takes an ounce of perception to tell whether something is full of Holy Spirit power or is merely in the flesh. Flesh just doesn't "feel" spiritually right – especially when you're right in the flow. It's kind of obvious!

Mark Virkler, author of *"Dialogue with God"*, calls the prophetic stream, a flow. It's like jumping in a river and moving along with the current. Because we want Holy Spirit to lead, it's a good idea to invite Him to take the helm. We are the vehicle and He is the driver. The vehicles responds to the driver's steering etc., and so too must we.

OK, how can you "get into" the flow in the first place? Mark Virkler advocates to firstly quieten yourself down, - i.e. you must firstly to get out of your *own* thoughts, focus on Him, and *then* tune to "flow". What is Holy Spirit saying, or doing and how is He moving? Following the Holy Spirit necessitates hearing His voice, seeing what He does, and sensing where He is moving. Only once we comprehend those things, can we *then* respond to His directions.

Remember that even Jesus *only* did what He *saw* the Father do, and said *only* that which He *heard* the Father say. We, as children of God and joint heirs with Christ, can and should do the same as Jesus did. We can tune in and see, hear and sense what the Holy Spirit is doing and where He is taking the worship. (I encourage you if you haven't done so already, to either read Ps Mark's book or to watch one of his videos series about hearing the voice of God.)

As with any Holy Spirit gift or skill, practicing with the Holy Spirit can only improve it.

For example: If you are learning how to give a prophetic word, you would be learning to recognise His voice, and trying it out as often as you could - getting feedback so that you can hone in more skilfully in discerning His voice from all the other spiritual voices.

It's the same with leading worship in the flow. It get's better with practice. Try at home in your own worship. Then practice in a place where mistakes don't matter, rather than in front of a full church. (I personally used half our practice night for rehearsal of new material and the other half in worship. It was in this safe environment that aspiring worship leaders would practice leading the group in worship. They had to pray about the songs or how how the Holy Spirit was going to lead, before hand, and then lead in the same way they would on a Sunday. In this atmosphere they were free to make mistakes and to get feedback – there was no judgement, only encouragement. Some of those nights were just glorious nonetheless - so much so that non-music team members began coming just to experience the worship.)

God is not complicated. If He wants people to worship in Spirit and truth, then it must be easy enough for all His children to do. If I may put it simply, *worship leading is hearing/seeing what or where the Holy Spirit is doing or moving next, and then doing the same*. Jesus only did what He saw the Father do, (John 5:19). Likewise we only do/sing what we see or hear the Holy Spirit doing/saying.

When hearing the Holy Spirit's voice, intimacy is everything! Your time spent (not per time as on the clock but willingness to be still) in your prayer closet – in that secret place where you listen to Him daily, will determine how well you hear Him whilst you worship lead.

In the midst of the Sunday worship, some may hear a phrase of the next song. Some will hear a particular sound. There's also a sense in your spirit – a "*feeling or knowing*" if you like – that the music was speeding up or slowing down or becoming louder or quieter or even changing beat or groove, or completely stopping. You may even see yourself playing something on your instrument.

When you're in the "flow", there's a kind of weight or resonance on the music. It's almost vibrating in the Spirit realm. In fact, sometimes there will be a single note or phrase that definitely vibrates with heaven. Flow with that! Your backing singers and musicians should try and follow you. If the congregation is following well, they will pick up the musical phrase and like a choir, begin to sing, and it will be glorious.

What it is *not*, is enthusiasm, or recognising another song from the musical phrasing or wording of the current song, or figuring it out in your mind as you go! In fact, if you are working it out in your head, you're not following the Holy Spirit. The Holy Spirit talks to your spirit. You hear in your spirit what He is doing or saying. The head is not required nor should it enter in – the head is the place of man. Worship must always be in spirit and truth to be effective. We do not worship music, or feelings or even worship itself. We worship *God* in *Spirit* and truth!

If you cannot hear the Holy Spirit and the current song is coming to an end and there is no song list to fall back onto, then continue playing a chord progression, singing in tongues and ***focus your attention back on Jesus*** – not what the next song will be. (This is paramount!) Usually another song will automatically come.

If the free worship is coming to an end, move on to the next song on your list. If there is no other song, perhaps begin to simply pray in tongues without music and encourage the congregation to join in. (You could, however, also have the band continue playing chords softly during this time if stopping feels wrong.) From this point, with our hearts totally listening to the Holy Spirit without distraction, we may be led to another song or even Spirit led intercession, or even to finish up – depending on where the Spirit takes you.

As an aside here, if the people are not worshipping, or worse, are bored, then you, the worship leader, have still not carried out your function – i.e. to lead the congregation in worship. Always the worship leader must encourage and invite without bullying or berating, and create such an encouraging, loving atmosphere that people want to join in. With hungry hearts, people will jump into worship from the first note. Nevertheless, when leading a different congregation who are not use to deep worship, you will need Holy Spirit wisdom married to your ability to follow Holy Spirit's leading.

When speaking about the most important steps to preaching (and leading worship is applicable here too), Roland Baker said[24],

> *"I learned from Bob Jones. The thing to do is the sure-fire three steps to preaching:*
>
> *1. Show up*
>
> *2. Be on Time*
>
> *3. Be empty headed - that's important! If you have thoughts of your own, there's no room for God's thoughts.*
>
> *Your real job is not to be amazing, fulfil yourself, find your destiny, or be all you're called to be. Your real job is to become nothing at all so that Jesus can become everything in you."*

We must not try or be or do anything of ourselves, but just allow Him to use us. We are His tools. Remember, it's not what we can think up, or what song we want to sing next, but what the Holy Spirit is saying/doing that's important.

So how do we know what song to use next? When another song does pop into your head *while still focussing on Jesus*, use that – it's most likely the Holy Spirit prompting you. In fact, if your congregation is unfamiliar with free worship, being able to move from one worship song to another is a great way to keep the flow moving without causing offence, and still be Spirit led.

Theme Jumping

Often there is a *common theme* that comes forth from the songs. In fact, so many times when I ran with the theme that the Holy Spirit wanted to use for that service, the sermon covered that very topic – a perfect dove tailing. This is what we should expect if both worship leader and preacher have both waited on God for His message for the day! Needless to say, the *Holy Spirit does not change His mind willy-nilly and choose a different message with each song* all through the worship. If there is a change, there is usually a gentle transition.

Personally, because I think the words we are singing are important, I find that songs that jump from theme to theme are very distracting. For example, if the current song is focused on the overcoming warrior aspect of Christ and is then followed by an intimate song about the heart and His love, or vice versa, followed by another focussing on joy or surrender, it can be difficult to know where to focus attention. We don't want to engage our heads but our hearts, but songs that jump all over the place, bring us back into our minds.

Further, this jumping about rather than following a simple flow, suggests that something like a musical phrase, a few words etc. from the current song, merely *reminded* the song leader of another song, so they ran with it, instead of being completely immersed in the Holy Spirit "flow". **This is *not* hearing from the Holy Spirit** any more than just any thought that comes into your head through the day is the Holy Spirit talking to you.

Of course, if the current song *is* wrong, you will need to change it, but the occasional change to a differently themed song is far removed from constant theme jumping. The Holy Spirit doesn't jump about from theme to theme.

Merely getting louder or faster doesn't mean it's Holy Spirit ordained either. It could be that your musicians are becoming excited and pre-empting the flow rather than hearing the direction. It could also be a song that excites or speaks to them personally, and hence, they naturally want to go with that song. However, that doesn't necessarily mean it is of the Holy Spirit.

You're the leader! It's your job to lead. Don't be afraid to rein it in if you feel it's *not* where the Holy Spirit is moving. On the other hand, if you're listening to no avail, and one of the musicians or singers picks up the spiritual song or sound, AND if it has Heaven's weight on it, *let them go on.*

On the other hand, if you know the current song *is* incorrect and/or needs to be changed, but you can't get to that place of hearing just what song/theme the Holy Spirit wants to run with - if you're "stuck", or if it just doesn't make sense to you, start praying/singing in tongues. This is a spiritual act and not one of the head. When you are spiritually engaged, it is easier for the flow to commence or re-commence. If tongues are unacceptable in your church, just use normal English words of adoration to a repeatable chord sequence. Just let it flow from your heart while you are totally transfixed on Him alone. Don't start thinking, just worship. A song will generally come. It may come from someone else in the team or even someone in the congregation! If you regularly practice this freer style of worship during your team meet-ups and rehearsals, you will become far more skilled.

As I've stated before, the Holy Spirit is not out to trick you. If you have sought the Lord about the songs on your list and feel confident you have it right, any last minute changes or changes on the fly are not necessarily to do with you, but could be because of many other reasons. Besides you getting it wrong, another possibility is that the Holy Spirit may need to be deal with some issues (personally or corporately) first, but will not force people to respond one way or the other. Needless to say, their response will have a flow-on effect in the worship. There could be several reasons for a last minute change of strategy, but He's definitely not out to trick you or catch you out, or make you look foolish. He wants to work with you for everyone's edification and building up.

Of course, if you may have not heard correctly the first time and have not waited long enough to hear His response to your list, He may change the direction you are taking the congregation. So be ready for *His* leading. Naturally, this is why intimacy and surrender are paramount!

If you are still having trouble hearing the Holy Spirit in the midst of worship, visualisation (the way that Mark Virkler discusses – that is in the Holy Spirit) may be a very useful tool for you, especially in free worship. First visualise/see your instrument and then ask the Holy Spirit to show you where to place your hands next, or to help you see the notes (if you read music), or simply just hear the pitch or sound. It's important to follow what He shows you, because this leads to more.

When praying for the sick, Stewart Gramenz explains that he often visualises himself as the jumper leads connecting a sick person to the real power - God! Mark Virkler visualises Jesus's power running through him to the sick person. Other people *imagine* God's hands superimposed over their own.

Likewise, when we worship in the Spirit, it can be useful to imagine the sound of the Holy Spirit springing up like a fountain from deep inside and out through your mouth. Just allow Him to give you the picture that works for you and let Him teach you how to move on from there, whether verbal or visual.

Throne Room Worship

As a worship leader, I of course had encountered this to some degree, but never heard it given a name nor spelled it out descriptively. Neither had I ever devoted an entire worship session to this, but my desire or goal was more often than not, that the congregation would approach the throne in worship before the we arrived at the next portion of the "Sunday service. So when Dr Mark Virkler asked me whether I had ever heard of Throne Room Worship", I had to say, "No!" However, upon further investigation, I had to agree that I do recognise this as yet another aspect of worship. It is therefore worth mentioning here.

Depending on your church and just how open it is to the things of the Holy Spirit, "Throne Room" worship is yet another aspect of worship available to all the worshipping saints. Unfortunately, this is not widely discussed or practiced - seeming to some, to be a little intimidating or even "out there on the fringe". Nevertheless, it is very real, as the many that have experienced throne room worship will attest.

Although I will very briefly outline this here, one of the better descriptions of this can be found in a blog by Dr Mark Virkler, author of "*Dialogue with God*", (more recently named: "*4 Keys to Hearing God's Voice*") on the CWG Ministries website. This blog can be found at: https://www.cwgministries.org/blogs/leading-worshipers-throne-room

Another blog worth checking out and also on the CWG Ministries website is by Jeff Duncan, who, after having heard Ps Mark speak on the subject, decided to outline in practical steps, how this can be achieved. Here's where to find it: https://www.cwgministries.org/blogs/which-these-four-places-do-you-gaze-you-worship-only-one-correct-jeff-duncan

A brief outline: Throne Room Worship begins by setting your mind on things above. You begin focussing on Almighty God who sits on the throne, ruling and reigning high above every power and principality. You could read a Scripture that describes this scene in Heaven, or sing a song reminding people of the same, or say a prayer about this. Use whatever helps to set people's focus on God.

Then with eyes focussed on the King in all His glory, by faith and with boldness approach the throne of grace. Let your worship mingle with the saints and angels around the very throne of God, while at the same time being open to whatever the Holy Spirit wants to do.

Don't be quick to move from this. Allow the Holy Spirit to have His way. You may even encounter a time of silence when people are communing with God individually, or perhaps deep ministry in people who are getting real with God. Whatever happens in this time of worship, don't be in a hurry.

If your church has only 10-15 minutes allocated to worship, it is probably not appropriate to pursue this during a Sunday service, but is something you could use during your worship practice or prayer group. People need time to get out of their heads and focussed on the Father reigning in awesome power and glory. They then need to allow the Holy Spirit time to do whatever He desires. It cannot be hurried!

This kind of worship has the capacity to do some deep ministry in people's lives, so listen carefully to the Holy Spirit.

Free Worship

Free worship is a time for everyone present to simply express their love and worship to God in their *own* way. It can be sung praise from one's heart, singing in tongues, shouting praise in English or tongues, or even praying quietly. It may be clapping, or dancing, or waving banners. It can be playing one's instrument. It could be even kneeling or laying prostrate before the Lord. It is free for each person to express themselves without restrictions. However, this freedom may be restricted by the codes of conduct set down by your church, and it is up to you to respect those restrictions as you comply.

What it is *not* is your chance to jam musically with the group.

Worship is God centred and He alone gets the glory. Even though it is free, you are still listening to the Holy Spirit and following where He leads. In order to facilitate this, you will need to have some kind of musical backing that allows everyone to sing together.

Is free worship Biblical and acceptable? Paul Says:

> "*[15] What am I to do? I will pray with my spirit, but I will pray with my mind also; I will sing praise with my spirit, but I will sing with my mind also.*" – **1 Cor 14:15 ESV**

We worship God freely in our personal quiet time. So of course, free worship is acceptable to God!

How can this be done? Musically the worship team are merely producing a platform or vehicle that everyone can choose to use (or not) from which to sing their own love song, or dance before, the Lord. Although it is free expression, it needs some sort of canvas just like the painter needs a canvas. The music is merely that. What people put on that canvas is up to them!

To achieve this, often the final musical cadence can be repeated until Holy Spirit moves on from this, but there are some chord progressions that are easier for congregational singing than others.

An example of a final cadences typically used in songs is:

IV, V^7 & I (i.e. 4, 5^7, 1).

From this cadence you can simply use these variations:

[4, 1]; or [4^{maj7}, 1^{maj7}]; or even [4^m, 1].

These two-chord progressions are very easy for congregations to use and can build or diminish with ease as the Holy Spirit dictates. From that same ending cadence, another two-chord progression can be:

[2, 1] or [2/7^b, 1].

Some other longer common chord progressions that kick off song endings are:

[4, 5⁷, 1, 6]; [4, 5⁷, 1, 3]; [2, 5⁷, 1]; [4, 5, 6]; [4, 2, 6]; [6/4, 6/5, 6]; [4, 5⁷, 1, 6]; [2, 5⁷, 1, 6] and even [2, 4ᵐ/5, 1, 6].

Some progressions are less distracting than others and possibly even have a mood attached to them (as music often does.) For example, some have a very majestic sound, others reverential. Some sound of victory and the mightiness of our God, while others sound like intimacy and love. Some even have a sound of brokenness and repentance, while other chord progressions sound like surrender. If you use some of these, be sure you've heard from the Holy Spirit before hand. Of course there are many "neutral" progressions that are suitable to commence the free worship, but listen to where the Holy Spirit is leading.

The most common neutral chord progression I find used today is: [1, 5, 6, 4]. There are so many songs written using that progression is uncanny. (I tried to avoid it though, because it's easy to over-use progressions and end in a rut musically.) Another that had popularity in the past was [1, 6, 4, 5] and that became very tired after a while as well. It's ok to use neutral progressions that are popular, but change them up often.

Progressions that have a certain sound are: (Note that these are the base or basic progressions that can be used but variations of these can sound great too!)

Warfare:	[1, 7ᵇ, 4, 1–5]
Victory:	[1, 4–5⁷]; [1, 6, 2, 5⁷]; [4, 5, 6]; and [1, 7ᵇ, 4].
God's Greatness:	[1, 3ᵈ 4, 5⁷]; [1, 6, 4, 5⁷]; and [1, 4–5⁷]
Authority:	[6ᵇ, 7ᵇ, 1ᵐ]; [1, 7ᵇ, 6ᵇ, 5⁷]; [1, 7ᵇ]; [4, 5, 6]; and [1ᵐ, 1ᵐ/4, /5, /6ᵇ, /7ᵇ]
Majesty:	[1, 7ᵇ]; [1, 7ᵇ, 6ᵇ, 5⁷]; [1, 6ᵇ]; [1, 6ᵇ, 7ᵇ]; and [1, 6ᵇ, 4];

Healing: $[1^{maj7}, 4^{\,maj7}]$; $[1, 2]$; $[1, 4, 1, 5]$; $[1, 6, 4]$; and $[1, 6^7, 2^7, 5^7]$.

This last sets have some interesting variations such as $[1, 6, 2, 4^m/5]$; $[1, 6, 4, 5^7]$ and $[1\text{-}5/7, 6, 4^{maj7}, 5^7]$

Another interesting progression is: $[6^7, 2^7, 6^7, 2^7\text{-}3^{7aug}]$; and some that feel as if rising are: $[1, 2, 3, 4\text{-}5]$; $[1, 2, 4, 5]$; $[1, 3, 2, 5]$; and $[1, 5, 4]$.

Of course these are just a few. There's nothing hard and fast here, just suggestions. Use what works for you and experiment a little in rehearsals. Free worship doesn't have to follow a particular progression at all. It may be something completely different. The lead musician, worship leader, or the person who has the message may just choose something that flows appropriately. If the choir or band cannot follow that person, stop! Don't be a distraction to what God is saying or doing!

Vocal Gifts & the Song of the Lord

Singing in Tongues

Before I begin, and to both clarify and dispel any mysticism surrounding tongues, I'd like to point out that there are a few main uses for tongues.

- To pray and edify **oneself**. (1 Corinthians 14:2,4)

- To be able to **pray for others** from a spiritual perspective, especially in cases where the head may just get in the way. Because it is a spiritual act, it can also position us to "hear" spiritually and receive insight into the heart of God for others or a particular situation. Praying in tongues for others may happen privately but sometimes may be over and for others.

As an example: I was driving home alone from the Gold Coast back to Brisbane one night when I felt very strongly compelled to pray in tongues. I had no idea why. There was practically no traffic – only about 3 cars travelling in my direction and nothing at all in the other. Nevertheless, my understanding is not required – only obedience. (1 Corinthians 14:14) The Holy Spirit knows all.

A few minutes later I realised the reason for the urgency of the prayerful tongues. There was a major multiple car accident on the other side of the road. There were many ambulances and police cars, people being treated for injuries, and others running around helping. I even noticed a sheet covered gurney as I passed going in the other direction! There were also cars banked up for miles behind the crash site on the four-lane freeway heading towards the Gold Coast.

Eventually after some time of praying in tongues, the urge to do so, lifted. I have no idea what I was praying for, but the Holy Spirit needed me to intercede, so I did.

Another example: A couple of years ago I told the Holy Spirit He could do whatever He wanted with my tongues no matter how silly people thought I was being. Well, He took me at my word. There was a bubbling up when I prayed for people, which gushed out without provocation and often loudly. Many of the people for which I prayed, told me later that they had heard the interpretation in their own minds while I did this. Some even heard declarations. My point in telling you is not to big note myself but to say that the Holy Spirit can use prophetic tongues as well. (Unfortunately, the response I received from some onlookers who had no idea was rather negative and I had to apologise to the Holy Spirit and discontinue allowing this to occur – though it still spills over from time to time despite my best efforts! When you're in the flow – you are in the flow! So if you do this, be prepared for possible negativity from those who do not understand what is happening.)

- To **prophesy in a corporate setting**. Here Paul has given us definite guidelines to maintain order and peace during the service: that any prophetic tongues must be interpreted and only 2-3 different messages at most, and if there is no interpretation, the speaker should remain silent. (See 1 Corinthians 14:27-28)

- As a **sign for unbelievers**, (1 Corinthians 14:21-22)

- For the **singing of praise** (1 Corinthians 14:15)

(Please Note: I do not want to conduct a full study on the topic here, but 1 Corinthians 14 is a great place to start your study. Just be mindful that Paul talks about speaking, praying and prophesying in tongues, and you may even need to check the original language to see which is which, as the English translations may not be accurate either. Without making these distinctions, it is easy to become very confused as to what kind of tongues he is referring. Also bear in mind that Paul is thankful that he speaks in tongues more than them all - 1 Corinthians 14:18)

When singing in tongues, the Holy Spirit can use all forms powerfully as we praise God, pray over the congregation, declare His will over the church, and speak forth healing power. Singing in prophetic tongues can also edify the church once it is interpreted. This interpretation can also be sung.

Music combined with a prophetic word can be powerful because not only does it carry the anointing of the worship, but the weight of the prophetic word as well. This is called the Song of the Lord.

In the Bible we see the Song of the Lord has a few different labels.

Spiritual Songs:

> *"18 And do not get drunk with wine, for that is debauchery, but be filled with the Spirit, 19addressing one another in psalms and hymns and **spiritual songs**, singing and making melody to the Lord with your heart"* – **Ephesians 5:18-19 ESV**

> *"16 Let the word of Christ dwell in you richly, teaching and admonishing one another in all wisdom, singing psalms and hymns and **spiritual songs**, with thankfulness in your*

hearts to God." – **Colossians 3:16 - ESV**

A New Song:

*"Praise the Lord! Sing to the Lord a **new song**, His praise in the assembly of the godly!"* – **Psalm 149:1 ESV**

*"Oh sing to the Lord a **new song**; sing to the Lord, all the earth!"* – **Psalm 96:1 ESV**

*"Sing to Him a **new song**; play skillfully on the strings, with loud shouts."* – **Psalm 33:3 ESV**

*"He put a **new song** in my mouth, a song of praise to our God."* – **Psalm 40:3a ESV**

*"Oh sing to the Lord a **new song**, for He has done marvellous things! His right hand and His holy arm have worked salvation for Him."* – **Psalm 98:1 ESV**

*"I will sing a **new song** to You, O God; upon a ten-stringed harp I will play to you"* – **Psalm 144:9 ESV**

His Song:

*"By day the Lord commands His steadfast love, and at night **His song** is with me, a prayer to the God of my life."* – **Psalm 42:9 ESV**

The Lord's Song:

*"How shall we sing the **Lord's song** in a foreign land?"* – **Psalm 137:4 ESV**

Song of the Lord

What exactly is the *"Song of the Lord"*? It is a spontaneous new song that Holy Spirit bubbles out of your heart. It is prophetic in nature, i.e. it may be a message in tongues and/or an interpretation, or simply a prophecy. The prophetic "Song of the Lord" is NOT simply repeating a few lines of the current song over and over unless the Holy Spirit says to do so. It's looking for the *prophetic word* the Holy Spirit is speaking to the church, but its delivery is via music. That is, whoever is delivering it, will be singing it.

The Song of the Lord will usually contain encouragement and edification - the Holy Spirit is people building (e.g. "*God is pleased*", "*His love is upon His children*", "*keep doing what you know to do*", "*stand strong for breakthrough is on its way*", etc.). However, it may also contain:

- **Insight** - the Holy Spirit is revealing things that are happening within the church that are of a spiritual nature (e.g. "*God is accelerating people*" or "*pouring out healing*" etc.)

- **Foresight** - the Holy Spirit is revealing where He is taking the church or what lies ahead! (e.g. "*It's a new day*", or "*I am raising up people*" etc.)

There are times when the Song of the Lord may contain elements of thanksgiving, adoration, exaltation, celebration, healing, intercession, warfare, and victory, as well. It may simply be an invitation to deeper intimacy and worship. Of course this list is not exhaustive by any means.

Though it can vary in expression, the message of the Song of the Lord is usually to the church, and the same checks and balances that we have for the prophetic, also apply here. The words will never contradict the Biblical word, and its ultimate aim will be to build up the Bride of Christ not tear her to shreds!

In the same manner as prophecy, you must wait on the Holy Spirit and, as Mark Virkler says, you "*tune to flow*" - the Holy Spirit flow - only this time, with the added dimension of music. This can make it a little scary or intimidating if you are not a songwriter, but remember that the Holy Spirit will use whatever is in your hand. If you can only sing the tune of the last line of the previous song, He can still use that. I suggest you practice at home or even small groups as you gain confidence, before you try at church.

For the musicians and backing singers, it is their responsibility to follow to the best of their ability – not racing ahead but following! This is great if you have a skilled team who can pick up chords and harmonies and can easily follow where the music is flowing. However, if this is not the case, it is better to stop and let the worship leader keep flowing using their lead instrument only or be totally unaccompanied.

The tune and style of music can vary. It may (in part at least) depend again on the skill of the musicians to follow, but the Holy Spirit may use whatever He feels is appropriate. It may be that the melody of the current song becomes the melody of the prophetic song (as mentioned), but more often than not, it can simply become a springboard to a new melody for the Song of the Lord.

As with free worship, perhaps there's a chord progression that seems to flow on from the last song, or perhaps just one chord! Sometimes there can be a definite style that comes through the free worship. It may be that the Holy Spirit is trying to draw the people's attention to something in particular, whether it is warfare or intercession for a particular nation or culture. Definitely flow with that!

The Song of the Lord may occur as a complete prophecy or (tongue which then is interpreted) or line-by-line, repeated by the congregation until everyone is singing the entire song. There can be a very potent message blossoming from these beginnings if you are willing to launch out. It's a powerful way the prophetic word can, not only get into our spirits, but our memory as well. People may even go home singing the song to themselves for the rest of the day. Now that kind of prophecy makes an impact!

Although you don't have to wait until you feel some kind of "goose bumps" to launch out, you still need to wait on the Lord as it is Holy Spirit enabled.

"All of them were filled with the Holy Spirit and began to speak in other tongues as the Spirit enabled them." – **Acts 2:4 ESV**

Congregational Led Spiritual Songs

Though this can happen, I do urge discernment and caution when doing this.

At times, the Song of the Lord may even come from a person in the congregation. This is a harder to work with if you are not used to this occurring, especially if that person is a visitor. (The question: *"Do you let just anyone up to prophesy over the church?"* applies here. This depends on the wishes of your headship who may wish to only use those prophetic people he/she knows are trustworthy and reliable!) I do know of a church where the entire song service is not worship team led only, but the congregation are encouraged to sing whatever song or prophetic song the Holy Spirit puts on their hearts. (I guess you could compare it to a prayer group where each intercessor brings whatever prayer the Holy Spirit is prompting them to pray.)

This can work very well where everyone is listening to the Holy Spirit but is a rare thing indeed. As mentioned, I do advise caution, or not to go there unless absolutely certain God wants this! It only takes one or two people who like to hear themselves sing, to create something very unwholesome and performance oriented.

To prevent this you could try letting people know in advance how the service is run, and that if something is not of the Holy Spirit, the team will retake control of the music. However, in these situations great wisdom is called for, and you, as the worship leader, need to know when to override this behaviour, and when to let it run its course. You don't want to grieve the Holy Spirit either by a fleshy display OR by cutting off someone who was totally in the flow. Generally you will know straight away, as it will "feel" wrong, but if you are not use to the style of a particular person, it may feel awkward to you regardless of whether they're in the flow or not!

How do you intercept and shutdown the discordant "spiritual" song? The easiest way to override a very much out of order voice (and I ask you to take care doing this) is to encourage the congregation to all join in singing their own song to the Lord whilst ramping up the intensity of the music backing itself. The reason for the caution here is that by doing this, it may seem a little rude and hurtful to the person if they are innocently and genuinely singing what they feel is of God.

You can see why it is a rarity and I personally tend to err on the side of caution. Don't use this approach unless you really know God is on it. I still, personally, love the idea nevertheless! Discuss this with your senior pastor if you want to do this, as it is not your church that you are left to clean up the mess or aftermath. Headship definitely has the final say!

Spirit Led Dancing

So what is happening during Spirit led dancing? You might be surprised to know that the Holy Spirit's leading is not that different to His interactions with music and singing.

My daughter is the spiritual dancer with whom I am most familiar. She has always danced since she knew how to walk and was always making up dances to perform at Sunday school or to dance for the family at home. Because I was music director at my church, the entire family came to rehearsals. One son played guitar, the other drums, my husband operated the sound and Amelia spent her time worshipping in dance. No one told her to worship in dance, it was natural for her to do so. All that time in the anointing, she learned much of the Holy Spirit flow.

As well as worshipping corporately, as a teenager, she often danced alone with God in her room and sometimes even took her music and flags and worshipped in the paddock where no one would see her – just her and God. Needless to say, through all this, she became a very anointed dancer.

At first she did not want to dance up front at church. For her, the dancing was private and intimate worship between her and God – not a spectacle. Nevertheless, when people witnessed her dancing, the Holy Spirit ministered to them profoundly.

This is how she experiences Spirit led dancing:

Relaxing into the flow and leaning into Him is a big thing. There are a couple of ways you can "hear" for want of a better word. As a spiritual "feeler", I feel drawn in a direction. This is not easy to explain especially to people who are not spiritual feelers. It almost feels like the path of least resistance spiritually speaking, while other directions feel "heavy" or "less easy".

(It's like when you hear something that it doesn't feel quite right, and other times the words seem to have the weight of heaven on them. In a similar manner when dancing some movements or directions don't quite feel right either, and some just do! - KMG)

That's the touch-based way of navigating the Spirit flow, but a dancer may also receive an image of the next movement. For me, these can be harder to synch with when and where the Holy Spirit wants them, but for the more visual person, it works well, and I guess the more you do it the more proficient you become.

The drummer is very important to the dancer because dancing relies on the beat, the groove and the feel. So having a prophetic drummer who flows well in the Holy Spirit anointing, makes the prophetic dance just take off – the dancer's job is so much easier.

The style of dance doesn't really matter so much. God will just use whatever you have in your repertoire, whether it's trained or not trained. Obviously the more skill and movements you have mastery over, the more tools Holy Spirit has available with which He can work. When I add movements to my dance repertoire for fun, they can often come back out in my worship.

When singing in free worship, you can sing personally to God, or God can speak prophetically to the church through the song of the Lord. Dance too can be used in the same way. You can simply express your heart to God, or your dance can be used to illustrate God's message to the church. That is, God can speak through you, though dance.

Used on the platform, dance definitely has a heavier corporate anointing whilst ministering to the church. I remember when I was at a youth event, the associate pastor asked me to come up on the platform and minister during worship and the level of anointing was so much heavier than in the congregation. It was very obvious to me at least.

There's definitely a grace that comes with dancing on the platform and ministering to the church. There is a stronger sense of His leading and less licence to do your own moves whilst on the platform. There's a real sense of His leading, His glory and His drawing into various movements. The corporate anointing is so much stronger.

With regard to other corporate anointings, I have not personally been used in the healing anointing through dance, but I have heard of many others who have experienced this kind of miracle when they obeyed Holy Spirit and danced around the sick. It was pretty cool! Anyhow, I'd say obedience is the key thing there.

Flags & Banners

Using flags and banners in dance is an extension of Spirit led dancing. However, they definitely add something extra to it - another layer. It's like an amplifier if you like. It just makes the Holy Spirit message so much more evident. I can dance without them and still be in the anointing, but when I do so, the worship then feels more personal and more intimate. On the other hand, when I use the flags in the dance, they have a more corporate feel. It's like they are being waved over the body to minister to the church at large, or like a standard - rallying for an army. That need not be the case every time, but I feel that they are more corporately oriented as a general rule.

Flags are interesting because of the way they change the atmosphere and I feel that's the biggest part of what they do. I do recall attending a worship event that New Hope Church was hosting a little while ago. There were some people using flags up the front, but I was worship-

ping with my eyes closed in the church proper at the time. Suddenly I started getting images of a lion in my mind. When I opened my eyes, lo and behold, someone had picked up a flag with a lion image on it and was waving it. It had bought something into the atmosphere that even with my eyes closed, I had picked up on spiritually.

Flags and dance can minister to individuals when done among the congregation (as opposed to on the platform.) People have said before that they were ministered to when they watched me dance. Unfortunately these people did not go into specifics so I can't tell you exactly how the Holy Spirit ministered to them – only that it happened.

Many years ago at a different church, I was dancing up the back. Spiritually speaking, the area felt "cold" initially, but as I started to dance, the area began to warm up, so to speak. That is, I noticed a considerable change in spiritual atmosphere within that dancing area.

Another example happened soon after coming to Glory City Church, Brisbane. I was dancing at the side behind the curtain (it was when the sanctuary faced in the other direction). A pastor came over and started wandering around just outside where I was dancing. Later he told me that there was an anointing in that area and he was just using that anointing to help him prepare for whatever he was doing on the platform that night.

Remember the verse in Jeremiah where he says he couldn't NOT prophesy because it was like a fire shut up in his bones? Sometimes I have that same experience. I have moved in various anointings with dance, but warfare in particular, seems to be the strongest. It has a real effect on me. In the past, when the worship began to flow in that direction I tried to just sit it out, but simply couldn't. I became sort of shaky, with a strong "got-to-get-it-out" compulsion. I can definitely relate to Jeremiah in that regard!

Even my old faithful flags that I've had for over 15 years, have many anointings on them because they were all I had in the beginning and I used them for everything. Even so, warfare seems to be the strongest anointing on them. Technically their colour (pink-mauve) usually signifies intimacy but because the Holy Spirit will use whatever you've got in your hand, they've picked up various anointings over the years.

Warfare, which you might consider to be a serious kind of battle/dance, can also be a joyous kind of dance when it's more focussed on victory.

The fire of God is an interesting anointing. When you use the fire flags, you can actually feel like you are getting physically hotter as well, but that could just be my spiritual sense of "feeling"/touch.

Colours and Anointings

I have a set of light blue flags, which represent peace and so on. Though I don't use them often, I remember pulling them out one service and a pastor, who before this was not at all convinced about their usefulness in worship, reported to me later that she had a sense that they were exactly right when I started using them – they perfectly befitted the moment and added to the Holy Spirit atmosphere.

Although certain flags represent different things, they can be used for multiple anointings – whatever the Holy Spirit has in mind. When I was making a set of orange chiffon flags that had a silver wavy line through the material, I had repurposed them in my own mind and was adamant that I was not going to use them as fire flags. However, God had another idea, and even when we were sewing them they started to feel hot! I can't even remember why I didn't want them to be fire flags, but they definitely are now! So He can use whatever He wants for whatever He wants.

Most of the flag colour charts that you can find online and in books and so forth, are based on Bible references, or prophetic dreams and visions. So there are base lists out there, but keep in mind that God is also very flexible in just what He can and will use.

I had a dream about using red flags that were much longer and thinner than the standard flag. So I went ahead and made them, and it works well for the flow of blood cleansing us from all sin. I realise there are particular shapes that can have various functions, but I haven't explored that much. Because God gave me this in a dream, I assume He has specific purposes for me using them.

There are flags with negative meanings – like the black flag (sin and death), but as to when an appropriate occasion to use them is anybody's bet. I have considered constructing a white flag with a white centre that has red streaks shooting out of it, and black edges. These flags would represent the blood of Jesus removing the sin and death at salvation and replacing it with righteousness. So in a sense you can combine black with other colours to shift it to a more positive message.

For those starting out

The most important thing I would say to someone wanting to start worshipping this way is that it is actually worship and not performance! Be God focussed and allow the Holy Spirit to lead! When you start it can feel kind of cold and forced, but if you relax into it and just keep going, there comes a point when (to use the words of a person who was at one time watching me) the Holy Spirit "grabs" you. Yeah, so just relaxing and just doing, is the best way to get started. For some people it will be that you need to start at home where others are not watching and distracting you, until it becomes a little more of an automatic extension of your worship. For others - maybe not so much.

For me, when I was young, I had lots of dreams about fighting with dual short swords. (Note from mum: Amelia was home-schooled and did not watch violent TV, movies or games that might fill her mind with such things.) *I look back now and think that those series of dreams that I had from quite a young age, were all pointing to my use of flags. So God had already set me apart for this kind of ministry from the start.*

I think if you're wanting to try dance as personal worship, you should absolutely go for it! That's your heart expressing love to God. However, for the corporate aspect, that's Him flowing through you to the body, and you need to be following His leading – and particularly in regards to being on the platform, you need to be in right alignment to the authority of the church, and called by God to minister in that way. In one church, I was asked to stop dancing by the leadership. That was their decision, and God has asked us to honour our leaders, so although I didn't wish to, I did stop as an act of love to God. (Note: That church did not want anyone using flags!)

When you set out to worship, sometimes you need to "break through" the atmosphere (for want of a better phrase). This can be on a personal level (whether just getting out of one's head and the day's activities and beginning to focus our attentions on God, or something more spiritual) but other times it can be a spiritual atmosphere within the church, or combination of the two. Obviously the Holy Spirit wants to work with us, so any "barrier" probably emanates from us – i.e. we can be that barrier.

Whatever "it" is, you can definitely feel that change in atmosphere and the Holy Spirit take over. I often think of it as cold to warm, or grey and colourless to a honey colour – it's a little hard to describe, as it is more of a sensation than any of those things. (I have only ever sensed this in my spirit and never had to define it before so my apologies there.)

I'm not suggesting that the flags and dancers alone are responsible for this. It's the music team together with the worship of the people and the dancers etc., that together make room for the Holy Spirit to come in and take over the meeting!

At any rate, for that reason I often use flags to start with, and then move into some personal dance, and later stop dancing and drop to my knees and do some heart to heart worship. It's quite common for me to do that, but I often start with flags because they are great at shifting atmospheres.

One particular service I had left my flags at home, but I had an image of God giving me a flag to use for that moment. It was gold handled with a navy blue flag that had a gold border just offset from the edges. (I guess to others it would have looked like I was dancing the way I normally dance with flags except they weren't physically there!) So He can do that as well – i.e. He can provide a spiritual equivalent!

Be aware of the enemy's tactics!

A caution is that the enemy will throw thoughts to your mind that you are just attention seeking and performing, because he wants to distract you and even stop you altogether. However, you know in your heart of hearts that you want to honour the Lord and worship only Him. So you have to just put it out of your mind and put your thoughts back on Jesus. I have used imagery in the past to help me do this. For example, I have imagined myself dancing before the throne of God in an empty throne room – just Jesus was watching me worship. That sense of doing it for His pleasure alone can help overcome those distracting thoughts.

The other image I have used is the Holy Spirit flowing around me – like wind or fire as I dance – particularly if I'm doing any spinning. That's a really nice image that keeps me focussed on Him and not the negative comments from the enemy.

Sometimes when I dance in worship, I have a sense of Jesus dancing with me. I can almost sense where He is standing and moving. It's far more "intimate" or personal than the corporate-oriented dance.

Another caution is that dancers must dress respectfully and ensure that any movements and poses used in their dance do not reveal things they would rather remain covered. Not only can this become a distraction to others but you need to honour your church's code of propriety and conduct as well.

Choreography

Although much of my own dancing has been spontaneous, there are some dance teams that have used Spirit led choreography to create dances as items – not performances as such, but pieces that can be used at particular events and times to illustrate a message that the Holy Spirit is impressing on the church at that time. It's analogous to singing a set song as opposed to free worship. Each has its place. Technically, a dance team could have set choreographies for many particular songs and simply pull them out as Holy Spirit instructs during the regular worship.

I personally had a prophecy that in my own dancing, each movement would be like a vocabulary – that I would be speaking things through the movements. I have noticed since then that certain movements will mean certain things.

Stuff that is coming right from my spiritual heart tends to come from my stomach area and not my physical heart, which many have said is the seat of the Holy Spirit, so most of the movements reflect that.

Most of my movements will match up with the meanings of the songs, as you'd expect if everyone is flowing in the Holy Spirit together, but the bulk of those movements emerge from the prophetic dance vocabulary that I've developed with Him.

Even so, you are dancing in partnership with the Holy Spirit. You might interpret what He is doing in a certain way and He'll say, "Sure we can do it that way!" There is an interweaving if you like, between what He is doing and what you bring to the table for Him to use. He is not opposed to your suggestions unless He has something completely different in mind. That is, it depends on what He is doing as to how much license He'll give you in the dance. The important thing is to remember is to always follow Him in preference to your own ideas.

The Inner Workings of a Spirit Led Team

Firstly, this book is not a "how to run a band" book. Those books are readily available elsewhere. I want to explain how to run a team who listens to, and is obedient to follow, the Holy Spirit, and to foster an attitude that not only pleases the Holy Spirit, but one that He can use every week. However, there are some people and relationship issues that must be covered here. Your priority is unity and having a cohesive team that is willing to flow together with the Holy Spirit. This necessitates that certain things must be addressed first and foremost.

Lead as Christ Leads

As the leader of the worship team, a music director must, above all, treat the team as Christ does. Leading is not so much to do with authority, as leading with love and respect. These are children of God, who are filled with God. (It is no longer I who live but Christ in me! Jesus and the Father are one. And these people are also Holy Spirit filled.) Therefore, you have no rights over them, nor is "lording over them" acceptable. Your team are volunteering their time and efforts because they love what they do and they love doing it unto the Lord. They don't have to be there and they do not have to follow you. They instead have given you permission to lead them, but they are joint heirs with you and God has no favourites.

Love them, befriend each one, and choose to spend "down time" with them – just getting to know them and building unity and team spirit. I use to run an annual music team camp, where we would have great worship times together, but we would also just chill. Doesn't have to be expensive or long. Might just be a day retreat where you all get away to worship together and encourage one another.

Be inclusive – especially to the shy or those lacking confidence in their abilities, knowing that the Holy Spirit is able to also advance them, and probably will. Encourage and build up! Organise with those that are struggling over a song or instrumental section, to stay back after rehearsal, after church or whenever is convenient, to help them master it. Above all, do not be judgmental in any way.

Think Well of Your Team

Because of the nature of the ministry, there will always be those who speak negatively or who pass judgments on your members – especially judging actions as pride. Be careful not to join in that negative chorus. Sometimes an overactive person has a very sanguine personality and may not actually be attention seeking as many suppose. Yes, you need to reign in those that do look for attention from anywhere other than Christ, but sometimes teaching on a person's new creation identity and how much God loves them is far more effective than berating or embarrassing them in front of the team. Your job is to encourage them to grow in their gifting and not destroy their confidence. Anything negative you say about another can also act as a word curse, so just don't! All leaders are responsible before God for how they treat those they lead and the words they speak over them.

Just about everyone will have to endure troubles, trials and grief. That's life! At these times a person may need more love and reassurance than they would normally. Yes, it's easy to point the finger and glibly say that these people need to draw their strength from God alone, so get over it. While that may be true to an extent, it is never an excuse for giving someone the cold shoulder with an attitude of, "Their attention seeking will not be facilitated by me!"

Put bluntly, we wouldn't need a Holy Spirit Comforter if there were not times in our lives that cause us to need comfort and reassurance. If Holy Spirit comforts, so should we. We are to be Jesus to one another. We are called to love, and as fellow spiritual family members, we are also responsible one to another. This is part of loving the brethren.

There are other times when stress and pressure, or even marriage upheavals, can make people "act a little crazy". You may be totally unaware of what is pre-empting their strange behaviour. Don't be quick to assume a person's actions are merely a display of attention seeking motivated by pride.

If they are willing and open to talk to you about what is happening behind the scenes, it may make your decision-making concerning them, easier. Nevertheless, especially if they remain silent on the matter, ask the Holy Spirit for wisdom and guidance as you approach the subject of their behaviour with them (and you will need to address this if it is affecting the team). Perhaps this person needs to take some time off to sort themselves out, but then again, maybe not. Treat each person individually – case by case, but don't be quick to judge and shun. Love them! Be Christ to your team. Ask yourself whether Christ would do something before you decide to do it.

I have seen and experienced first hand, judgements and prejudices, which were totally unfounded, and totally ugly and unwarranted Christian behaviour – not just to me, but to other team members as well. Let me give you my own first hand example:

Many years ago I joined an amateur musical theatre company because I enjoyed musical theatre and it was a good way for me to shine Christ in a place few Christians are able to go. (I will add that this kind of musical theatre was also family oriented and wholesome!)

The "Christian" backlash from that exercise was severe! So many people accused me of preferring the limelight than serving God, and told me I had no business being in such a place. I was rather shocked by this attitude. Who can minister to these people if we do not move among them?

I was using what I loved doing as a means of reaching the lost, and by doing so, I was able to minister to one of my fellow principle players who came down with a debilitating migraine headache just prior to her entrance. She complained that once these migraines took hold, she was normally incapacitated for several days at a time. So I prayed for her and Holy Spirit immediately healed her. She was then able walk on stage on cue. That opportunity would never eventuated had there not been a Christian there to be Jesus to her.

Besides all this, my heart was definitely not looking for outside attention. Anyone that knew me well would have known this. My heart was always to see the miraculous breakout during the worship through the move of the Holy Spirit, and still is. That cannot happen if the leader is looking to take all the glory. That glory is God's alone! My involvement with musical theatre had nothing to do with glory seeking, nor was it connected to worship leading in church! One is helping the saved worship their King, the other helping the lost to *know* the King so that they too can worship Him. It was simply my way of being Christ to the lost.

Nasty judgemental and under-handed comments about your team members have the capacity to cause even further division. I've seen that too! Nip any criticism you hear, in the bud as soon as possible. Don't be quick to agree with the judgements of others, no matter who is making them! There will always be plenty of people offering their opinions about the members of the music team, but don't be one of them. Your job, as a leader, is to love and build up – not judge and tear apart. Therefore, encourage your team members, and support them.

Having said that, you may find that the behaviour of a particular member *is* unacceptable according to your church's platform behaviour code. The Senior Pastor will see this as your responsibility, and you will need to address it. Obviously, you talking to the offending party in private about this, is second only to praying for them and asking God for wisdom in how to conduct your conversation with them. The entire episode may simply be a misunderstanding, or that person may not even realise they are doing anything wrong. If they are gracious and respond by changing their behaviour, great! If they refuse to listen, or have a contemptuous attitude (God forbid!) you will need to work through the Matthew 18 process.

> [15] *"If your brother sins against you, go and tell him his fault,* **between you and him alone.** *If he listens to you, you have gained your brother.* [16] *But if he does not listen, take one or two others along with you, that every charge may be established by the evidence of two or three witnesses.* [17] *If he refuses to listen to them, tell it to the church. And if he refuses to listen even to the church, let him be to you as a Gentile and a tax collector."* – **Matthew 18:15-17 ESV**

Hopefully no more than a warning will be warranted after phase two, but in those rare cases where a person will not listen to reason, you will either need to remove them from the roster for a period of time, or worst-case scenario, be forced to ask them to leave the music ministry altogether. As mentioned, it is not your church and all members of the team must abide by the church's platform code of conduct. There is no middle ground on this, particularly if your headship has told you this behaviour must stop! The good news is that most people are reasonable and will listen, especially if you have developed a close friendship with your team members. *Let love be your guiding light, and wisdom have it's way.*

If a member is always late and subsequently holding up practices or pre-service sound checks, you may need to talk to them about serving and respecting others. They may have a legitimate excuse that begs you to be gracious for their sake. However, if it is obvious that they don't really care, try to ascertain why they are there. What is their motivation for being on the team? Any ministry carries a certain amount of sacrifice, (ministry = service). It's not all about being up the front of the church for all to see. There's a pile of work and preparation that goes on behind the scenes. If a person desires ministry they must be aware, or made aware, of all the work that is required of them. You can't have one without the other – it's a package deal. Being punctual is such a trivial thing to ask of any team member.

I heard a pastor once recall a story about a friend of his that could never arrive at church on time. For him it was such a chore getting up in the morning to go to church. That is, until he discovered scuba diving. Then he was up every morning before dawn and off to the beach or wherever the diving was taking place. It's a very potent reminder that we will happily give of ourselves when we truly love something.

Serving in music ministry is our way of serving the church and bringing glory to God. It's not a matter of "feeling like it" as if it is some task we can pick and choose at will. There is also some level of commitment to the other members of the team, for we love them, and love being a part of the ministry. It doesn't matter if the consistently tardy team member is the most skilled musician or singer in the team. If they cannot or will not love their team members by honouring them in this small way (that is by being punctual and attentive when there), it is obvious that music ministry is not a priority for them.

Love is manifested in action. It is obvious. Consequently, if they do not/cannot change after you've discussed this matter with them, again, you may need to ask them to leave. It sounds harsh, but if you allow this behaviour to continue, it may cause ill feelings - even resentment - between them and other team members. As music directors, we are working towards love and unity that allows the Holy Spirit to move. That cannot happen if division within the group causes the Holy Spirit to be grieved. Therefore, any divisive behaviour is to be avoided at all costs. This includes disruptions at the rehearsals as well. Hopefully a word or two with that person will be enough for them to lift their game a little.

Even if you have to ask a member to resign, please do it in a loving manner and ensure that they understand the issues. It's not about them on a personal level, but about behaviour and unity. They can always approach you at some future time and try out for the team again.

Pray for each one – not just their musical ability, but for their life's journey and growth in Christ. Ask God for divine strategies to help each one. Pray together as a team and ask the Holy Spirit for more anointing over each one and the team as a whole, and that you all might hear His voice and see His directions far more clearly!

Back-Up Singers

The task of the back-up singer is to provide vocal instrumentation and enhancement to the musical backing, and to emphasize or frame what the leader is doing. In essence, the back-up singers are likened to another instrument in the band. They will only "lead" a song if they are invited to do so, since that is not their function as "back-up" singers.

Because the back-ups are not leading, it only makes sense that they should not try to push the music along in tempo, or sing loudly so that they can in essentially lead from the side-lines. There can be only one leader and that is the person who has been delegated or appointed for that service. (Take note of this if you, the music director, decide to do backups whilst someone else is designated worship leader for the service!) Let love reign in your hearts through every circumstance. It doesn't matter if that leader has "missed it" or sung the wrong part. The back-up singer's job is to back-up (strangely enough!) and support – that is all!

You are a team. Each person has a particular function and responsibility to the rest. In this way you perform as a cohesive unit – just like the inner workings of a wind up clock. A cog can't suddenly try to be a spring and expect the clock to still function as it aught. Bottom line: You do well as a team or you do badly as a team.

Any back-up singer who insists on leading from the side-lines needs a heart check. Tough words but I've said it! Being submitted to one another, and preferring one another, is part of being a Godly team and remaining in perfect unity one with another. We are there for God's glory, and in everything our motivation must be love or it's not worth anything!

It is difficult enough for the worship leader to hear and see what the Holy Spirit is doing without also dealing with prima donnas and conflicting personalities. These issues become a sound that the Holy Spirit cannot use because the people making it are not a cohesive, unified, Christ-minded team. Unity is what brings the blessing! Division grieves Him!

> "*30 And do not grieve the Holy Spirit of God, by whom you were sealed for the day of redemption.*" - **Ephesians 4:30 ESV**

Any thing contrary to Jesus' teachings and contrary to the way of love, can easily grieve the Holy Spirit. Loving one another was not only commanded by Jesus, but defines us as Christians.

> "*34 A new commandment I give to you, that you love one another: just as I have loved you, you also are to love one another. 35 By this all people will know that you are my disciples, if you have love for one another.*" – **John 13:34-35 ESV**

"Love" is *who* we are because God is love and He now lives in us. The Holy Spirit is grieved when there are factions or "unwholesome" relationships/feeling between team members, or between members and the leader. You are brothers and sisters in Christ who love unconditionally as He loves us. So to clarify: there is no place for envy and jealousy (e.g. because someone else was picked to do the solo part), and equally no place for contempt for those who don't measure up to a certain standard. You are part of a team. You must have the same mind and heart. It's not about what we want after all. We are serving the church together under the Holy Spirit direction. There is no place for pre-eminence, pettiness, unkindness and selfishness!

In worshipping as a team, our hearts and minds should be

centred upon God and not other personalities within the team. God is worthy of praise whether or not the person next to us is singing off key or too loud, or the song being sung is one we really don't like. Praise and worship are God's dues at all times, and are not dependant upon our surroundings or circumstances. He is the King of kings and Lord of lords at ALL times; now and forever more.

"Where the brethren dwell in unity the Lord commands a blessing." When speaking of music ministry, this blessing often comes in the form of a special anointing over that ministry - unseen because it occurs on a spiritual level. That means that for the team to be truly effective ministers of the anointing, the team must be unified and in one accord.

Note: Although it should go without saying: In order for a team to "lead" worship as a unit, not only worship leaders must be worship-ers, but also the individual worship team members. Although there are some very anointed leaders around who could lead everyone (including the team) into some wonderful worship, it is the entire team's responsibility to seek the anointing and spend time worshipping God in their private time. This also facilitates ease of flow when you come together, because each person will also recognise the Holy Spirit's leading.

The Real Qualifications for Back-ups

We've all seen the very polished worship teams of big TV churches and many local churches feel they need to aspire to those standards. However, smaller churches can also enjoy the benefits of beautiful harmonies and the refreshing sounds of smaller worship teams, and I believe, should be encouraged. The smallest of churches can produce beautiful worship music with even a small number of people. Just two or three singers accompanied by a piano or guitar can lift the worship to great heights; so don't be discouraged by numbers, lack of equipment and limited amplification. It doesn't matter that you have only two singers and a piano. It can still sound brilliant and be ultra anointed if the Holy Spirit is all over it.

So much emphasis is placed on technology, when much of the time it is totally unnecessary. For example, I have seen people set up a full band in a very small classroom sized room when it was totally unnecessary, and from a hearing point of view, bordering on deafening – quite literally! There is nothing wrong with acoustic bands in small areas. At most a microphone for the leader is all that is required, but not so it drowns out all else. Think of it, teachers for centuries have been teaching in rooms this size without any amplification at all, and quite effectively, AND (as mentioned previously) it has been proven that people who can hear themselves sing will join in more readily than those who can't hear anything but the band!

While the latest technology or big numbers are not essentials to produce a successful singing group, there are a few prerequisites that should be considered:

Humility of heart - God's glory not ours: After a great service where the Holy Spirit ministered with such power, it is very tempting for those running the service to beat their chests with pride, and think to themselves, "*Wow! Look what we achieved here today!*" Though a team may follow what they see the Holy Spirit doing, whose power is it, and who deserves the glory? All the glory is His alone! If Holy Spirit had not turned up, there is no way you could have done the same on your own.

The team's function is to give glory where it is due; to God the Father, Jesus, and the Holy Spirit, not the church, not the team or individual members. It's your job to give space for the Holy Spirit to minister and to encourage/welcome the congregation to participate. That is all we can do. The rest is the Holy Spirit's work not ours.

Those with humble and contrite hearts will be able to lovingly glorify Jesus, and not be self-seeking. Pride, on the other hand, grieves the Holy Spirit and will destroy the anointing. It may be far easier to find talented people, than talented humble people. However, it is better to work with a small number of people who may not be exceptionally talented, than to try to teach people how much they are loved by Father God, and that His attention is the best attention they could ever ask for – well above any other. This really is the Holy Spirit's task, and to a lesser extent, the preacher's job as well.

Being a part of a music ministry should be seen as a great honour and privilege. To view this ministry as anything less, will produce less than our best for God. "*Our Utmost for His Highest!*" Our best for His glory! This is also a great testimony to the onlooker and non-believer, and is pleasing to God.

However, each team member should soberly remember that God has no favourites and that they are all doing their particular role in this ministry for the greater benefit of the body as a whole. (The toe is no less than the eye; nor can the eye do without the toe!) Before joining a team, possible members should be prepared to honestly answer the question of why they want to join this ministry.

An ability to sing in tune: If you are on a team to sing, then it is logical that you *can* actually sing; otherwise why are you there? While sounding like a professional is less important compared to correct attitudes and anointing, we want to give the King of kings the very best we have to offer. If the attitudes and heart are right, but the person seeking to sing cannot sing in tune, (or for that matter, the one wanting to join the band cannot play their instrument sufficiently to keep up with the rest of the band), I suggest there is real need for soul searching prayer to ascertain if this is exactly the ministry in which God desires that person to be involved. I honestly do believe that God *does* equip His saints to do the task He calls them to do. Therefore, if a person is inadequately equipped, what is the conclusion here?

If a person still has a strong desire to sing with the team after you have turned them down, singing in tune can, for most people, be learnt, (especially with God's help), but it can be laborious and requires a dedication to practice. (I use to believe that anyone could be taught to sing, let alone sing on pitch, until I met someone who was totally tone deaf and it did not matter how much time and effort I gave to this person, they simply could not hear the correct notes.) If someone is not up to scratch, do not belittle them but gently tell them that with a little practice they may be good enough to join. Then only after this person achieves at least this fundamental skill (i.e. singing in tune or being able to play to a standard), should they be considered for the worship team. (A discordant choir member can be more of a distraction, and therefore, a hindrance to the flow of worship, than enhance it. Therefore, it may be better to do with fewer people than to let this occur!)

An ability to sing harmonies or hold melody against harmonies: The whole point of having a choir/singing group is to add the richness and fullness of sound of harmonies and counter melodies. It is one thing to have a great sounding soloist voice, but another to hold a part. Again, this is a learnt ability and just takes practice.

At first a person may need to learn their part away from the others and concentrate on singing it in tune when the choir/group comes together, but eventually, the person should be able to sing the correct part while listening to the others. It is helpful to 'hear' the chords and cadences throughout the song, to be able to keep pitch and anticipate the next note. (Playing a polyphonic instrument such as guitar or keys can assist in developing this if used in one's personal practice time.)

Blend: These days where the sound technician is responsible for individual volume levels, this may seem an irrelevant point. However, one voice sounding quite different from the others can destroy the overall sound and be a nightmare for the technician. The team must sound like one team with one voice. This means that people need to listen to one another and try to 'blend' or adjust their voice colour (i.e. tone or volume, though still maintaining the natural qualities of the voice without straining). Keep in mind the unity of the group, and the overall quality of sound produced by the group as a whole. Going acoustic on the odd rehearsal night in order that people learn to "hear" one another may be of value here.

Timing: An out of time team with people finishing (especially words ending in 's') or beginning lines (especially those starting with hard consonants), at different times, can be as ugly to the ear as a badly coloured picture with colouring out of lines is to the eye. When backing singers are in perfect time, (every word perfectly together), it becomes as one voice, or instrument, and very pleasing to the ear.

Improving skills and talents: As mentioned, I believe that we should be offering our best to the King of kings and as such investing in the talents He entrusts to us. (See the parable of the talents in Mat 25:14-30. Note: Jesus speaks this to believers, and not to the unsaved.) The allocated weekly practice will not achieve this rapidly, if at all. Even one's daily practice at home is limited by the skill required for the music's mastery. (Thankfully, most choruses are not that demanding.) The best way to improve is by receiving some sort of formal training, i.e. singing lessons. Though not essential, I believe, those that are serious, even if already capable, should consider this kind of investment.

Practicing at home: This is not only a responsibility of each member, but is essential to the progress and finished sound of the team. It is very difficult for the leader to take the team on to new or better songs if he/she must continually stop, correct or re-teach parts. Rehearsal times at church are usually very limited and must cover a lot of ground in a short period of time. By practicing at home a member can be an asset and not a hindrance to the choir's progress. This may mean recording church practices if one cannot play an instrument or read music.

The more important task of the rehearsal night is to practice worship. If the Music Director has to constantly stop to correct during the song practice, there is a risk of over-run and eating into your allocated worship time, and I can't stress enough how important it is to set aside this time to worship together. Therefore, team members should act responsibly by making their own private practice a personal priority, and not put it off until the last minute in preference to other activities.

Worship together often and become acquainted with how the flow feels in the spiritual sense. To be Spirit led, you must hear/feel/see where He is taking you, and the best place to learn this is behind closed doors where no one else but God sees – in your rehearsal time together.

Platform Codes: It goes without saying, the worship team is not on stage to parade or entertain. We cannot hope to compete with the entertainment freely available to people in today's world. (Big churches where people and resources are plentiful - perhaps!) However, for the rest, even at best, church music without the anointing in merely second rate entertainment, since it does not give glory to God, and does nothing to lift the worship, nor does it encourage and minister to believers. Without the Holy Spirit, performing on the platform is not worth being a part of. It doesn't matter how showy, how dressed up it tries to be. Therefore, anything that merely draws attention to the worship team and not to Him is useless and unfruitful, and merely demonstrates an orphan spirit instead of one that is hungry for God.

This brings us to dress code and platform behaviour – two awkward subjects that no one wants to talk about, since leaders are reluctant to put restrictions on team members. Nevertheless, if we are to minister on another's platform, then we must be in submission to the way ministry is conducted from that platform. For some churches, a dress code and etiquette for platform work has already been set and therefore, should be adhered to. For the rest, here are a few tips.

1) Dress Code: A choir 'uniform' may have some merit in the right setting. Nonetheless, it is not always possible, and may even look out of place in most churches. Thankfully, there are other ways to dress that do not draw attention away from God. That is, one's appearance should be neat, modest and understated. I'd advise against sparkling earrings, bracelets or necklets since they can

attract the eye and so distract. (Just my opinion here though.) Totally avoid plunging necklines or "mostly unbuttoned" shirts, high cut hemlines, large open splits in skirts and dresses, or tight clothes that show off every contour.

Whilst I was participating as part of the congregation in one particular service, the female worship leader who was dressed in a relatively short skirt, sat at the keyboard to lead. She was a wonderful leader, but the entire congregation had the complete view up her dress. Need I say where the attention of many of the men folk was that service!

The bible suggests women (men, you're not excused) to dress modestly. This was an "at all times" command, and not a when you feel so inclined or when the fashion permits. How much more so when we are in the eye of the entire congregation! If the problem is that of sitting in full view, as in the above example, perhaps a modesty cloth can be attached to the front of the keyboard stand. It only takes a little forethought. Ask yourself, "*What messages does my appearance convey?*" or "*How are the congregation viewing this?*" The worship team should always seek to focus people's attention on God and not themselves.

2) <u>Platform Behaviour:</u> Talking unnecessarily, laughing or joking, or even not paying attention to the proceedings of the church service, can be a big distraction to the congregation. A less obvious distraction is that of looking morbid, or not meaning what you are singing. We all have off days, but God is still the King and worthy of our praise whether we feel like it or not. On these occasions, the '*sacrifice of joy*', (i.e. rejoicing even though it's the last thing we feel like doing), is a great gift to God, and says to Him that He is above even our feelings. This is also a strong witness to the non-believers who may visit. (Note: To be joyful or "*rejoicing always*" is not a believer's personal option but a repeated exhortation throughout the New Testament!)

Of course, these guidelines are not limited to the back-up singers, but to all team members including the band members.

The Band/Instrumental Backing

Again, I will state that this book is not about how to run a band, but how to follow the Holy Spirit in worship. I could tell you that the bass and drums must work together to create the song's "groove", or that the vocal leader leads the melody, not a single instrument. I could also tell you about the importance of keeping time, and so the list goes on, but those things, you, as a worship-director, should already know! So let's talk about the band cooperating with the Spirit.

Firstly, there is not one instrument more important than the rest. All are important to create the overall sound. Each instrument can be likened to different colour paint in the artist's hand, but only together, is the picture is created. Sometimes a particular colour will stand out, in a particular picture, just like the Holy Spirit may highlight and anoint a particular instrument for a particular purpose, but overall, the art work is created while all the team members cooperate together. God created us as beings that love variety because He does. So while not all works of art are blue (for example) not every song will feature one instrument only, (or even style for that matter!) Every team member/instrument is important to the Holy Spirit.

If you, the leader, are requiring a certain sound or style - especially for a quick change of pace or even key - a reasonable level of skill will be required of your team members. Nevertheless, keep in mind that the Holy Spirit will not try to use abilities that are not currently present within the group. Just practice with what you have and always encourage the members to go further – building on what skills they have already, even if it means professional lessons (and I definitely encourage this).

Above all, the band should be listening out for where the Holy Spirit is moving and what He is about to do. They should also be listening to one another in order to maintain musical cohesion whilst simultaneously listening to and watching the leader for when to move. While there will be times when individual musicians will be highlighted to play solo, generally it's all about listening and following. (Note: band members that worship on their instruments at home are more likely to be the ones that the Holy Spirit highlights and uses during the service.) In order to follow successfully, the playing of one's instrument needs to be second nature. Being Spirit led is a multi-tasking operation. Again this requires practice, both at home and band rehearsals. In fact, team practice/rehearsals where each member learns to play as one band under the headship of the Holy Spirit, is vitally important.

Final note:

If your members are more about showing off the latest lick in their repertoire rather than co-operating with the set-up etc., something is out of alignment and needs adjustment by you – the team leader. In a music team, at the risk of sounding cliché, there really is no "I" in team! You are working towards cohesion and unity – preferring one another in love.

Special Training Sessions

It may well be worth your time to ask another leader from another church or a well known worship leader to come and share their own insights. Worship conferences are also a great place for team members to get a bigger picture and be inspired to go for more! Conferences can be expensive, however, but careful planning (for example: members putting in a couple of dollars each rehearsal, or putting on a fund raiser dinner or concert at church) may raise enough funds to enable those that can't afford the cost to attend. Most are well worth the expense and effort.

While it may be expected that every member attend to their own skills by taking regular lessons themselves, if the skill level of a particular instrument needs help or is non-existent within the church, a training day with someone who is expert on that instrument can be extremely beneficial, particularly if it is hands-on and with some time spent one-on-one with the teacher – a master class if you like.

Of course for the bigger churches that already have the luxury of so many people wanting to join the team that they hold regular auditions with strict constraints, this would be irrelevant. All your members will have a level of expertise before they join the team.

However, in the smaller local churches, it may be difficult to find someone not only capable and willing to play/sing during the worship, but who is also willing to be rostered on regularly. Therefore, holding training sessions to inspire the "up-and-coming" is of great advantage.

As an example: In our church, there was a distinct lack of drummers at one point. (Although we did have a few on the team, they were not always available.) Therefore, my husband who is also a drummer, took and extra set of drums to church for a couple of Saturdays in a row so that anyone wanting to learn could do so. He even brought in a professional drummer to talk to and teach them. This was very successful. Many of those that came to those training sessions were inspired to continue. Many went on to take lessons of their own accord, and can now play quite skilfully. Yes, it meant that the spare set of drums did the rounds until people could afford to buy their own, but by being committed to the ministry no matter what the cost, the worship team and the church benefitted overall.

Harmony training sessions can also be useful. Singing lessons may help the aspiring singer to hold a tune, but learning to hold that tune against harmonies, or to provide harmonies against the melody, may not be so easy for some. So ensure your singers can at least hold a tune, and then teach them harmonies.

Sound Engineers and Technical Support

When considering the worship team, rarely do the sound techs and words projection operators come to mind, but only those who regularly appear on the platform. Nevertheless, these people are also vitally important to the smooth running of the worship service, and should be included not only on your regularly scheduled rehearsal nights but also in other worship team activities if they are to feel included in vision of this ministry and not just some congregational volunteer who rocks up once in a while.

As a worship team, you want the congregation to have their eyes on God alone, so that they can worship. If the sound mix is bad, it can be very off putting/distracting to the congregation, so it should be done well. If the volume is too loud or too quiet, it can also be a distraction. Likewise, if someone is constantly slow changing the words slides, it can also be very distracting.

It is most unfortunate that the only time these people are noticed is when something goes wrong. They are rarely praised for their consistent giving and diligence! However, they are the very people that undergird your ministry and make the rest of you "sound good"! They deserve your respect and honour! They also deserve your consideration when you are considering hosting training nights, or exclusive ministry nights for the music team. How many times have churches had visiting ministries come to minister specifically to the music team and the techies are not included.

Be kind and inclusive to these people. Treat them as vital members of this ministry and they will go the extra mile for you. Ignore them and the attrition rate for those tasks will be high!

If you have no one in your church who can capably do sound or words projection, it would be very advantageous to organise training days for them as well. Not only does this make these people feel important enough to be included, but will benefit the team as a whole! It's a win-win and highly advisable.

Signals and Cues

If you want your team to follow your lead and the Holy Spirit requires some deviation from the rehearsed list or song flow, you need to be able to give accurate cues verbally or with hand signals. There are various versions of hand signals out there. Just make sure the system you use is unambiguous, and clear to *all* in the team – including the words projectionist (As mentioned, these people are only noticed when they mix up slides, or lag behind the words being sung, so ensure they can have the correct slide up in time so that people can continue singing.)

The idea is to ensure that the congregation have their eyes on God and are praising Him without distraction, and not in creating a show. Many in the congregation will have their eyes closed whilst they worship. Verbal signals can be very useful at this time. However, there's not always time between lines to give verbal cues, and hand signals will be necessary.

Some common hand signals are:

- Cupping the hand like a "C" for chorus,

- One finger (index) up for first verse, two fingers for the second verse (and so on),

- Closed fist for the end of the song, or to stop,

- Twirling upward pointed finger for "repeat this section"

- Pat down for "become quieter"

- Single flat hand with "lifting up" motion for louder

- "L" shaped fingers for last line /end tag,

- Pointing to singer or musician for a Spirit led solo

And so on! I don't believe you need to hide these signals (as mentioned, the projectionist rely on these as well as your band), but at the same time, these signals should not be big and flashy, or worse – distracting!

Above all, don't expect your team are mind readers or so skilled they can chop and change in an instant. That simply is not fair to them. Yes, many times your team will also "hear/know" where the Holy Spirit is leading and naturally flow that way, but not always. If they are finding a passage difficult or even just concentrating on getting that right, or are even distracted by something happening in the congregation, they may not be so spiritually insightful.

I mentioned before that other worship leaders may lead slightly differently to one another, so to expect that they will hear every spiritual cue in the same manner as you do, is unrealistic. There will also, no doubt, be times when you are not really sure what comes next. Consequently, you may decide to repeat a verse or chorus because you are waiting to hear Holy Spirit move. At this point, team members may "hear" before you do, but don't assume anything! The giving of cues only makes sense if you want your band and singers to follow.

Dancers & Flag Bearers

Not too many worship ministries think of dancers and flag bearers as part of their ministry. Nevertheless, they are part of the worship and carry the Holy Spirit anointing as well. As Music Director AND worship leader, it's your call as to when to use dancers as part of the up front ministry. Being sensitive to the Holy Spirit with this is critical. You do not wish to create a spectacle, but at the same time, you do not wish to leave out another vital aspect of the worship ministry, or the giving to the Holy Spirit something else He can use. It may feel foreign to you, but you can become accustomed to this when the Holy Spirit is saying, "*Now!*"

The best way to train yourself in how and when to incorporate dance, is to practice! It may be difficult to have dancers turn up to your usual rehearsals, but I would suggest you assign a once a month (or at least every second month) worship night with the entire team (including dancers) so that you can simply worship together. Become accustomed to each other and the way the Holy

Spirit can use the various aspects of worship to His Glory! What is it like to all flow together with the Holy Spirit? You just can't hope it will work come Sunday. At the very least, the dance troupe leader should be given the list of new songs you will be introducing so that they too can choreograph and practice these songs. While there is a place for free expression, when you are dealing with a team of dances, they need to dance cohesively together. This means well choreographed and Spirit inspired team dance movements.

You may not be a dancer or flag bearer, and therefore need to appoint competent leaders for them, but all leaders, whether sound desk or dance etc., should be under the one Music Director since this is all part of the worship ministry. Ultimately, as Music Director, the buck stops with you for how this ministry is run, so getting to know your team is very important.

The dancers too, need to know how you will use them and be accustomed to your way of running the worship. If they are relegated to the *"use only when a special event calls for an item"* or *"people can do it for themselves in the congregation but not the platform"* category, it is the church as a whole that is missing out.

The levels of anointing and ministries available have already been mentioned. It is worth considering how you can incorporate all these elements cohesively and effectively in the Sunday service – using them to their full potential. To that end, spending time in worship with them outside the Sunday service, makes sense.

Get to know well the people/person you put in charge of the dance worship. They need to understand what you expect of them – how you think, just how they are to be used, and how they can fit into the overall vision you have for the worship.

You may even need to set out guidelines of where dancers can dance and flag bearers can use banners and flags, and to what extent they can interact with the congregation during worship or prayer times and lines. This might be something you want to discuss with your senior pastor first to ensure you do not overstep any unspoken boundaries, or vision for the church. Better to know what is expected and the teams boundaries and limitations well before you are pulled up by your headship to answer the *"Please explain!"* coal raking.

Running a Holy Spirit Led Team

The Importance of Worship Practice & Team Work

By far the best way for your team to achieve skilful navigation in the flow of the Spirit is to practice. Yes, practice! It seems incongruous to practice worship, as it is a natural heart response to our revelation of God. Nevertheless, setting time aside to worship simply as a team, without the congregation, is utterly vital!

We are not fond of that word "practice", but training is important in just about any activity in which you desire some level of skill and competence! As with any gift in the Holy Spirit, especially the prophetic (of which this is a form) you become more skilled the more you use it. If you run a team, this is essential when you come together to rehearse each week.

As an army trains regularly, so we too must train regularly. A mere 45 minutes three times a month (or for however long or frequent church teams meet) will not train up a skilled group of warriors, or new worship leaders. (I suggest a minimum of a three-hour rehearsal session each week!) We quickly forget what we have learned, unless we reinforce it by hearing and doing it again.

Also practicing the mechanics of the music at home is therefore, not just essential to the outcome, but a part of being responsible to each other, over and above scheduled weekly rehearsals. (That is, when we come together, others won't have to redo songs or passages because we haven't mastered it yet.) This provides more time to perfect our teamwork and flow in the Holy Spirit during these rehearsals.

I believe, now more than at any other time, we must push into the things of God fervently, letting go the inessentials. In today's modern world, there seems to be an emphasis on the perform-ance and *"getting things right"*. To facilitate this, many worship leaders will concentrate their efforts on chord changes and how they want the music to sound, during the time before the service rather than at a designated weekly rehearsal time apart from the Sunday service. To be honest, this is one of those inessentials.

Pre-service time is better served with sound checks and warm-ups, plus "tops and tails" for ease for transition, but more im-portantly with prayer – inviting the Holy Spirit to be our guide even before the music begins. A little worship together before service may set the tone, but a full service rehearsal is not good for a number of reasons!

One such reason is that for the people coming into the church, the sound can be too loud to converse with others, making it hard to forge relationships between brethren. However, the main rea-son to not have pre-service rehearsals is this: if you haven't gotten it right in rehearsals, even an in-depth practice before church only serves to tire voices, not fix the problems with the song. Anyone who has performed extensively in any music arena (whether church or secular) will attest to this fact! Practice at home is the place we ultimately master the music, followed by rehearsal on a designated rehearsal night where we can play with the entire band/team.

The other reason to not use pre-service as your only rehearsal time is that there is little time to naught, to practice worship to-gether, or give pointers to help your team, or even to train up worship leaders - which if we are honest here, should be a part of your Music Director job description!

I realise that some music directors prefer to do the hour before service to bring it all together, because they don't want to burden the team with another night out, or that the team members are already too busy. However, it is worth noting that to be a part of a team, each member must be prepared to shoulder their re-sponsibility and do what it takes. This is ministry – that is service!

(As mentioned already: "Ministry" literally means "*service*"!) It's neither duty nor performance! Nor is it something we do because we feel like it or are entertained by it. We love to serve the brethren in this manner, in order to bring glory to God, because we love to worship God! It is a privilege motivated by our love for Him, and not something we do lightly!

I realise that team members are volunteers. However, any ministry costs. Jesus said for us to take up our cross and follow Him. Is this ministry worth the cross of dedication and commitment, to practice at home where no one but God sees, to invest your talents in the hope of a larger return, and to give some priority to rehearsal nights over other activities?

Above all, worship ministry is a team effort. The worship team is a Holy army sent before the battle. They must work as a team in order to be used effectively by the Holy Spirit. This means practicing as a team. It means learning to blend harmoniously, no voices or instruments standing out above the rest, but all working together as one. It means following the appointed captain for the service.

While it is the worship leader's *responsibility* to get before God and find out what God wants to do, the team's responsibility is to *follow the leader*. The members cannot afford to be doing their own thing, anymore than an army would be able to fight and win, if the soldiers made their own choices concerning when, where and how to do battle. For the team this means that members need to be watching for signals and be ready to do the unexpected. You are a worship team not worshipping individuals.

The Word of God tells us to be submitted to those in authority over us, and submitted to one another.

> "*17 Obey your leaders and **submit to them**, for they are keeping watch over your souls, as those who will have to give an account. Let them do this with joy and not with groaning, for that would be of no advantage to you.*" – **Hebrews 13:17 ESV**

*"**Submitting to one another** out of reverence for Christ."*
– **Ephesians 5:21 - ESV**

Therefore, in light of this, team members must flow with the person appointed to lead, whether or not you consider they have missed the mark or not, or "done it differently" to the way we thought it should be done.

This also means that if a team member has a prophecy or song or whatever, and the leader says, *"Not now!"* then that team member, in humility, should submit, deferring to the leader's judgment, and not vying for their way or the highway. Trying to lead and over-rule from the sidelines is definitely out of order, and God will not honour this!

Likewise, as we come together on rehearsal nights, even the music director must also be submitted to God and give the Holy Spirit time to teach the team how to follow His lead – a task far more important than learning a new song. Therefore, make time for worship on these nights!

****

As a small less important side note (more of a suggestion): Although most modern worship leaders merely use chords and mimic/copy another's recorded song when learning that new song, merely copying someone else, can in itself, stifle your own creativity, especially if you are not trying to push the boundaries and learn more musically in order to improve! I get it – you want to be true to the song and the composer, or perhaps learning a song as it is recorded gives everyone on the team a common point from which to launch. That's great! However, don't park there!

I have even heard people copying the spontaneous worship from live albums and singing them as part of the song. *What?!!* Is that truly following the Holy Spirit or trying to mimic what He did another time, despite the fact that it may not be what He is saying in the Sunday service for today? Things that were happening on the night the album was recorded had to do with what the Holy Spirit was doing with those people and on that particular night. Now that recording may also minister to those who purchase and listen to the album – the Holy Spirit knew who would be listening to that album sometime in the future. However, to copy word for word, note for note, something that was happening in the spirit then, and try to replicate the atmosphere is nothing more than ignorance at best or presumption at worse! I'm sorry to have to say that!

You and your team are individually and uniquely gifted by God. As such, using your own creative talents honours both your talent and the Creator who made you that way. You are being true to yourself – authentic - and not mere copycats! God hasn't created robots who all do exactly the same thing in exactly the same way! He created us all with diverse and wonderful differences/giftings that together produce an amazing symphony of worship before Him. A brass band has very different skills and sounds to that of a stringed quartet, but it would be ludicrous for the brass band to try and sound like the quartet. It would not even be kind to the people to whom the performance was directed! I encourage you to use your own giftings to create your own unique and glorious style!

I once saw a video of a tribe in Africa that worshipped using a well-known worship song. The big difference, however, was the way the song was "played". The only "instrument" was a large gear ring from a piece of machinery that the player struck with a metal object to make it ring like a triangle. Sounds simplistic, but the worship was glorious! No one was trying to copy any style, or sound or anything else. They were all just singing from their hearts and touching heaven. No, I am not suggesting we dispense with the instruments! By no means! The point is that we can get so caught up in the mechanics of the song and ensuring that we perform it correctly, that we can forget to just let it flow from our hearts.

If you are not sure how to be creative, consider learning about various harmony constructions, counterpoint backing melodies or just instrumentation or groove that can be complementary. More importantly, don't be afraid to just allow a song to flow out of you and your team. Spirit led worship comes from the Holy Spirit flow. It doesn't copy another.

As leader of the team, it's, of course, your call. Copying other well-known worship leaders and their style may be safe and easier to co-ordinate on a team level, and even afford some level of professionalism to which team members can aspire. However, your team may just surprise you with their creative suggestions if you give them opportunity. Don't be afraid to make the worship uniquely yours, (that is: you as a church.) Remember that you always have the final say and can decide not to go with any suggestion put forward if you don't feel comfortable. Keep in mind though, that if you are on track/in step with the Holy Spirit during the service, He may suddenly change something Himself, so be prepared for that!

Musical Temperament

It is often said that singers and musicians are temperamental (sensitive and moody) and can be easily offended, taking any criticism to heart. They feel like their creativity is part of them – an expression of who they are, and so take offence if they are pulled up on something. (You may have found this out already.) What usually follows is that music directors tiptoe around these people in an effort not to upset them - give them some space to do their own thing, in order to prevent any upset. However, you are the leader and cannot compromise the Holy Spirit's task at hand. There are two very important points here:

1) Temperamental out-bursts that occur after an attempt to correct "off" notes or timing, generally arise because the person who is making the error feels as if they are being berated personally and/or being made a fool of in front of the whole group. Therefore, they take offence at being corrected. However, the leader concerned, nine times out of ten, is merely pointing out the mistake in order to correct it, not

trying to attack a team member on a personal level.

In this situation, the temperamental member needs to be able to differentiate between criticism of personal character, and that of one's performance. The first (personal criticism, name calling, or any verbal abuse) wounds the heart deeply. The second (being told we have made a mistake) is outside the realm of our identity and should not be blamed for our emotional state. Put simply, we are not what we do! Maturity is being able to differentiate between the two and get on with life!

2) The bible tells us that one of the fruits of the Spirit is self-control, (Gal 5:22,23). Part of maturity, both spiritual and of character, is being able to be master of one's emotions and not the other way around. While it is important for people to retain their sensitivity, it is the sensitivity to the Holy Spirit's leading that is essential, and not a sensitivity that creates an emotional flare-up.

As well as these points, the Bible also tells us that love is not easily provoked (1 Corinthians 13:4-7) and does not readily take offence.

> "*4Love suffers long and is kind; love does not envy; love does not parade itself, is not puffed up; 5 does not behave rudely, does not seek its own, **is not provoked, thinks no evil;** 6 does not rejoice in iniquity, but rejoices in the truth; 7 bears all things, believes all things, hopes all things, endures all things.*" – **1 Corinthians 13: 4-7 - ESV**

My old pastor used to say, that **offence is very rarely intended, but far too often picked up**. That's because, it's far easier to blame others for negativity than to take responsibility for our own beliefs about our self. Do we stand strong in the knowledge of who God says we are? The bottom line is that it is a choice to become offended or not.

Nevertheless, as Christ's representatives, our first command is to love, for love overlooks offence and forgives. This should be our heart also, especially if we are to remain in unity and of one mind.

That is not to say that a music leader has the license to criticise team members whenever or however, and feel justified. (Love does not behave rudely - above) A worship leader should lead as Christ leads His church – with love, grace and forbearance, respect and kindness. (Leaders also be aware that you too must be humble to accept constructive criticism if you are not performing the song correctly. Don't assume that because you have been assigned leadership that you can't be wrong sometimes. Please remain humble and loving toward your team!)

A Question of Skill & Ability

Lack of musical ability can be limiting because your focus is on the doing and not the hearing. If you are leading from an instrument, you have to be able to handle both your instrument and sing simultaneously. This can be tricky for some but a little practice and it can be mastered. Those that can only play with sheet manuscript are rather limited because reading the music can be distracting, but again it can be mastered. Most modern worship teams use chords only or learn by heart off recorded music. This too can be limiting and distracting until a song is mastered. (Obviously, again practice is important – not necessarily for perfect performance but so that you need give little attention to those things and more to the Holy Spirit!)

Is skillful playing important? Scripture sheds light on this.

> "*Moreover David and the captains of the host **separated to the service** of the sons of Asaph, and of Heman, and of Jeduthun, who should **prophesy** with harps, with psalms, and with cymbals: and the number of the workmen according to their service was:*
>
> "*Of the sons of Asaph; Zaccur, and Joseph, and Nethaniah, and Asarelah, the sons of Asaph under the hands of Asaph,*

*which **prophesied** according to the order of the king.*

*"Of Jeduthun: the sons of Jeduthun; Gedaliah, and Zeri, and Jeshaiah, Hashabiah, and Mattithiah, six, under the hands of their father Jeduthun, who **prophesied with a harp**, to give thanks and to praise the LORD.*

"Of Heman: the sons of Heman; Bukkiah, Mattaniah, Uzziel, Shebuel, and Jerimoth, Hananiah, Hanani, Eliathah, Giddalti, and Romamtiezer, Joshbekashah, Mallothi, Hothir, and Mahazioth:

*"All these were the sons of Heman the king's seer in the words of God, to **lift up the horn**. And God gave to Heman fourteen sons and three daughters.*

"All these were under the hands of their father for song in the house of the LORD, with cymbals, psalms, and harps, for the service of the house of God, according to the king's order to Asaph, Jeduthun, and Heman.

*"So the number of them, with their brethren that were instructed in the songs of the LORD, even all that **were skilled**, was two hundred fourscore and eight."* - **1 Chronicles 25:1-8 KJV**

From these verses we see that those chosen to minister in music were specially separated for this task and were also *skilled* players who could also prophesy on their instruments. That is, they were in touch, and in the flow of, the Holy Spirit, because the Scripture says that they were also *skilled* in the Song of the Lord.

We notice in this Scripture that David and his men *selected* the players/singers for service to their God. We do know that David often demonstrated that he wanted to give only the best to God. His God is an awesome King! He deserves the very best. It follows then that these people would have been the best musicians /singers of the Levites, that David could find. It does not say this implicitly but it would be out of character for David to just choose anyone for the job!

For us, the best is our heart, but there's nothing to stop us from becoming more skilled in all the areas of our worship - Spiritual and physical. David could have just let the people praise God verbally, but he understood the power of his own musical and prophetical gifts when used together with the Holy Spirit. He wanted nothing less in the house of God. He choose the most skilled players who were also trained in the prophetic, and whose training had been passed down and watched over carefully by their fathers before them. Our heart attitude should be like David, that God must have our best! What is our King worth to us?

Remember, we are vessels or tools in the Holy Spirit's hands. The sound you produce will be dependent on how skilled you are. There are a few special times when He will take you beyond your skill for some purpose, but more often He will simply use you and your current level of skill. While it's true that a non-skillfully produced song can be just as anointed and hard hitting as a very skillfully produced piece of music, your task is to ensure your team is as useful to Him as they can be, as well as continue to be anointed. Are we effective tools in the Masters hand, able to produce something worthy of a King - and not just any King - the King of Kings!

A cavalier, or *"It'll be alright on the day!"* attitude suggests a deeper look is required to ascertain whether motivation and heart are out of order. True love gives! It goes to great expense. *"For God so loved, He gave His Son"*. (John 3:16) God's love is not only extravagant but costly. What is your love worth? Does it give the very best?

This is not some manipulative argument I have cunningly devised to have teams practice more. If playing worship music in church was only about excellence and performance, leaders might have reason to cajole team members to improve, but worship is about the heart. If we give our left overs and not our best, what does this say about our heart and love? If we want Him to have our best because we love Him above all else, then surely we want to improve our skills so that He has the pinnacle of what we have to offer at His disposal and not just our "get-around-to-it" efforts. Worship team members would do well to think regularly about their motivation and how they are responding to His love.

The Anointing

King David was not only skilled, but also anointed. As he played, the evil spirits departed from Saul.

> *"14 Now the Spirit of the Lord departed from Saul, and a harmful spirit from the Lord tormented him. 15 And Saul's servants said to him, "Behold now, a harmful spirit from God is tormenting you. 16 Let our lord now command your servants who are before you to seek out a man who is skillful in playing the lyre, and when the harmful spirit from God is upon you, he will play it, and you will be well." 17 So Saul said to his servants, "Provide for me a man who can **play well** and bring him to me." 18 One of the young men answered, "Behold, I have seen a son of Jesse the Bethlehemite, who is **skillful** in playing, a man of valour, a man of war, prudent in speech, and a man of good presence, and **the Lord is with him.**"*

> *19 Therefore Saul sent messengers to Jesse and said, "Send me David your son, who is with the sheep." 20 And Jesse took a donkey laden with bread and a skin of wine and a young goat and sent them by David his son to Saul. 21 And David came to Saul and entered his service. And Saul loved him greatly and he became his armour-bearer. 22 And Saul sent to Jesse, saying, "Let David remain in my service, for he has found favour in my sight." 23 And whenever the harmful spirit from God was upon Saul, David took the lyre and played it with his hand. So Saul **was refreshed** and was well, and the **harmful spirit departed** from him." -* **1 Samuel 16:14-23 - ESV**

Although David was clearly skilled, it was the anointing that caused the evil spirit to depart, not David's skill! Because of the state of Saul's heart, the spirit had the legal right to remain. However, it could not stay in the presence of a Holy God. Our worship also does battle in the heavenlies when it is Holy Ghost anointed. We need the anointing. Worship teams should seek this above all else. Where the light is, the darkness cannot stay. Where there is a real anointing on the worship, God can have His way in hearts, and the devil cannot stand in His way.

> *"²¹ And when he had taken counsel with the people, he appointed those who were to sing to the Lord and praise him in holy attire, as they went **before** the army, and say,*
>
> > *"Give thanks to the Lord, for his steadfast love endures forever."*
>
> *²² And when they began to **sing and praise**, the Lord set an ambush against the men of Ammon, Moab, and Mount Seir, who had come against Judah, so that they were routed." -* **2 Chronicles 20:21-22 - ESV**

Praise is a powerful weapon that can defeat our enemy, but our praise must be full of the Holy Ghost anointing.

So what is the anointing exactly?

There are several answers to this, all of which are correct. Some say it is God's stamp of endorsement on what is being said/done. That endorsement comes with power, just as if God were saying/doing something. Some say it is the power of the Holy Spirit that comes from a special calling to be that kind of minister - i.e. the minister is doing what he/she is called by God to do. Others say it is the presence of the Holy Spirit. Still others claim that the minister, knowing who he/she is in Christ, by faith allows Christ to minister through him/her. (I like that one.) Without a shadow of doubt, however one describes the anointing, it is something that we seek when we minister. We want to be like David in his worship. Without the anointing, our music and singing is just a performance and nothing more.

The only way to gain anointing is to first realise who you are, to pray for anointing to co-minister with Christ, and by faith be able to release it. Finally then, to spend time worshipping in His presence. He is your audience of one, and He looks favourably upon your willingness to give your talents to Him alone where no one else sees.

Skill & Anointing

Putting the two together: Skill and anointing are not necessarily mutually exclusive. You can have skill without the anointing, and anointing without skill, but David had both and used them **both together** to the glory of God. This is the standard to which we aspire to attain. Be skillful, but be anointed even more so. Pursue both diligently!

If your team members are skilled enough at what they do, and the anointing is upon them for that time, do not be afraid to allow them to lead that song or play their instrument as a lead instrument whilst the free worship is continuing. The Holy Spirit wants to use all the arrows in your quiver. Do not be afraid to release them at His beckoning. This also encourages your team members to reach for more and to train for more as well. It's a win-win for all!

Raising Up Worship Leaders

To raise-up worship leaders is not really an option you can choose or not choose. You may feel that your job is simply to lead the team and that's the end of it, but I would say you are wrong. Leadership in Christian circles includes building up and raising-up people in their giftings and potential, so that they can be released into their destiny. You are not only caretaking God's kids, but have a responsibility to pass on to your people anything the Holy Spirit teaches and entrusts to you, so that His legacy continues – not for your benefit, but for the church. The most important aspect of your role as a music director is to grow your people both in skill and in their ability to partner with the Holy Spirit.

It may seem a daunting task, especially if you are new to this whole team leadership thing. Rome wasn't built in a day as the saying goes, so start small. Giving others the opportunity to help behind the scenes, communicates to your team that you trust them and are willing to work with them. It also allows them the privilege of giving and serving, which many may want to do. So delegate tasks, and allow your people to learn what needs to be done!

Delegate!

Though your heart may be in the right place, you may still be holding on to a fear of failing and, as such, doing everything yourself to ensure it's all done correctly. Don't let fear be your motivation for anything you do in Christ. John tells us that perfect love casts out all fear. Hate is not the opposite to love – fear is. Fear prevents us reaching out to others, and from fulfilling all God wants us to achieve! Love moves us forward.

I can understand the desire to do everything yourself. After all, you have been doing it longer than everyone else, and can probably do it better and faster than everyone else too. Nevertheless, if you try to do everything yourself, you will burn out. (Ask me how I know this!)

Naturally you want to give your best, and ensure the congregation experiences the best worship each service. However, worship is not about perfectionism, but love. Yes, we practice and keep learning, but I am not merely talking about skill and excellence here. Perfectionism is a fastidious attitude that demands everything be precise in an almost religious or legalistic manner. I believe it was Bill Johnson that said that where there is a lack of love legalism abounds. If you are to love well, relax a little and believe in your team enough to involve them in the many tasks required to run the team.

Teach others to build the roster. Teach your team to care for and respect the equipment, knowing that it is the church that pays for the sound system etc. and that should be honoured, not taken for granted. Teach others to set up and pack away – even the most expensive equipment. Teach responsibility! Build trust! This is super important if your want a team to follow your lead.

You may think, *"What's this got to do with leading worship?"* True, it looks more like teaching another to lead the team from an organisational point of view, not to actually lead worship, but those that are willing to help will make the best followers of the Holy Spirit, and won't be there to build a following for themselves.

Developing People who will Follow Holy Spirit

Not everyone who can sing will want to learn how to lead worship, so you will need to look to those who do desire to lead, or to whom the Holy Spirit is highlighting. There may be fear that is holding a person back at this point in time, but that doesn't mean they do not have any potential to lead. Just encourage but don't push.

The raising-up of leaders happens during team rehearsals and team time. Someone will have expressed the desire to lead or have been highlighted by the Holy Spirit, or simply caught your attention as having great potential. The next step is to get to know them better. Talk to them, find out their hearts desires, and especially why they decided to be a part of the music ministry. Befriend them. Invite them into your home and your activities. Pray about them before the Lord. How does He feel about the choice?

When you have the green light in your mind and heart, train them. Give them pointers (See chapter on worshipping in the "Holy Spirit flow"). Discuss with them the finer points and even give accounts of your own experiences and mistakes. Let them know the lessons the Holy Spirit has taught you. Share with them other worship leader's videos and books that you have found particularly helpful. Most of all pray with them and for them.

The next step is to allow them to lead at worship rehearsals – right from the production of a spiritual song list, to its execution. (You will have had to have discussed this with them before hand.) Tell them what to expect and what you expect. Remember you are there to encourage and build them up. Let them make mistakes – give them space to do so, but also build them up if they fail. It is up to you to provide a safe place for them. If their leading "fizzles out", be encouraging and give them some pointers in a very kind manner – even privately. If they follow the Holy Spirit well and worship is delightful, honour them for their diligence, even to the point of having the team to do the same.

Exhort the other team members to be gracious and encouraging, and as much as is possible, to work with the trainee, allowing them space to fail without complaints or negative comments. Let your team be a place of love, family and unity always!

It may take time before your trainee becomes proficient but slow and steady wins the race. Don't roster them on for service until they are competent and feel ready. On the other hand, if they are ready and want to do so, but are fearfully reluctant, you may have to throw them in the deep end in a loving manner.

If you have a few people who want to train, you will have to roster them on different rehearsal nights, which may take a lot longer before you can roster them on the platform. For that reason, only take two to three at most, per time. Batches of trainees are better than trying to "give everyone a go" and achieve little. People easily forget and need to practice often. To worship effectively in the Holy Spirit flow requires skill, not head knowledge. Skill acquisition requires practice. If you are trying to train up too many people at a time, the practice times available for each person's worship leading skills is sparse.

You also cannot spread yourself that thin. There are many things that require your attention and personal giving of your time. This is do-able when you have a small number, but not with a huge group! Remember that Jesus had twelve apostles out of His many disciples and followers, but only had Peter, James and John in His inner circle! They accompanied Jesus everywhere and not only got to see the Master at work in all the miracles He performed, but to ask Him questions about them.

There may just be a team member who wants to be a worship leader and whom you really feel is wrong for this task. Firstly, I suggest you spend some time in prayer about this. It can be tricky to handle especially if you have already let them lead once or twice at worship rehearsals. It's very important to let all candidates know that if you feel they need to concentrate on being part of the team for the time being rather than lead, even if they have had a chance to lead at rehearsals, then there's nothing personal going on here. You simply do not think they are ready.

Keep the communication open and act in a loving manner towards them. Otherwise, your lack of communication may be taken as personal bias. This then can produce grumbling and grumbling is never silent. It always finds a listening ear, and has the potential to cause great division within the team – most often festering behind the music director's back until it's too late! The lesson here is to be completely open with your members and invite discussion where necessary.

A cautionary note: Be careful when judging the potential worship leader's skill in the flow of the anointing, (especially if you merely sitting in the congregation of another's church under another worship leader that day). Different worship leaders have different skill sets and life experiences, which make them unique in their expression, presentation and style. I may interpret the flow of the Holy Spirit differently because of my unique way of seeing both the world and spirit realm, but God will still use my understanding and skills to communicate the same message to His people as the other worship leader who is leading the people using his/her own style etc. It may mean that a worship leader may use a completely different song or way of leading to what I would have used.

This does not mean that one leader got it right and the other did not. Both are right! God will work within the skills and understanding a worship leader possesses, because He delights in partnering with us. Plus, that particular Holy Spirit message may have only had the impact it did because of the way that leader arrived at it. Thus, worship leaders can lead differently and still end up in the same place – the place where Holy Spirit wanted to take the congregation.

Therefore, be encouraging! Even if the worship leader "misses it" for whatever reason, be sure to be the encourager and not the criticising person. Perhaps you, as the Music Director could offer some suggestions at a later time when they are more receptive to hear. In everything you do, ensure you build up and not tear down. These people are God's own, full of the Holy Spirit, made in His likeness, no longer the old man but now a new creation with Christ living in them. Therefore, any time you criticise, be mindful of just who you are unwittingly criticising.

Note: Being picky or judgemental about how worship is being led when you are not rostered on will only stop you from enjoying His presence. Remember, where there is unity, God commands a blessing. Just sit back and enjoy Him in worship. That is why you came to church in the first place.

Above all pray with your team members and for them – especially those you are raising up as leaders. Lay hands on them asking the Holy Spirit to impart what they need to do the job. Prophesy over them if you are able (encouraging things only!!!) Invest in your people as much as is possible. No, I don't mean that you should pay for lessons, but give them your time. Listen to their stories and their hearts desire. The better you know your team, the easier it will be to work with them and grow them.

Consider how the Holy Spirit leads you and try to be like Him in His leadership, whilst simultaneously allowing Him to lead and teach you how to lead.

Always be a leader who treats team members with love and respect, and those you lead will treat you in the same way. Not only that, but they will try to be just like you when they lead others.

Appendix

Appendix A

How to Hear God's Voice – By Dr. Mark Virkler

She had done it again! Instead of coming straight home from school like she was supposed to, she had gone to her friend's house. Without permission. Without our knowledge. Without doing her chores.

With a ministering household that included remnants of three struggling families plus our own toddler and newborn, my wife simply couldn't handle all the work on her own. Everyone had to pull their own weight. Everyone had age-appropriate tasks they were expected to complete. At fourteen, Rachel and her younger brother were living with us while her parents tried to overcome lifestyle patterns that had resulted in the children running away to escape the dysfunction. I felt sorry for Rachel, but, honestly my wife was my greatest concern.

Now Rachel had ditched her chores to spend time with her friends. It wasn't the first time, but if I had anything to say about it, it would be the last. I intended to lay down the law when she got home and make it very clear that if she was going to live under my roof, she would obey my rules.

But...she wasn't home yet. And I had recently been learning to hear God's voice more clearly. Maybe I should try to see if I could hear anything from Him about the situation. Maybe He could give me a way to get her to do what she was supposed to (i.e. what I wanted her to do). So I went to my office and reviewed what the Lord had been teaching me from Habakkuk 2:1,2: "I will stand on my guard post and station myself on the rampart; And I will keep watch to see what He will speak to me...Then the Lord answered me and said, 'Record the vision....'"

Habakkuk said, "I will stand on my guard post..." (Hab. 2:1). The first key to hearing God's voice is to go to a quiet place and still our own thoughts and emotions. Psalm 46:10 encourages us to be still, let go, cease striving, and know that He is God. In Psalm 37:7 we are called to "be still before the Lord and wait patiently for Him." There is a deep inner knowing in our spirits that each of us can experience when we quiet our flesh and our minds. Practicing the art of biblical meditation helps silence the outer noise and distractions clamoring for our attention.

I didn't have a guard post but I did have an office, so I went there to quiet my temper and my mind. Loving God through a quiet worship song is one very effective way to become still. In 2 Kings 3, Elisha needed a word from the Lord so he said, "Bring me a minstrel," and as the minstrel played, the Lord spoke. I have found that playing a worship song on my autoharp is the quickest way for me to come to stillness. I need to choose my song carefully; boisterous songs of praise do not bring me to stillness, but rather gentle songs that express my love and worship. And it isn't enough just to sing the song into the cosmos – I come into the Lord's presence most quickly and easily when I use my godly imagination to see the truth that He is right here with me and I sing my songs to Him, personally.

"I will keep watch to see," said the prophet. To receive the pure word of God, it is very important that my heart be properly focused as I become still, because my focus is the source of the intuitive flow. If I fix my eyes upon Jesus (Heb. 12:2), the intuitive flow comes from Jesus. But if I fix my gaze upon some desire of my heart, the intuitive flow comes out of that desire. To have a pure flow I must become still and carefully fix my eyes upon Jesus. Quietly worshiping the King and receiving out of the stillness that follows quite easily accomplishes this.

So I used the second key to hearing God's voice: As you pray, fix the eyes of your heart upon Jesus, seeing in the Spirit the dreams and visions of Almighty God. Habakkuk was actually looking for vision as he prayed. He opened the eyes of his heart, and looked into the spirit world to see what God wanted to show him.

God has always spoken through dreams and visions, and He specifically said that they would come to those upon whom the Holy Spirit is poured out (Acts 2:1-4, 17).

Being a logical, rational person, observable facts that could be verified by my physical senses were the foundations of my life, including my spiritual life. I had never thought of opening the eyes of my heart and looking for vision. However, I have come to believe that this is exactly what God wants me to do. He gave me eyes in my heart to see in the spirit the vision and movement of Almighty God. There is an active spirit world all around us, full of angels, demons, the Holy Spirit, the omnipresent Father, and His omnipresent Son, Jesus. The only reasons for me not to see this reality are unbelief or lack of knowledge.

In his sermon in Acts 2:25, Peter refers to King David's statement: "I saw the Lord always in my presence; for He is at my right hand, so that I will not be shaken." The original psalm makes it clear that this was a decision of David's, not a constant supernatural visitation: "I have set (literally, I have placed) the Lord continually before me; because He is at my right hand, I will not be shaken" (Ps.16:8). Because David knew that the Lord was always with him, he determined in his spirit to see that truth with the eyes of his heart as he went through life, knowing that this would keep his faith strong.

In order to see, we must look. Daniel saw a vision in his mind and said, "I was looking...I kept looking...I kept looking" (Dan. 7:2, 9, 13). As I pray, I look for Jesus, and I watch as He speaks to me, doing and saying the things that are on His heart. Many Christians will find that if they will only look, they will see. Jesus is Emmanuel, God with us (Matt. 1:23). It is as simple as that. You can see Christ present with you because Christ is present with you. In fact, the vision may come so easily that you will be tempted to reject it, thinking that it is just you. But if you persist in recording these visions, your doubt will soon be overcome by faith as you recognize that the content of them could only be birthed in Almighty God.

Jesus demonstrated the ability of living out of constant contact with God, declaring that He did nothing on His own initiative, but only what He saw the Father doing, and heard the Father saying (Jn. 5:19,20,30). What an incredible way to live!

Is it possible for us to live out of divine initiative as Jesus did? Yes! We must simply fix our eyes upon Jesus. The veil has been torn, giving access into the immediate presence of God, and He calls us to draw near (Lk. 23:45; Heb. 10:19-22). "I pray that the eyes of your heart will be enlightened...."

When I had quieted my heart enough that I was able to picture Jesus without the distractions of my own ideas and plans, I was able to "keep watch to see what He will speak to me." I wrote down my question: "Lord, what should I do about Rachel?"

Immediately the thought came to me, "She is insecure." Well, that certainly wasn't my thought! Her behavior looked like rebellion to me, not insecurity.

But like Habakkuk, I was coming to know the sound of God speaking to me (Hab. 2:2). Elijah described it as a still, small voice (I Kings 19:12). I had previously listened for an inner audible voice, and God does speak that way at times. However, I have found that usually, God's voice comes as spontaneous thoughts, visions, feelings, or impressions.

For example, haven't you been driving down the road and had a thought come to you to pray for a certain person? Didn't you believe it was God telling you to pray? What did God's voice sound like? Was it an audible voice, or was it a spontaneous thought that lit upon your mind?

Experience indicates that we perceive spirit-level communication as spontaneous thoughts, impressions and visions, and Scripture confirms this in many ways. For example, one definition of paga, a Hebrew word for intercession, is "a chance encounter or an accidental intersecting." When God lays people on our hearts, He does it through paga, a chance-encounter thought "accidentally" intersecting our minds.

So the third key to hearing God's voice is recognizing that God's voice in your heart often sounds like a flow of spontaneous thoughts. Therefore, when I want to hear from God, I tune to chance-encounter or spontaneous thoughts.

Finally, God told Habakkuk to record the vision (Hab. 2:2). This was not an isolated command. The Scriptures record many examples of individual's prayers and God's replies, such as the Psalms, many of the prophets, and Revelation. I have found that obeying this final principle amplified my confidence in my ability to hear God's voice so that I could finally make living out of His initiatives a way of life. The fourth key, two-way journaling or the writing out of your prayers and God's answers, brings great freedom in hearing God's voice.

I have found two-way journaling to be a fabulous catalyst for clearly discerning God's inner, spontaneous flow, because as I journal I am able to write in faith for long periods of time, simply believing it is God. I know that what I believe I have received from God must be tested. However, testing involves doubt and doubt blocks divine communication, so I do not want to test while I am trying to receive. (See James 1:5-8.) With journaling, I can receive in faith, knowing that when the flow has ended I can test and examine it carefully.

So I wrote down what I believed He had said: "She is insecure."

But the Lord wasn't done. I continued to write the spontaneous thoughts that came to me: "Love her unconditionally. She is flesh of your flesh and bone of your bone."

My mind immediately objected: She is not flesh of my flesh. She is not related to me at all – she is a foster child, just living in my home temporarily. It was definitely time to test this "word from the Lord"!

There are three possible sources of thoughts in our minds: ourselves, satan and the Holy Spirit. It was obvious that the words in my journal did not come from my own mind – I certainly didn't see her as insecure or flesh of my flesh. And I sincerely doubted that satan would encourage me to love anyone unconditionally!

Okay, it was starting to look like I might have actually received counsel from the Lord. It was consistent with the names and character of God as revealed in the Scripture, and totally contrary to the names and character of the enemy. So that meant that I was hearing from the Lord, and He wanted me to see the situation in a different light. Rachel was my daughter – part of my family not by blood but by the hand of God Himself. The chaos of her birth home had created deep insecurity about her worthiness to be loved by anyone, including me and including God. Only the unconditional love of the Lord expressed through an imperfect human would reach her heart.

But there was still one more test I needed to perform before I would have absolute confidence that this was truly God's word to me: I needed confirmation from someone else whose spiritual discernment I trusted. So I went to my wife and shared what I had received. I knew if I could get her validation, especially since she was the one most wronged in the situation, then I could say, at least to myself, "Thus sayeth the Lord."

Needless to say, Patti immediately and without question confirmed that the Lord had spoken to me. My entire planned lecture was forgotten. I returned to my office anxious to hear more. As the Lord planted a new, supernatural love for Rachel within me, He showed me what to say and how to say it to not only address the current issue of household responsibility, but the deeper issues of love and acceptance and worthiness.

Rachel and her brother remained as part of our family for another two years, giving us many opportunities to demonstrate and teach about the Father's love, planting spiritual seeds in thirsty soil. We weren't perfect and we didn't solve all of her issues, but because I had learned to listen to the Lord, we were able to avoid creating more brokenness and separation.

The four simple keys that the Lord showed me from Habakkuk have been used by people of all ages, from four to a hundred and four, from every continent, culture and denomination, to break through into intimate two-way conversations with their loving Father and dearest Friend. Omitting any one of the keys will prevent you from receiving all He wants to say to you. The order of the keys is not important, just that you use them all. Embracing all four, by faith, can change your life. Simply quiet yourself down, tune to spontaneity, look for vision, and journal. He is waiting to meet you there.

You will be amazed when you journal! Doubt may hinder you at first, but throw it off, reminding yourself that it is a biblical concept, and that God is present, speaking to His children. Relax. When we cease our labors and enter His rest, God is free to flow (Heb. 4:10).

Why not try it for yourself, right now? Sit back comfortably, take out your pen and paper, and smile. Turn your attention toward the Lord in praise and worship, seeking His face. Many people have found the music and visionary prayer called "A Stroll Along the Sea of Galilee" helpful in getting them started. You can listen to it and download it free at www.CWGMinistries.org/Galilee.

After you write your question to Him, become still, fixing your gaze on Jesus. You will suddenly have a very good thought. Don't doubt it; simply write it down. Later, as you read your journaling, you, too, will be blessed to discover that you are indeed dialoguing with God. If you wonder if it is really the Lord speaking to you, share it with your spouse or a friend. Their input will encourage your faith and strengthen your commitment to spend time getting to know the Lover of your soul more intimately than you ever dreamed possible.

Is It Really God?

Five ways to be sure what you're hearing is from Him:

1)   **Test the Origin (1 Jn. 4:1)**

Thoughts from our own minds are progressive, with one thought leading to the next, however tangentially. Thoughts from the spirit world are spontaneous. The Hebrew word for true prophecy is naba, which literally means to bubble up, whereas false prophecy is ziyd meaning to boil up. True words from the Lord will bubble up from our innermost being; we don't need to cook them up ourselves.

2)   **Compare It to Biblical Principles**

God will never say something to you personally which is contrary to His universal revelation as expressed in the Scriptures. If the Bible clearly states that something is a sin, no amount of journaling can make it right. Much of what you journal about will not be specifically addressed in the Bible, however, so an understanding of biblical principles is also needed.

3)   **Compare It to the Names and Character of God as Revealed in the Bible**

Anything God says to you will be in harmony with His essential nature. Journaling will help you get to know God personally, but knowing what the Bible says about Him will help you discern what words are from Him. Make sure the tenor of your journaling lines up with the character of God as described in the names of the Father, Son and Holy Spirit.

4)   **Test the Fruit (Matt. 7:15-20)**

What effect does what you are hearing have on your soul and your spirit? Words from the Lord will quicken your faith and increase your love, peace and joy. They will stimulate a sense of humility within you as you become more aware of Who God is and who you are. On the other hand, any words you receive which cause you to fear or doubt, which bring you into confusion or anxiety, or which stroke your ego (especially if you hear something that is "just for you alone – no one else is worthy") must be immediately rebuked and rejected as lies of the enemy.

5) Share It with Your Spiritual Counselors (Prov. 11:14)

We are members of a Body! A cord of three strands is not easily broken and God's intention has always been for us to grow together. Nothing will increase your faith in your ability to hear from God like having it confirmed by two or three other people! Share it with your spouse, your parents, your friends, your elder, your group leader, even your grown children can be your sounding board. They don't need to be perfect or super-spiritual; they just need to love you, be committed to being available to you, have a solid biblical orientation, and most importantly, they must also willingly and easily receive counsel. Avoid the authoritarian who insists that because of their standing in the church or with God, they no longer need to listen to others. Find two or three people and let them confirm that you are hearing from God!

The book *4 Keys to Hearing God's Voice* is available at www.CWGMinistries.org

Appendix B

The Book's Back Story

I suppose this began after I had written up some worship teaching notes for a Supernatural Glory School. Around this time someone who knew nothing about the teaching notes I'd written, prophesied over me that I would be teaching Spirit led worship far and wide; so get ready!

As I was reviewing those notes, the Holy Spirit suggested I share this information with the world in the form of a book. To be honest, I was not overjoyed at the prospect. My first book, also done under the instruction of the Holy Spirit, took 2 years to research, compile and write, and did not experience large sale numbers at all. Was this to be any different? Nevertheless, I did as the Holy Spirit had instructed me. Thankfully, it wasn't a long write, as all the information pretty much flowed out of my own experience and much of what the Holy Spirit had taught me over the years.

Then, just after I had put the book up on Amazon, I had a prophetic dream. Now please before I am accused on putting myself on a pedestal here, keep in mind that this was just a dream and a prophetic dream at that.

In the dream it was my job to finish dressing a beautiful bride. As she walked into the church building and into the Bride Room, she was already dressed in her beautiful white gown. She walked confidently with her head held high as the royalty that she was. Behind her flowed a long blood red scarf that had a line of remembrance poppies down the centre, from one end to the other.

Unfortunately there were people jostling as they came in behind her, and they were stepping on this scarf as it trailed behind the beautiful bride. I quickly intervened, scooping up the end of the scarf so that it no longer dragged on the floor, and put a little distance between the bride and the people entering, so that the scarf once again prominently fluttered high behind her as she walked.

There was a scene change as often happens in dreams. Suddenly I am in Heaven observing a very small group of people already seated at the table for the marriage supper, even though the ceremony had not yet commenced. Although they were happy enough, they were a little impatient, as they wanted the meal served then and there. It was then that some waiters came and took an empty table away from beside these people, and they were served a very small amount of finger food. That puzzled me.

Scene change again, and I was with the bride in the Bride Room, putting the finishing touches to the bride to make her ready. I placed on her shoulders a kind of thick, weighty, silvery, furry stole/shawl – a mantle if you like.

Here is how I interpreted the dream: God at the time had been telling me to make some teaching videos based on the book so that it could reach even further.

Now in this dream, to me it felt like God had given me the responsibility of clothing the Bride of Christ further with deep heart felt worship, out of which loving obedience would flow.

The red scarf obviously represented the blood of the saints gone before and those who will yet be added to their number – those that had paid the ultimate price for the kingdom. Unfortunately there are those who take this sacrifice for granted, but God says, "*No more! They not only deserve a place of honour and respect, but the reason they sacrificed their lives must also be respected!*"

The "pre-wedding supper" to me seemed like those Christians who have lived fairly selfish Christian lives – always wanting the blessing and not wanting to reach out in God's love to others and help build the kingdom.

This can also relates to our worship. We can be like those who just want the blessing in worship and to enjoy His presence. While there is nothing wrong with that, since in His presence there is fullness of joy (**Psalm 16:11**), true intimacy gives birth to life, and not selfish living. Enjoying God's love is wonderful, but in order to be the kind of love God seeks from us, our love for God must be demonstrated in our obedience and in our love for one another and to the lost and broken world. (See **1 John 4**) We must live as Jesus did.

(Think of the *cross* as a memory help. The top of the cross points upward to heaven, the arms reach out to others. It stands solidly on the Rock (which is Christ), secured firmly by obedience to His Word and unable to by washed away by the storms and pounding waves of life.)

Although those people that were seated at the table still received their tip-bits of food as a precursor to the wedding feast, (God's kindness and generosity still covers them), there is no longer any room for that kind of lifestyle. There is now a more urgent call to pull out that last bit of reserve to sprint to the finish line to receive the imperishable crown of life – as Paul describes in **1 Corinthians 9:24-27.**

Finally, the finishing touches to the bride are made. She has a mantle (and mandate) to reach the world, but this begins from a place of intimacy and worship. The silver colour, according to *The Prophet's Dictionary*[27] means wisdom. So in this end-days' ministry, Holy Spirit wisdom will belie all the Bride ministers to the world. Then she will be ready!

The dream confirmed the Holy Spirit nudging I had felt to promote and release it even further afield.

Appendix C

About the Author

Karen, herself, describes her pre-ministry and pre-salvation years:

> "*I have always been singing and creating music since I was preschool. My first recollections were at the age of about three years old, sitting in the sand at the base of some jungle gym equipment in the park, wondering about singing and the construction of songs. Obviously the thinking ability of a three year old was not advanced, but I remember it vividly nonetheless.*
>
> "*What followed was a life of song writing and singing. Even in primary school I was creating songs and performing them in front of the class. When I was eleven, my brother who was teaching himself to play the guitar, taught me a few basic chords, and I taught myself a few more from there. What followed was my first penned song with actual music accompaniment. Strange as it may seem, I can still recall the song clearly – sounded almost country in style! Ha!*
>
> "*After this, I spent a great deal of time teaching myself even more chords and styles. However, I also wanted to play the piano, now that I had a taste for the instrumental side of*

music. I would bang on the piano trying to make it sound musical – much to my mother's dismay. In the end, realising this was <u>not</u> a phase that was going to go away, and no doubt to be kind to hers and everyone else's ears, she decided to pay for piano lessons for me. At least the banging would stop! (Laugh) Although, I still had to compete with my brothers who would quickly put on a music album before I could clamber to the piano after school to practice.

Later, once my voice had matured enough, I received vocal training to performance (A. Mus. A.) level for classical singing, though I am not so keen on classical music, but the technical training was very useful!"

At the age of fifteen Karen was invited to play guitar and sing in a small church folk group. A couple of years later (and by then very much saved by the blood) she was running it, as well as playing and worship leading for other groups and events in her home town of Ballarat. This ministry blossomed, and over the space of nearly thirty years Karen directed music & worship, and raised up worship leaders whilst doing so.

"As "music director" at my old church, it was my job not just to run the team and ensure there was music each service, but to train up more worship leaders – not to do myself out of a job as I often joked, but to help the new worship leaders leap from my shoulders into their destinies, while using all the skills I had learned from the Holy Spirit."

She was also invited to speak at worship conferences, ran conferences, and organised intercity & inter-church large worship events, and now has written this insightful and useful book – a book that any aspiring worship leader, and even those who have been leading for some time, can grasp and use to propel their leading into greater heights of worship.

She has also written over 200 Christians songs with an album released over a decade ago and according to the prophetic, has more on the way.

Today, Karen still worship leads at various events when asked, but is not part of any particular team. Her focus now is on training the next generation into leaders of glorious worship.

To book Karen, please contact author-KGray@KMGPublications.com.au

Karen's own story, together with her other books, literary papers and even a small selection of her songs, can be found on her website: www.KarenGray.com.au

References and Bibliography

[1, 2 & 5] Retrieved from an article by Steven Hawthorne, "*The Story of His Glory*"

[3] Robert Rayburn, *Come Let Us Worship*

[4] James B Torrance, *Worship, Community and the Triune God of Grace*, Published by IVP Academic, 1997 (page 60)

[6, 12 & 22] W.E. Vine's "Complete Expository Dictionary of Old & New Testament Words" by W.E. Vine, Merrill F. Unger, & William White, Jr. Published in 1940 and without copyright. Subsequent editions have been published in other forms and titles. The copyright for the latter belongs to the various publishing houses that have since produced their own printings of the works.

[7, 9, & 21] "*The Ministry of the Psalmist*" By Tom Inglis. Copyright © 2012 - Tom Inglis. Copyright © 1982 by Thomas Nelson.

[8] "*Gifted Response: The Triune God as the Causative Agency of our Responsive Worship*" by Dennis Ngien, Copyright 2008, Paternoster publishers. ISBN: 1842276107

[10] *The Practice of Praise*, (Waco, Word, 1992)

[11 & 15] *Let Judah go up first: A study in praise, prayer, and worship.* By Dr. Roy Blizzard. Copyright © 1989 Center for Judaic-Christian Studies, ISBN-10: 0918873010, ISBN-13: 978-09188730196 Retrieved from https://en.wikipedia.org/wiki/Yadah October 2018

[13] *The New International Dictionary of the Bible*. 1st Edition edited by Merrill C. Tenney and Published by Zondervan (1967). More recently by the work was chiefly edited by J.D. Douglas.

[14] *Worship Is...What?!: Rethinking Our Ideas About Worship.* Copy-

right © 1996 Tom Kraeuter. Published by Emerald Books ISBN-10: 1883002389, ISBN-13: 978-1883002381

[16] Retrieved from https://en.wikipedia.org/wiki/Yadah October 2018

[17] All definitions are referenced to Francis Brown; Samuel Rolles Driver; Charles Augustus Briggs (1898). Brown-Driver-Briggs. Clarendon Press. p. 392.

[18] Geoffrey Wainwright, *"The Praise of God in the Theological Reflection of the Church,"* Interpretation 39 [1985], 35

[19] J.I Packer

[20] *"God has Spoken"* by J.I Packer, Copyright © 1979 Ebook ISBN 978 1 473 63708 5

[23] *Dialogue with God: Opening The Door To Two-Way Prayer* by Mark Virkler, Copyright © 2001. Published by Bridge-Logos Publishers; ISBN-10: 0882706209, ISBN-13: 978-1862630062

[24] January 13th, 2017 at Glory City Church Brisbane, Friday night service.

[25] The blog from Ps Mark Virkler can be found at: https://www.cwgministries.org/blogs/leading-worshipers-throne-room

[26] The blog by Jeff Duncan can be found at: https://www.cwgministries.org/blogs/which-these-four-places-do-you-gaze-you-worship-only-one-correct-jeff-duncan

[27] *"The Prophet's Dictionary"* by Paula A Price, Ph.D, © 1999, 2002, 2006 by Paula A Price. Published by Whitaker House, New Kensington, PA, 15068, USA

Also by Karen M Gray:

Save Your Marriage

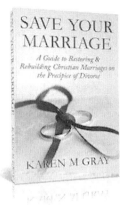

This masterfully created and thoroughly researched book is a must for any marriage whether facing problems or just starting out. It is a resource that you could find yourself using again and again.

Answering tough questions whilst giving wise insight and understanding, this books not only deals with many of the problems facing Christian marriages today and how to overcome them, but provides ways to help marriages to heal and rebuild, even after suffering immense hurt and betrayal.

"*Save Your Marriage*" is available through Amazon, Apple ibooks and Barnes & Noble.

Made in the USA
Las Vegas, NV
03 August 2023